Matter in the Floating World

Matter in the Floating World

Conversations with Leading Japanese Architects and Designers

Hitoshi Abe · Tadao Ando · Jun Aoki · Masayo Ave · Shigeru Ban · Shuhei Endo · Terunobu Fujimori · Kenya Hara · Eriko Horiki · Sachiko Kodama · Kengo Kuma · Toyo Ito · Oki Sato · Kazuyo Sejima · Reiko Sudo · Takaharu Tezuka · Akira Wakita · Makoto Sei Watanabe · Yasuhiro Yamashita · Tokujin Yoshioka

Blaine Brownell

Princeton Architectural Press · New York

*In memory of Tomio Abe, John Hancock, and Allan Walker—
who each shared his own special Japan with me*

Published by
Princeton Architectural Press
37 East 7th Street
New York, New York 10003

For a free catalog of books, call 1-800-722-6657
Visit our website at www.papress.com

© 2011 Princeton Architectural Press
All rights reserved
Printed and bound in China
14 13 12 11 4 3 2 1 First edition

No part of this book may be used or reproduced in any
manner without written permission from the publisher,
except in the context of reviews.

Every reasonable attempt has been made to identify
owners of copyright. Errors or omissions will be corrected
in subsequent editions.

Editor: Becca Casbon
Designer: Paul Wagner

Special thanks to: Sara Bader, Nicola Bednarek Brower,
Janet Behning, Megan Carey, Carina Cha, Tom Cho,
Penny (Yuen Pik) Chu, Russell Fernandez, Pete Fitzpatrick,
Jan Haux, Linda Lee, John Myers, Katharine Myers, Dan Simon,
Andrew Stepanian, Jennifer Thompson, Joseph Weston, and
Deb Wood of Princeton Architectural Press
—Kevin C. Lippert, publisher

Library of Congress
Cataloging-in-Publication Data

Brownell, Blaine Erickson, 1970–
Matter in the floating world : conversations with leading
Japanese architects and designers / Blaine Brownell. —
1st ed.
      p.   cm.
ISBN 978-1-56898-996-9 (alk. paper)
1. Architecture—Japan—History—21st century. 2.
Design—Japan—History—21st century. 3. Architects—
Japan—Interviews. 4. Designers—Japan—Interviews. I. Title.
NA1555.6.B76 2011
720.952'09051—dc22
                              2010029061

Contents

6	Acknowledgments	145	**FLOW**
8	When the World Floats: Material Buoyancy in Contemporary Design **Hiroshi Ota**	149	Recoding Materiality **Jun Aoki**
11	Substance and Transience in Japanese Architecture and Design	161	Pattern and Movement **Hitoshi Abe**
		173	Connective Tissue **Shuhei Endo**
19	**LIGHTNESS**	183	The Fluidity of Fabric **Reiko Sudo**
23	Expanding Boundaries **Takaharu Tezuka**	193	Liquid Architecture **Sachiko Kodama**
35	The Presence of Absence **Kengo Kuma**	201	**EMERGENCE**
45	Weightless Surfaces **Yasuhiro Yamashita**	205	The Emerging Grid **Toyo Ito**
57	A Small "!" Moment **Oki Sato**	217	Natural Logic **Makoto Sei Watanabe**
69	Strength in Weakness **Shigeru Ban**	229	Soft Interface **Akira Wakita**
		239	Summoning Nature **Tokujin Yoshioka**
83	**ATMOSPHERE**	249	The Sound of Material **Masayo Ave**
87	Information Architecture **Kenya Hara**		
99	Invisible Architecture **Kazuyo Sejima**	256	Image Credits
111	Substance and Abstraction **Tadao Ando**		
121	A Canvas for Light **Eriko Horiki**		
133	Evoking the Primal **Terunobu Fujimori**		

Acknowledgments

Although this book focuses on recent events, it has much earlier origins. In 1977, my father was granted a Fulbright Award to teach at Hiroshima University, and my family accompanied him for a yearlong adventure in Japan. As a second-grader at the time, the experience made an indelible impression on me, and I have been "drawn east" ever since. My indebtedness thus extends back to this opportunity and all who made it possible.

Given the subject matter of this book, it should come as no surprise that I pursued architecture and East Asian studies in college and graduate school, with a couple of summertime stints working and conducting research in Japanese architectural offices. These opportunities were made possible by the Princeton-in-Asia program and former *sensei* and longtime family friend Charles Kite—with support from a Woodrow Wilson Fellowship and a John T. Mitchell Fellowship.

When my research in emerging materials directed me eastward once more, I was granted the good fortune to become a Fulbright Scholar in 2006, and my own family accompanied me for an unforgettable year in Tokyo. I owe thanks to Bill Bain, John Casbarian, Jack MacAllister, and Jennifer Thompson for recommending me for this award, as well as David Adams, Adam Broder, and John and Marga Hancock for supporting my application process. My affiliation at the Tokyo University of Science was made possible by the efforts of longtime family friend Shunichi Watanabe, as well as Kazuhiro Kojima and Kaori Ito. I would like to thank David Satterwhite, Mizuho Iwata, and the employees of the Japan-United States Educational Commission—as well as members of the Council for International Exchange of Scholars—for ensuring that I would have the best possible experience as a Fulbrighter in Japan. I am eternally grateful for the enduring hospitality of Fulbright host family Keimi and Takako Harada, hosts Teruaki and Nobuko Kunitake, and Kaori Ito and her students in the Ito Lab at the Tokyo University of Science.

My Fulbright research was greatly enhanced by recommendations, contacts, and support offered by Dana Buntrock, Florian Idenburg, Kaori Ito, Charles and Yuriko Kite, Toshiko Mori, Hiroshi Ota, Ari Seligmann, George Wagner, Steve West, Julian Worrall, and Gretchen Wilkins. I am deeply indebted to all of the interviewees presented in this book for their time, effort, and commitment to this project, as well as Hiroshi Ota for his thoughtful essay. I am also thankful for the critical assistance provided by Tohru Horiguchi, Atelier Hitoshi Abe; Antoine Moriya and Tamao Shichiri, Tadao Ando Architects & Associates; Yuko Machida, Jun Aoki & Associates; Tamaki Terai, Shigeru Ban Architects; Ken Sogawa, Endo Shuhei Architect Institute; Naoe Kowatari, University of Tokyo; Mutsumi Tokumasu, Nippon Design Center; Mayumi Hosoo, Eriko Horiki & Associates; Eriko Kinoshita, Toyo Ito & Associates, Architects; Mariko Inaba, Kengo Kuma & Associates; Akihiro Ito, Nendo; Florian Idenburg and Etsuko Yoshii, SANAA; Satoko Tanazawa, Takaharu + Yui Tezuka Architects; Reiko Shimada, Makoto Sei Watanabe Architects' Office; Chika Muto, Atelier Tekuto; and Kei Ueda, Tokujin Yoshioka Design. I am also grateful for the help of Hideo Arai and Masanobu Iwata; Mark Dytham and Emi Takahashi; Masatoshi Iji; Kazuhiro Kojima and Kazuko Akamatsu; Shinji Ohmaki, Masumi Sasaki, and William Galloway; Kenji Nakamura and Kohei Nishiyama; Yoshi Shiraishi and Kazuo Hayakumo; Yoshinobu Tsujikawa; and Riken Yamamoto and Minako Ueda.

I received significant assistance in the development of the manuscript from Suma Pandhi, who translated and transcribed conversations conducted in Japanese; Kelly Day, who transcribed conversations conducted in English and assisted me in preparing the manuscript; and Laurie McGinley, who assisted me with photography and image management.

I also received help from the University of Michigan graduate students in my Matter in the Floating World seminar: Kanwal Aftab, John Beck, Emily Corbett, Glenn Ginter, Emmett Harrison, Pai-Kai Huang, Juliet Kim, Mary Martin, Adrienne McDaniel, Rebecca Morello, Reiji Moroshima, Amanda Olczak, Suma Pandhi, Ivelisse Ruiz, Matthew Soisson, Tyson Stevens, Tiffany Wang, and James Witherspoon. Elizabeth Turner also provided assistance during her independent study on Japanese housing at the University of Minnesota.

I would like to thank Renee Cheng, Tom Fisher, and the rest of the faculty, administration, and staff at the University of Minnesota School of Architecture for their support of this endeavor. I would also like to thank Kevin Lippert, Jennifer Thompson, and Becca Casbon at Princeton Architectural Press for believing in this project and seeing it through to completion.

In closing, I would like to convey my deepest gratitude to my wife, Heather, and sons, Blaine and Davis Brownell, who patiently accompanied me on countless architecture tours, museum trips, and exhibition visits in Japan and beyond. Their love, support, and willingness to share my personal exuberance for all things architectural and Japanese have made my life experience truly magical.

When the World Floats:
Material Buoyancy in Contemporary Design

The authenticity of materials is no longer guaranteed. The constructed world was once dominated by wood, stone, brick, iron, and bioderived fibers. However, we have now entered an age in which countless new materials are added to the patent database every day, and these materials are being harnessed by research laboratories, product manufacturers, and design firms to create new applications within the built environment. The fibers of our clothes, the tips of the ballpoint pens we use to write, and even the ingredients in the food we eat are constantly subject to change. To discount these alterations is to underestimate the significance of the massive material transformation currently underway.

In 1986 sustainable design expert Ezio Manzini clearly articulated this trajectory in his book *The Material of Invention*. Using the term "light recognition," Manzini addressed the loss of meaning in contemporary materials and instead emphasized materials' "performance-related identities."[1] His prediction came to pass, and we are now surrounded by objects like biodegradable plastic, transparent concrete, and sensory touch screens—products we don't understand in terms of material origins, but rather in terms of functional attributes. In 1995 architecture and design curator Paola Antonelli contributed to the critical assessment of contemporary materiality in her influential Mutant Materials exhibition at the Museum of Modern Art. Stating that "the mutant character of materials, as expressive as it is functional and structural, generates new forms and a more experimental approach toward design," Antonelli exposed the newfound freedoms in material production, proposing that the emphasis has shifted from material capabilities to the potentials of the human imagination.[2] In her assessment, Antonelli established the extent to which contemporary materiality is testing us, alluring us, and enthralling us.

Blaine Brownell's work here highlights this significant change in material culture from the perspective of Japanese contemporary design. In Japan, material is called *sozai*, which means "pure" or "white" matter. Traditionally, materials are consecrated when they are handled or altered, and are regarded as a rich source of inspiration. Craftsmen, carpenters, and even sushi chefs listen to the "internal voice" of materials, seeking to extract their intrinsic logic in order to fashion new objects. As clearly introduced in this book, this idea is alive and well in the work of contemporary Japanese architects and designers, who derive the syntax of designed objects and spaces from the hidden physics of materials. A major purpose of this book is therefore to communicate an awareness of physical transcendentalism in Japanese culture, which may certainly influence the international design sphere.

In his direct conversations with interviewees, Brownell successfully reveals the transient and ephemeral nature of the projects at the forefront of contemporary Japanese design. For example, in Tokujin Yoshioka's Venus chair—which incorporates the phenomenon of crystallization within the aesthetic of the object—there is no longer a distinct division between material and form, or *hyle* and *eidos*. It is much more indicative of Heraclitus's philosophy of *panta rei*, or "everything flows," reminding us that design is just a moment within a continual state of material flow. Materials like plastics, concrete, or liquid crystal displays are all employed for their characteristic state of liquidity, thus revealing the inherent inconstancy of matter in its various physical states. Moreover, the dynamic changes in today's society demand that materials become more changeable, reactive, and elastic. As a result, terms like dematerialization, ephemerality, and instability are frequently employed in the contemporary design process. This is an irreversible tendency seen not only in Japan, but also throughout the globalized world. Design must therefore uncover new possibilities within a constantly shifting context.

In our reading of *Matter in the Floating World*, we witness the ways in which matter also causes the world to "float." The many imaginative projects presented here defy our preconceptions toward expected material behavior in design, and project ephemerality through substance. This book is a record of the ways in which Japanese designers, researchers, craftspeople, and manufacturers are currently pursuing this preternatural buoyancy. It reveals a confidence in design intelligence, a passion for material sensitivity, and a "pure" and "white" attitude directed toward our common future. For this reason, I believe this book will make a distinct mark in its appraisal of humanity as well as materiality.

With respect to the contributors and author.

—Hiroshi Ota, Architect and Associate Professor, Institute of Industrial Science, the University of Tokyo

---

1 Ezio Manzini, *The Material of Invention* (Cambridge: MIT Press, 1989), 34. Manzini states: "In this case the new identities of image and/or performance, springing from various materials and various combinations of materials, would become the new words in a language of objects. They would lose, however, the 'weight' of meaning that words such as 'marble,' 'wood,' and 'steel' once had. The new recognizability of materials is destined to be a 'light recognition.'"

2 Paola Antonelli, *Mutant Materials in Contemporary Design* (New York: Museum of Modern Art, 1995), 17.

Kengo Kuma & Associates' Oribe Teahouse

Substance and Transience in Japanese Architecture and Design

> Many new buildings in Japan remind us of the poignancy of things on the verge of disappearing or, conversely, on the point of emerging. Experiencing them is a process of suspending architecture in a perpetually evanescent and temporary state of "in-between" where becoming and fading away, growth and decay, presence and absence, reality and fiction, silence and speech take place simultaneously—or perhaps are one and the same thing. It is in this sense that many of these designs evoke the images of elusive phenomena, of twilight, shadows, clouds, or mirage, and gain a certain ephemeral or fictive quality.
> —Botond Bognar, *The New Japanese Architecture*

Japanese architecture and design have long fascinated a global audience. The masterful combination of aesthetic elegance, functional pragmatism, technological sophistication, and precision in craft that characterizes exemplary works from Japan has exerted a strong influence abroad, especially during the last two centuries. The stylized organic forms of art nouveau, for example, were inspired by the inundation of Japanese wood-block prints and other artworks in Europe during the mid-nineteenth century.[1] Frank Lloyd Wright was profoundly influenced by Japan, and his celebrated Prairie Style works exhibited qualities reminiscent of the structures and spatial logic found in Japanese architecture.[2] Bruno Taut was also taken with the art of building in Japan, and his publicized acclaim for the Katsura Detached Palace, Ise Shrine, and other revered monuments established a new framework for understanding Japanese architecture from a Western perspective.[3]

In these and other examples, the enduring significance of Japanese architecture and design for foreign audiences has revealed a fascination with something deeper than mere visual or organizational qualities. The product of a homogeneous culture that developed in relative isolation over millennia, the Japanese creative process is connected to deeply embedded traditions and philosophies that define space and time as particularly precious commodities. As a result, Japanese design embodies a heightened awareness about the ephemerality of existence and the significance of the present moment. Japanese artists and craftspeople therefore approach their work with an acute interest in perception, seeking to enhance the viewer's multisensory experience. It is not enough for a creative work to be attractive or functional; it must also readjust expectations about reality. This elevated state of consciousness is possible when one is simultaneously aware of the physicality and ephemerality conveyed by a work, resulting in a vacillating condition of permanence and impermanence, emergence and dissolution, reality and illusion.

Artists and architects have long appreciated the value of uniting the concrete and the abstract. Creative endeavors are born somewhere within the inscrutable realm of consciousness and eventually assume physical form with the investment of labor and material. The process through which this exchange occurs remains a singular mystery, and eminent minds have attempted to give it definition. Louis Kahn wrestled with what he called the "measurable and the unmeasurable,"

12   Matter in the Floating World

Shokin-tei tea pavilion, Katsura Imperial Villa, Kyoto

Eriko Horiki & Associates' Mino Washi no Sato Kaikan

Ise Jingu

declaring that "the measurable is only a servant to the unmeasurable."[4] Japanese architect Kiyonori Kikutake incorporated physicist Mitsuo Taketani's theory of three elements—the phenomenal, the substantial, and the essential—as *ka*, *kata*, and *katachi*, proposing a parallel for the design process.[5] Inherent in these perspectives is the notion of a conduit that links consciousness to substance. Craft, procedure, and technique are tools used to bridge mind and matter, projecting ideas onto material. Although this marriage of concept and corporeality is an inherent part of the design process, it is a much more difficult prospect to create work that preserves a connection to the realm of ideas. As Kahn declared, "A great building, in my opinion, must begin with the unmeasurable, must go through measurable means when it is being designed and in the end must be unmeasurable."[6]

The Japanese creative psyche exhibited this approach long before Kahn's pronouncement, and the Japanese creative arts have captivated a global audience with their adroit embodiment of ephemerality within substance. This sensibility is evident in early works of Japanese architecture constructed for the worship of Shinto, Japan's native polytheistic religion. Ise Jingu, the Grand Shrine devoted to the goddess Amaterasu and originally constructed in the mid-eighth century, is the most-heralded example of Shintoism. As architect Kenzo Tange writes, "Ise came into being through the sublimation of symbols into a basic form"—a manifestation that "partakes of the primordial essence of the Japanese people."[7] A persistent program of rebuilding sustains this embodiment of religious symbolism. With the exception of a few historical lapses, Ise Jingu has been relocated and rebuilt every twenty years, alternating between two adjacent and identical sites. This cyclical reenactment of origins preserves the presence of the "unmeasurable" in a state of permanent suspension—a concept similar to what Martin Heidegger calls the "temporality of falling."[8] According to architect Arata Isozaki, "We are forever being lured toward whatever may be lurking in a beginning endlessly repeated."[9]

The spirit of Ise Shrine's frequent renewal resonates throughout Japanese art and architecture. In the eighteenth century, influential literary scholar Motoori Norinaga coined the phrase *mono no aware*, which has been translated as "sensitivity to things" as well as "awareness of the transient beauty of nature." In this simple expression, Norinaga captured the essence of Japanese attentiveness to the present moment, and the concept became a critical aesthetic principle in Japanese art and culture until modern times.[10] The celebration of transience was fundamental to the development of the *cha-no-yu* (tea ceremony) as well as Japanese garden design, in which seasonal changes were accentuated and embraced. Reveling in ephemerality was also a central theme in *ukiyo-e*, or "pictures of the floating world," which were produced in the latter seventeenth century to depict an evanescent, dreamlike realm of entertainment and beauty—in contrast to the banal experience of daily life. These developments relied upon articulating distinctions between corporeality and spirit, as well as reality and illusion.

Historians and critics have underscored the contrast between substance and permanence in Japanese art and architecture as a way of clarifying different physical, cultural, and conceptual attitudes. One dichotomy surfaced in the 1950s Jomon/Yayoi dispute, which juxtaposed the differing styles of the Japanese

Jomon (10,500–300 BCE) and Yayoi (300 BCE – 200 CE) archaeological periods. Painter Taro Okamoto, who sought to label the distinction between the abstract and concrete as "oppositionalism," characterized the earthy, rugged beauty of Jomon earthenware as populist and the clean, sophisticated terra-cotta works of Yayoi as elitist.[11] Okamoto's interpretation influenced architects like Kenzo Tange, who distinguished a raw, earth-bound architecture from one defined by lightness, refinement, and elevation.[12] Another schism developed between the different approaches for temple and teahouse construction. *Miya daiku,* or temple builders, were concerned with the structural resolution of large buildings that emanated a particular gravitas; meanwhile the *sukiya daiku*, or teahouse artisans, focused on crafting small-scale, delicate structures that seemed to float or disappear within their context.[13] More recently architect and historian Terunobu Fujimori has promulgated another dichotomy between what he calls the "red school" and the "white school."[14] According to Fujimori the red school is defined by mass, rawness, and realism, whereas the white school is characterized by lightness, elegance, and abstraction. Intended to illuminate the dissimilarities between contemporary architects like Arata Isozaki (red) and Fumihiko Maki (white), Fujimori proposes that red signifies earth, nature, and the body, while white symbolizes sky, artifice, and the mind.

Although these dichotomies establish stark contrasts, reality is decidedly less clear. Despite the fact that Fujimori feels that the white school is ascendant in contemporary Japanese design, he adds, "Nevertheless, we cannot clearly divide all architects into red and white. There are red elements in Maki's work and white is mixed into Isozaki's work."[15] Thus, the truth lies somewhere in the assimilated combination of the two tendencies. Moreover, differing sides are not actually engaged in cutthroat competition, but rather in a respectful dialogue about divergent viewpoints. After all, assimilation is a fundamental theme throughout Japanese history, and contrasting sides have often found common ground in a society that values social harmony and mutual respect. Architect Kisho Kurokawa's philosophy of symbiosis, for example, advocates a balanced coexistence of contrasting elements that are able to maintain their individual viewpoints without compromise.[16] This inherent predisposition toward assimilation helps explain Japan's remarkable ability to weather significant changes since the mid-nineteenth century, including Westernization, industrialization, modernization, post–World War II reconstruction, and the wholesale transformation of building construction from wood to steel and concrete. In the wake of such massive disruptions, the fact that Japanese architects and designers continue to address fundamental Japanese concepts today—despite the fact that their projects bear little or no resemblance to past works—is profoundly impressive.

Matter in the Floating World addresses the connection between materiality and transience in the work of twenty renowned contemporary Japanese architects and designers. The conversations presented here relate firsthand knowledge about the design methods, strategies, and ambitions they apply to create groundbreaking work. The dialogues also reveal personal insights about these remarkable human beings, exposing their struggles, surprises, aspirations, and successes—stories that dispel cultural barriers and transcend geophysical boundaries. All of these discussions bring to light a collection of common

15   Substance and Transience

Great Buddha Hall, Todai-ji, Nara

Dior Omotesando, SANAA—indicative of the white school

Genka-sen well, Kinkakuji, Kyoto

Shin-ken (Firewood Tearoom), Terunobu Fujimori— indicative of the red school interests, including material expertise and the precision of craft; a consideration for resources and the optimization of fabrication processes; a reduction of elements and simplification in approach; a connection to tradition with a focus on the future; an appreciation for multidisciplinarity and a respect for diverse backgrounds; and an open-mindedness and fearless enthusiasm for experimentation.

The conversations are organized according to four general themes that illustrate various approaches for embodying materiality and evanescence in architecture and design. Each theme has specific origins within Japanese culture as well as broad relevance for creative practices in other geographic regions. "Lightness" describes resource-sensitive approaches to achieving technologically sophisticated constructions via minimal material means. "Atmosphere" considers the formation of spaces that employ light and materials to stimulate curiosity and imagination. "Flow" examines spatial sequences that facilitate connectivity as well as multivalent surfaces that embody instability and transience. "Emergence" concerns the realization of complex structures and assemblies from the study of natural phenomena and ecological systems. Together, these themes convey the breadth of approaches employed by today's Japanese avant-garde to create exceptional works of architecture and design.

As the world continues to address seemingly intractable challenges, and proponents of design struggle to communicate its value, it is my desire that this collection of provocative discussions will provide wisdom and inspiration to a broad audience. I also hope that readers from all parts of the globe may find meaningful applicability of these visionary approaches to assimilating the measurable and immeasurable within their own work.

1 Debora L. Silverman, *Art Nouveau in Fin-de-Siecle France: Politics, Psychology, and Style* (Berkeley: University of California Press, 1992), 114.

2 Kevin Nute, *Frank Lloyd Wright and Japan: The Role of Traditional Japanese Art and Architecture in the Work of Frank Lloyd Wright* (London: Spon Press, 2000), 68.

3 Bruno Taut, *Houses and People of Japan* (Tokyo: Sanseido, 1958).

4 Louis I. Kahn, lecture to the students at the School of Architecture, ETH, Zurich, Feb. 12, 1969, reprinted as "Silence and Light—Louis I. Kahn at ETH 1969," in Heinz Ronner and Sharad Jhaveri, *Louis I. Kahn: Complete Works 1935–1974,* 2nd ed. (Basel, Switzerland: Birkhäuser, 1987), 6.

5 Kiyonori Kikutake, *Taisha Kenchiku Ron—Ka, Kata, Katachi* (*The Metabolic Theory of Architecture—Hypothesis, Form, Shape*) (Tokyo: Shokokusha, 1969).

6 "Voice of America—Louis I. Kahn. Recorded November 19, 1960" folder, Box LIK 53, Louis I. Khan collection, University of Pennsylvania and Pennsylvania Historical and Museum Commission.

7 Kenzo Tange and Noboru Kawazoe, *Ise, Prototype of Japanese Architecture* (Cambridge: MIT Press, 1965), 18–19.

8 Martin Heidegger, *Being and Time*, trans. John Macquarrie and Edward Robinson (San Francisco: Harper, 1962), 396. Arata Isozaki makes note of Heidegger in his essay on Ise (see next endnote).

9 Arata Isozaki, *Japan-ness in Architecture*, trans. Sabu Kohso (Cambridge: MIT Press, 2006), 146.

10 Robert E. Carter and Eliot Deutsch (foreword), *The Japanese Arts and Self-Cultivation* (Albany: State University of New York Press, 2007), 149. Carter and Deutsch explain that *mono no aware* emphasizes the fact that "the transiency of all things should only make them more precious in our eyes. The term refers to aesthetic sensitivity as an awareness of the richness and diversity of life where beauty and sadness as the awareness of the fleeting quality of all things meet."

11 Isozaki, *Japan-ness in Architecture*, 38–39.

12 Ibid., 39.

13 Thomas Daniell, *After the Crash: Architecture in Post-Bubble Japan* (New York: Princeton Architectural Press, 2008), 97.

14 Terunobu Fujimori, *Y'Avant-Garde Architecture* (Tokyo: Toto Shuppan, 1998), 16–17. Fujimori's model is intended to highlight contrasts in contemporary Japanese architecture, yet one can easily see its applicability to premodern examples. See also the conversation I had with Fujimori that appears in this book, pages 132–43.

15 Ibid., 17.

16 Kisho Kurokawa, *Intercultural Architecture: The Philosophy of Symbiosis* (Washington, DC: American Institute of Architects Press, 1991).

LIGHTNESS

Lightness has often been associated with modernity, in literal as well as figurative senses. In the book *All That Is Solid Melts into Air*, Marshall Berman captured the sweeping social changes caused by modernization, marking the dissolution of stable institutions and environments from advances in technology and industrialization.[1] Milan Kundera drew connections between a modernizing political sphere and personal freedoms in his novel *The Unbearable Lightness of Being*.[2] Architects like Buckminster Fuller embraced the enhanced strength-to-weight ratios made possible by modern engineering and sought to encapsulate maximum volume with minimal material in new constructions.

  Japan's affinity with lightness extends much farther back in time, as exemplified in elevated Yayoi-era structures or sukiya-style teahouse architecture. Even weighty, monumental buildings like the eighth-century Great Buddha Hall at Todaiji were articulated with nimble bracketing and graceful eave details, conveying an otherworldly presence. The delicacy and refinement exhibited by the seventeenth-century Katsura Detached Palace so impressed German architect Bruno Taut in 1933 that he celebrated its qualities in relationship to the emerging International Style, calling it "a masterpiece according to the measure of modern architecture."[3]

  The aesthetic predisposition toward lightness in Japan is connected to the nation's scarcity of natural resources—a limitation that influenced artisans and builders to develop consummate skill in working with materials. Lightness

Kengo Kuma & Associates' Pacific Flora 2004 Main Gate (opposite)

assumed enhanced meaning during Japan's post–World War II reconstruction, when a high level of resource productivity enabled the swift drive toward unprecedented industrial growth. The habitual transformation of drawbacks into opportunities in Japan has resulted in an association between frugality and prosperity—a relationship that resonates throughout contemporary Japanese architecture and design.

One strategy to achieve lightness is to reduce structure to minimal dimensions. The exaggerated, column-free spans of Tezuka Architects' buildings, for example, evoke surprise in their insubstantiality. The perforation of building envelopes with proportionately large, unobstructed apertures enhances this minimal approach by dissolving the boundary between inside and outside. Architect Kengo Kuma delights in this dissolution, intentionally blurring the edges between a building and its context. By investing considerable time in construction details, Kuma achieves lightness via a kind of material sleight of hand—making a glass-clad room appear to float on water, or a stone facade seem suspended in midair—in an effort to evoke a sense of unreality.

Another approach to lightness involves the fulfillment of multiple requirements with a minimal number of materials. This practical technique is seen in traditional Japanese devices such as the *hakokaidan*, or box staircase, which integrates a chest of drawers under a stair, or in *koshi*, or latticework, which supplies domestic privacy while affording light penetration. Atelier Tekuto's Cell Brick house exemplifies this multifunctional approach, with a series of thin boxes comprising structure, facade, and interior furniture. Design office Nendo endeavors to create uncommon functional pairings, such as a house enveloped by a communal library, or a bench that records the passage of time. These unexpected alignments of diverse uses inspire a small moment of surprise in the user—a kind of inner lightness that emerges during a moment of revelation. Also surprising is Shigeru Ban's realization of strong structures made with weak materials. His creation of complex, long-span vaults out of paper tubes—which are certainly among the lightest and most disposable of objects—astonished the architecture community in their apparent defiance of gravity. Ban also achieves lightness via low-impact approaches to material resources. His Nomadic Museum, for example, may be easily constructed in any major port, due to its utilization of plentiful, local shipping containers for structure and envelope. This heightened sensitivity to materials not only facilitates the realization of thoughtful and concise design approaches, but also the minimization of environmental impact.

---

[1] Marshall Berman, *All That Is Solid Melts into Air: The Experience of Modernity* (New York: Penguin, 1988).
[2] Milan Kundera, *The Unbearable Lightness of Being* (London: Faber and Faber, 1984).
[3] Arata Isozaki, *Japan-ness in Architecture*, trans. Sabu Kohso (Cambridge: MIT Press, 2006), 12.

Expanding Boundaries

A conversation with Takaharu Tezuka, Tezuka Architects

Takaharu Tezuka is convinced that buildings must push technological boundaries in order to be meaningful to society. This pursuit originates from a desire to integrate architecture more closely with its site through deeper connections between interior and exterior environments. In partnership with his wife, Yui, Tezuka bases building designs around these connections, with projects like House to Catch the Sea, Temple to Catch the Forest, and House to Catch the Sky. The result is a collection of extraordinary approaches toward envelope, structure, and aperture that achieve a closer association with nature.

Takaharu Tezuka was born in Tokyo in 1964. He earned a B.Arch from Musashi Institute of Technology in 1987 and an M.Arch from the University of Pennsylvania in 1990. From 1990 to 1994, he worked at the Richard Rogers Partnership in London, then returned to Tokyo to establish Tezuka Architects with his wife, Yui, in 1994. His firm has received international awards for projects such as the Roof House, Echigo-Matsunoyama Natural Science Museum, and Fuji Kindergarten. Tezuka has taught at the Musashi Institute of Technology (1996–2003), the Salzburg Summer Academy (2005–6), the University of California, Berkeley (2006), and Tokyo City University (2009–present).

Machiya House (opposite)

The first projects you and your wife designed after founding Tezuka Architects reveal the influence of your former mentor, Richard Rogers. However, as your work progressed, you seem to have developed your own distinct sensibility.

There's no doubt that Rogers's influence is quite clear and very difficult to disregard, but I knew we would have to develop our own language. With Richard Rogers, every detail has to be articulated beautifully, but Yui and I had to forget this approach because we wanted to make everything plain—and clean. Also, the funny thing is that Richard never liked to be called a "high-tech-style" architect. He is a modernist to the core, however, and he has always sought perfection and precision in architecture. Richard treated all of his employees like students, and as a result he would achieve things beyond his expectations.

Is that how you run your office as well?

Yes. This intern is making many models on her own initiative, for example [gestures toward employee]. She will make forty or fifty models and then I will join her and discuss various ideas. I always try to work with young architects with fresh ideas. I also let these architects run projects from the beginning to the end. Even inexperienced interns will eventually build up experience this way. Thus, our office is always changing. Of course, I supervise each design, and I have my own taste—however, I try to focus on the ideas. An ideal example is Louis Kahn. He did not simply give each architect a drawing or detail—he provided a way of thinking. His goal was to develop the logic for each project. So I always try to focus on the logic of each project with my employees. That is the most important thing, and that is what I learned from Richard Rogers.

This clarity of thinking is evident in your work. The Roof House, for example, doesn't require explanation—people immediately understand the way the roof is designed as a functioning, habitable space. The architectural diagram is incredibly clear. Your selection of materials is also very clear—materials are not merely applied; they support the logic of the project.

Actually, that is what we are trying to do. We can't be so pure all the time, however. You know, there are some really difficult clients and some challenges that prevent this kind of clarity. However, my belief is that we shouldn't attempt too many things on one project. If we were designing a city, it would be a different matter—but in that case, design variations should come from a variety of architects. I don't believe in the kind of fictional variety one sees in master-planned projects designed by one architect, for example.

When do you begin to think about materials in your projects?

Well, it is difficult to say when, because it really depends on the project. In the case of the Echigo-Matsunoyama Natural Science Museum, we decided upon Cor-Ten steel from the beginning.[1] When the competition was announced, we did a site visit and I immediately said, "I want to cover this in Cor-Ten steel." I wanted a material that would be durable and impart a monolithic feeling. Although concrete has these properties, it wouldn't have been as appropriate as steel for the long, thin shapes we wanted for the museum. The acrylic, however, was selected at the end of the competition.

The material for the windows? How did you determine that?

We couldn't find any other way to figure out the structure. We wanted one continuous, interrupted material for the window, but we wondered what could stand against the enormous pressure exerted by a heavy snowfall. My students and I were discussing this problem, and at the time we were drinking very strong Russian vodka [laughter]. I was really drunk and suggested many ideas. At one point, we discussed submarines, which have

---

[1] Cor-Ten is a weathering steel with increased resistance to corrosion due to a thin, protective layer on its surface. The first architectural application of Cor-Ten was in Eero Saarinen's Deere & Company World Headquarters, built in Moline, Illinois, in 1964.

Roof House (top), interior (middle), showing operable skylights (bottom)

We think that technology is the key to expanding the boundaries of architecture. Otherwise, if one always sticks to the same parameters, one can expect the same results.

Echigo-Matsunoyama Natural Science Museum (top), acrylic window night view (bottom)

Echigo-Matsunoyama Natural Science Museum, interior (above), acrylic window with snowpack (right)

acrylic windows.[2] So the whole idea came from a submarine. I asked, "Can we make it bigger?" Well, nobody knew, but it was just a competition at the time. Even if it would be impossible, we would never get sued just by proposing ideas. Also I knew it would be very expensive.

So we were a little nervous when we won first prize in the competition, because we didn't know if it would be possible. And it was very funny, you know. Legally, it was impossible.

Really?

Because acrylic is flammable, we would be endangering the visitors if we were to use it. However, we spoke to acrylic manufacturer Mitsubishi Materials, and they showed us a demonstration in which they burned acrylic in an oven at 1,500 degrees for thirty minutes. And the damage? Only 1.5 centimeters [0.59 inches] of material was burned away. Because once acrylic is thick enough, it cannot be burned—it is even stronger than glass. In this case, 75 millimeters [2.95 inches] of acrylic is stronger and less flammable than 5 or 6 millimeters [.2 or .24 inches] of plate steel. Despite this knowledge, our client was very concerned about the window's ability to support large snow loads. We were also nervous before the first winter, but the acrylic proved to be quite strong enough—even when completely blocked by snow. So you see, it's not easy to make a large acrylic window in a building, but you can do it. So far, ours is the only example of its size in Japan.

Amazing.

Currently we are designing a house for an art director, and we are searching for one material to use on the interior and exterior. So far, I think stucco is the only option. We could use concrete, but we also need insulation, which is easy to integrate with stucco. Also, stucco represents a kind of craftsmanship for us. So the project is going to be made entirely of stucco—every surface except for the floor.

Do you typically focus on one or two primary materials for each project?

---

2 According to German manufacturer Hydrosight Corp., the following three properties of acrylic are fundamental to its use in submarine windows: "1) Clear, distortion-free view; 2) Homogenous, monolithic character; and 3) Certified to be used for Pressure Vessels for Human Occupancy (PVHO-I)." www.hydrosight.com.

Yes—I don't like using many kinds of materials. Also, a material cannot serve as the primary concept. We have to be careful about this distinction. A material can be a great source of ideas, but it's just a starting point. A material is a kind of tool to achieve the end of design and should be a part of design. However, if the material dictates architecture, we overlook the importance of human beings.

Very interesting. Speaking of human beings, how do you involve clients in material selection?

Well, I tell them, "This is the best material," and when they don't like the material, I always get sacked.

Really?

Yes, sometimes I get sacked. Just the last few months, I have been sacked so many times.

Oh no.

It's not good news these days. But yesterday we formalized a new contract, so the work is coming back now.

Well, I certainly wish you luck. I imagine your approach requires a clientele with a stomach for risk, since you always want to push limits in architecture. From acrylic windows to cantilevered structures, you seem determined to exceed the common boundaries of material applications and engineering.

It's very important, because we think that technology is the key to expanding the boundaries of architecture. Otherwise, if one always sticks to the same parameters, one can expect the same results. We work very closely with the structural engineer, because good cooperation in the development of the structure usually leads to good design. I think almost all of our projects seek innovation in structure, because structure changes architecture—and space.

Could you please elaborate?

Take the example of a column-and-beam connection. If a column is moved just a little bit during the design process, a different space results—since columns define boundaries for internal space. Once we move just one column, the key element, we don't know where space stops. In our office building for Toyota, there is a span of 45 meters [148 feet].

That's significant.

You know, forty-five meters is not an easy span, and once we move a column just a little bit, the space becomes totally different. You cannot necessarily perceive that in photography, but if you go there, you will feel it. Some architects may not like to reveal the existence of structure, but if we design with structures, we can affect how structures will be perceived. New structures bring new perception.

I think of your Wall Less House, for example, in which several floors are cantilevered from an offset central core. The structural tension seems palpable. Do you begin every project thinking about how you can push structural boundaries?

Exactly. Whatever we design, structure comes with it.

And do you typically work with the same structural engineer?

Yes, actually. We used to work with one engineer who was very good, but he collapsed due to failing health and subsequently closed his office.

That's terrible.

Hiroshi Ono is in charge of our projects now—he used to work for the same structural engineer we worked with. We have been collaborating with him since the Roof House.

The continuity of this relationship must be very important to your work, so that when you get a new client, you can be prepared to break ground together from the outset. Do clients bring bold ideas to you, or do you interpret client needs in unconventional ways? With the Roof House clients, did you say, "You seem to like eating on the roof, so let's make a roof house," for example?[3]

---

3 The clients of the Roof House used to enjoy meals together on the roof of their previous house. Tezuka took inspiration from this activity and designed the roof of their new house explicitly for this purpose.

Toyota L&F Hiroshima (left), interior (right)

The electric pole is
the worst thing we have.
We should chop it up.

Wall Less House (above), interior (below)

I would say that I always get extraordinary clients. The Roof House was a special project. Over 70 percent of clients have no idea about architecture, so they just wait for the answer. However, 30 percent of clients have very strong ideas. So we have to work with them. If the client doesn't agree with the design, however, we try to get sacked [both laughing]. That's very important to the design, because otherwise my time is burdened by a project with limited potential.

It must take chutzpah to turn away work and keep an office going. What about environmental concerns associated with materials? Do clients address this issue?

Yes. We are living in the twenty-first century, and it's quite easy to find challenges with materials. Now the most important aspect of a material is not durability; it's how a material is considered. For example, some architects like to use aluminum, but they are not really trying to find an environmentally friendly material. Aluminum conveys a particular cultural attitude for them, and it can be used as structure. Really strong materials can be used to withstand earthquakes, and we now have sophisticated means of dampening seismic loads in buildings. However, you should know that most modern buildings are not destroyed by earthquakes, but by people's dislike for them. When we talk about architecture, we emphasize the word "fondness," because it is critical to buildings' longevity that they are beloved.

For example, there are old traditional houses in Kyoto whose owners care for them as a matter of habit. They have paper screens—thin paper—and if the screens break, their owners simply replace them. Paper is not a particularly durable material, but it has some meaning. However, architecture today has lost that kind of meaning for people.

Why is that?

Perhaps because we lost a lot of our culture. I think the worst thing that happened after World War II is that we lost a lot of traditional Japanese culture. When I was in elementary school, I was told that we needed to become more like the United States. Eventually, however, things changed—about five or six years after I finished elementary school. Now we know that Japan has so much to offer. That time period changed not only people's attitudes, but also our cities and towns. At the point we became aware of the importance of our culture, it was too late—we would have to rebuild. So I think the most important thing to build now—the thing that will really lead to a durable, long life—is architecture that can be lovingly maintained by people. That is sustainability, and that is the most important thing.

That's profound. You mentioned the need to rebuild—could you please explain that?

Sometimes we just don't know what we're rebuilding because we don't know the future. But the future is always constructed from daily life. The future cannot be planned. In the 1960s or 1970s, people used to say that our lives could be planned—but we know this isn't the case. We know that as long as people are aware of their culture, then they will naturally tend to rebuild their environment. It simply takes a long time. I think we need at least fifty years in Tokyo, which is still changing.

In what way do you envision Tokyo rebuilt? How would you prefer that it be transformed?

Well, I would imagine, as many people do, lots of green and many people in the street. You know, I think it's always a balance. If we focus only on greening, then the city planners start saying, "OK, we should set architecture as far back from the street as possible." Then we lose the contact between architecture and the street. So in the city, I always say that the walls should be right on the edge of the street.

---

4 The Environmental Protection Agency defines urban heat-island effect in this way: "As urban areas develop, changes occur in their landscape. Buildings, roads, and other infrastructure replace open land and vegetation. Surfaces that were once permeable and moist become impermeable and dry. These changes cause urban regions to become warmer than their rural surroundings, forming an 'island' of higher temperatures in the landscape." www.epa.gov/hiri/.

Fuji Kindergarten

Balcony House

> Most modern buildings are not destroyed by earthquakes, but by people's dislike for them. When we talk about architecture, we emphasize the word "fondness," because it is critical to buildings' longevity that they are beloved.

That makes the street alive, right? And green is the best way to cool the city down, you know?

Right—reducing the urban heat-island effect.[4] However, we shouldn't put green on top of architecture. There are so many wrong things about green architecture. But if you just plant a tree in the ground, you create a shadow and it makes the street more alive.

I would say that the electric pole is a problem. You know, the electric pole is the worst thing we have. We should chop it up.

You're saying that utilities should disappear altogether—be buried under the street? We are supposed to be a developed country, right? But we still have this ugly thing. The government always tells people to chop the branches off their trees so they don't endanger the utility lines. That's so stupid. So it's quite simple—we need more green, and a lot of people in the street.

Power lines tend to dominate the Japanese streetscape. Some of the minimalist dwellings designed by Japanese architects appear to be intentional refuges from the visual and aural noise of the city. Do you think this is a valid architectural response to a frenetic urban environment? Some projects are so pure that they act independently from the urban fabric. In Tokyo, this kind of purity and beauty stand apart—it's so obvious. However, we like architecture that connects with people—not only on the inside, but also on the outside.

Right. You also incorporate large apertures and interactive elements in your projects— like sliding doors, windows, or skylights— that bridge interior and exterior space. These devices play an important role in providing building occupants with superior control over their domain. They are also significant tactile interfaces. Yes, yes. Actually, we were thinking recently about the existence of the window. If you put a solid door in the middle of a clear glass

For many reasons, architects have used fixed windows. However, we always feel that to open a window has a stronger meaning and makes better architecture. And so I think our projects are really dependent on the window. The window must be open.

Floating Roof House (top), interior (above), at night (bottom)

Cloister House

window, it reads as a "window" so long as it is operable. So the function of the solid, operable door is stronger than the function of a transparent, fixed window. Thus, the window is really about the quality of architecture.

For example, let's assume you cut a section through a window wall. If there's no difference between the outside and inside, then you don't have a window; you have a hole. But if there is a difference, then you have a window. Do you understand what that means? "Window-ness" is not simply about adding a window; it is about achieving differentiation between outside and inside. It's about changing the quality of the architecture.

I see. By definition, a window changes the environment—the atmosphere.

If you just put a wall with a hole in the middle of a solid field, it's not a window at all; just a hole. But if the inside and outside are separated by a material, the aperture can become a window. It's not the same thing.

That means that the window itself represents the meaning of architecture and also the construction of architecture.

How does this thinking about the window inspire your current and future work? Are you attempting to expand the parameters of the window as you have done with structure?

Well, it's not difficult to foresee the future; we always try to do that [both laughing]. But the one thing I can tell you is that in Tokyo, we should be able to open the window. That is the only thing we are quite sure about. This operability changes the quality of architecture quite a lot. For many reasons, architects have used fixed windows. However, we always feel that to open a window has a stronger meaning and makes better architecture. And so I think our projects are really dependent on the window. The window must be open.

The Presence of Absence

A conversation with Kengo Kuma, Kengo Kuma & Associates

Not one for bland proclamations, Kengo Kuma has said he wants to erase architecture. This desire comes from an interest in designing buildings that fully blend with their surroundings. Utilizing simple forms defined by delicate structures of light-emitting filigree, Kuma's architecture appears blurry—as if frozen in a permanent state of becoming. Kuma is a master of material experimentation, transforming stone, wood, metal, and plastic into superthin, gravity-defying surfaces in an effort to define a new, ephemeral Japanese space.

One of Japan's most prominent architects, with a growing international practice, Kengo Kuma was born in 1954. He received an M.Arch at the University of Tokyo in 1979 and conducted research with the assistance of an Asian Cultural Council Fellowship from 1985–86 as a visiting scholar at Columbia University, New York. He established his office, Spatial Design Studio, in 1987 and Kengo Kuma & Associates in Tokyo in 1990. He has also taught as a professor of architecture at Keio University since 1998. Among his numerous awards are the Architectural Institute of Japan Award (1997), American Institute of Architects DuPont Benedictus Award (1997), Togo Murano Award in Japan (2001), International Stone Architecture Award in Italy (2001), and the International Architecture Award (2007). His internationally recognized works include the Water/Glass House (1995), Hiroshige Museum (2000), Stone Museum (2000), Plastic House (2002), Lotus House (2005), Suntory Museum (2007), and the Asahi Broadcasting Corporation Headquarters (2007).

Z58 office and showroom (opposite)

> Japanese architecture in the latter half of the twentieth century was largely preoccupied with a kind of formal exuberance, evident in the Metabolist projects or Japanese postmodernist structures.[1] I would characterize your early work in this way as well. After the initial projects, however, you completely changed course and have since emphasized the simplification of form and prioritization of material detail. I imagine such a transformation involved significant risk, since architecture that relies upon well-executed material details for the bulk of its success places a considerable amount of trust in the construction process and the faith of the client. During the design stage of your projects, do you ever grow concerned that the forms are too simple—perhaps bordering on the simplistic?

I am not at all afraid of things being too simple. This is because I am always making an effort to be simple. For example, I made such an effort with the Bamboo House. Its simplicity and clean appearance required a lot of time to develop, and so I was not ashamed of it. The project took a lot of time and I designed it with a particular determination. It may not seem apparent, but actually this simplicity was achieved by the effort of many—which is also something not to be ashamed of.

> I think this element of time is perceptible in your projects. Compared to other contemporary architecture, your work seems to require significant effort to produce.

Oh yes, it takes a lot of time [laughing]. With typical buildings, details are decided upon in the final stages. Because I decide on the details from the start, the work takes a lot of time at the beginning. With typical buildings, the site is chosen, then form, and lastly the details. By then, there is less time for the details—only standard details are considered because of the limited time. We do decide upon some details toward the end of the project, but we think about most of the details at the beginning. For example, if we have a year to design, we think about those details for a whole year. In that way, we do not leave things to the end.

> That's interesting! Your process would be counterintuitive for most architects, who focus on details at the end of a project. Since you mentioned details, I would like to discuss your idea of "particles" in architecture.[2] Many of your details are designed to dematerialize matter, allowing light to filter through perforated surfaces or delicate lattice structures. This theme is shared by projects having different programs and sites—such as the Takasaki Parking Building or Hiroshige Museum of Art—yet you alter the nature of this lattice for each project.

In the Takasaki project, I considered the surrounding space as well as the size of the particles and their relationship. I thought of the conceptual system as simple and finely grained—in the same way that the particles in the Hiroshige Museum are simple, small, and numerous. With the Takasaki project, however, the system became a kind of mess—meaning that the particles became random. I felt that balance could be achieved if the particles were a little larger, in equilibrium with the larger surface. The Takasaki project was designed this way so the details would be in balance with the larger facade.

> You described the Hiroshige Museum of Art as being a "sensor of light." Could you explain this concept? Is it related to the intentionally blurred figure-ground reading of the lattice?

If you change the openings of a space, light will come in. The way light enters changes. With a lattice pattern, there is contrast between the foreground and background. Depending on the light angle, the shift between foreground and background becomes ambiguous. For example, as you said with figure-ground, the particles of light can be either figure + ground, or ground +

---

1 Metabolism, a Japanese architectural movement begun in the 1960s, was interested in notions of biological growth and renewal. Its primary members were Kenzo Tange, Arata Isozaki, Kiyonori Kikutake, and Kisho Kurokawa.

2 See Kuma's description of "particlizing" in Botond Bognar, *Kengo Selected Works* (New York: Princeton Architectural Press, 2005), 16.

Great (Bamboo) Wall (top), stair (above), bamboo framing (left)

With typical buildings, the site is chosen, then form, and lastly the details. By then, there is less time for the details—only standard details are considered because of the limited time.

Lotus House (top), detail of stone curtain (above)

Takasaki Parking Building

Hiroshige Museum of Art (left), interior (right)

figure. This ambiguity allows architecture to become a light sensor. For example, a thin thread will move when the wind blows, but a thick piece of thread will not move. The thinner thread is more delicate and makes a good sensor.

> I presume that by using simple, thin elements, you can create architecture that harnesses light to create complex visual effects. I wonder if the delicate voids in your structures relate to the Japanese concept of *ma*—the strategic pause inherent in the timing of Noh drama or the intentional void spaces in Japanese art.[3]
>
> Do you apply the concept of ma to your work?

Ma is a very necessary thing. For example, a lattice is like a roof's pitch: you can see how much space is in between. This is microspace. At a bigger scale, there are two elements—the solid and the space in between. There are two buildings in the Hiroshige Museum. Going into the middle is the most important. In Noh theater, the stage and audience share a common space. Because this interior ma space is critically important, it must be the most beautiful space. It is therefore not an object, but space that I am focusing on.

> I feel that the void framed by the Shizuoka International Garden and Horticultural Exhibition is such a space. There is so much

material suspended in midair; it feels like a floating building. The structure appears to vacillate between an object and a space.

Yes, yes [laughs].

> With this and other buildings, there is a sense that the architecture is in the process of disappearing—or coming into existence but not yet fully formed. Your Water/Glass House creates a similar effect with different materials, for example. Where does this phenomenon of floating originate? You have written about artwork created during the ukiyo-e—or floating world—period in Japanese history.[4] Did this movement inspire your work?

No—but, yes, perhaps. Actually, I had not thought of it that way. *Fuyou-e* means floating world, but to a Japanese person ukiyo-e actually means something different.[5] But if you think about it—it can be a floating world. That's interesting [laughing]. I have a deep interest in

---

3 Ma is a concept that has many meanings and loosely describes an interval. Arata Isozaki defines nine aspects of ma in his book *Japan-ness in Architecture*. Some of the definitions are interstice, darkness, aperture, transience, and projection of the body. Arata Isozaki, *Japan-ness in Architecture*, trans. Sabu Kohso (Cambridge: MIT Press, 2006), 327–28.

4 See my description of ukiyo-e on p. 13.

5 Fuyou literally means "to float."

40 Matter in the Floating World　　　Lightness

> In Noh theater, the stage and audience share a common space. Because this interior ma space is critically important, it must be the most beautiful space.

Pacific Flora 2004 Main Gate

Water/Glass House (below),
pool detail (right)

Chokkura Plaza and Shelter

I have a deep interest in what is fictional. What I like is when something real is hovering just a little bit.

Something real has a little bit of mutability. Reality is only truly perceived in the presence of some unreality.

Steel House, interior

what is fictional. What I like is when something real is hovering just a little bit [demonstrates by raising teacup slightly above the table surface]. Something real has a little bit of mutability. Reality is only truly perceived in the presence of some unreality.

> Really? Why is something real only if it is a little bit unreal?

If it is a little unreal, there is a little bit of a surprise. If there is no surprise with something, it is not real, because it goes unnoticed. It might as well not exist. When I first realized this I thought, "Oh, things can be that way." It's very interesting.

> I agree. You seem to use many different materials in the service of this idea, including stone, wood, metal—even orange vinyl. What is your interest in using such a variety of materials?

I like designing experimentally.

> Are there any materials you refuse to specify?

I cannot really use concrete. It is not necessarily the strong material that people think it is. Before World War II, concrete was not very common in Japan, but then suddenly it became ubiquitous.[6] It is convenient and cheap, and has been overused. I think it has taken over the Japanese city. For this reason, I am always thinking about how to challenge concrete.

> Concrete does not seem appropriate for your particle theme. It may have positive qualities, but it also has weak points like high embodied energy and CO_2 production. What do you think about such issues? Japan has been an innovator concerning material resources, for example. Can Japanese architects provide leadership in combating global warming?

I think global warming is a very important problem. We need creative solutions. It's not effective to force solutions. I am interested in solving environmental problems creatively; otherwise it's boring for people. It's a small step, but when I use wood, CO_2 can be contained inside of it. We need many creative solutions like this one.

> How do you envision your future architecture? What will change in your work?

I want to pick up on the strengths of various places. Currently local character is being destroyed by mass standardization. By using local materials, I will relate to the qualities of a particular locale. I am interested in this kind of contextual approach.

> What would you define as a dream project?

When I travel to a new place, everything about it is a dream project. A new project is a dream place for me. A new site is always a space for dreaming. If there is a place I haven't been or a material I haven't seen, it is really a dream. It doesn't matter how small it is. Not a place for a museum, but a site where I could create a really small space would be interesting. It would be fun to do this somewhere I haven't been yet.

> I once had the chance to visit Le Corbusier's Petit Cabanon at Roquebrune-Cap-Martin. It had a really strong effect on me. I thought that by the end of his career Le Corbusier could design anything, yet for his final home he designed a tiny cabin for a minimal existence, facing the sea. I think that was his dream project.

That's true [laughter].

---

[6] Wood was almost completely replaced by concrete and steel in new structures. See Thomas Daniell, *After the Crash: Architecture in Post-Bubble Japan* (New York: Princeton Architectural Press, 2008), 46: "The use of wood, as both structure and surface, is the essence of Japanese architecture. In premodern Japan, wood was the primary building material, but following the firestorms that devastated Japan's cities during the final months of World War II, its use became almost extinct. Postwar reconstruction was primarily in concrete and steel, even for temples."

The Presence of Absence

A new site is always a space for dreaming. If there is a place I haven't been or a material I haven't seen, it is really a dream. It doesn't matter how small it is.

Z58 office, exterior detail

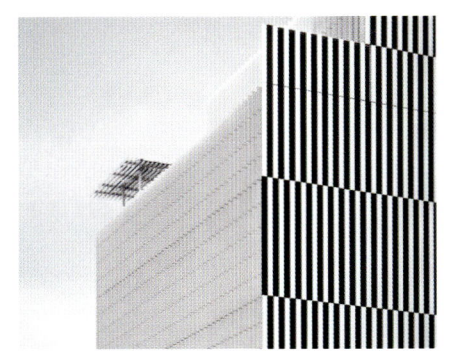

Suntory Museum of Art (above), exterior detail (right)

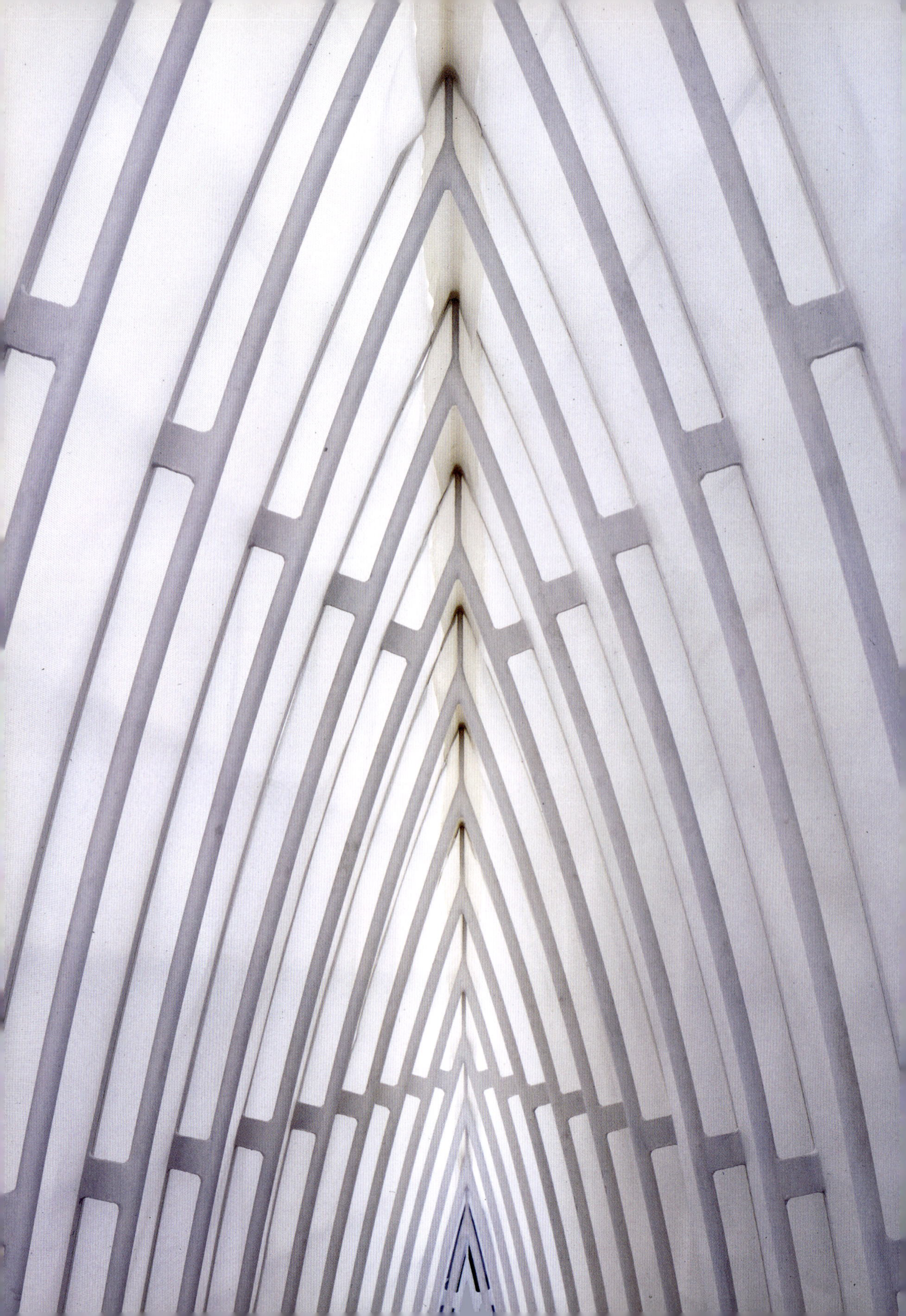

Weightless Surfaces

A conversation with Yasuhiro Yamashita, Atelier Tekuto

Architect Yasuhiro Yamashita perceives part and whole to be one and the same, and the intelligence of his buildings is reflected within their details. Yamashita's early career involved designing dwellings on tiny, residual sites—so-called "pet architecture" that treats limited circumstances as opportunities. As a result, Yamashita understands how to maximize space, daylight transmission, and other desirable qualities under challenging conditions. His works are characterized by multifunctional surfaces that integrate structure, aperture, cladding, and storage with minimal resources—thus conveying an exceptional lightness.

Yasuhiro Yamashita was born in Kagoshima, Japan, in 1960. He received an M.Arch from the Shibaura Institute of Technology in 1986 and then worked for Yutaka Saito Architect & Associates, PANOM, and Shunji Kondo Architects. He established Yamashita Kai Architectural Office in 1991, which was renamed Atelier Tekuto in 1995. Receiving international attention for projects such as the Penguin House (2002), Cell Brick (2004), Lucky Drops (2005), Reflection of Mineral (2006), and the Ethiopia Millennium Pavilion (2009), Yamashita has received the Good Design Award (2005), International Architecture Award (2008), and the Space Design Competition Gold Prize (2009). He has taught at the Shibaura Institute of Technology (1999–2007), the University of Tokyo (2008), and the Tokyo University of Science (2008–present).

Lucky Drops, FRP assembly detail (opposite)

Cell Brick, kitchen

I'm curious about how you create architecture from the mass aggregation of cellular units, as seen in the Cell Brick and Crystal Brick projects.
The part and the whole are the same thing. Like a cell in the body, the part signifies the whole.

So the intelligence of the whole is embedded in the modules?
Human beings are made completely of cells—for example, the brain has millions of nerve cells. It is through the connections between these brain cells that consciousness emerges. I think about space in the same way. The part and the whole are interdependent and have the same value.

Is it difficult to consider these different scales simultaneously?
No. In the Japanese Shinto religion, there are various spirits that reside within things.[1] I am not religious, but this is an interesting model. There is a degree of singularity in all things, so size is irrelevant.

I also noticed that the part does not have one purpose—it has many purposes. For example, the Cell Brick module functions as skin, shell, structure, and interior furniture.
Yes, the skin has a variety of functions, but these functions are accommodated by one element. If the budget is tight, one element can assume more than one role—like the movie actor Eddie Murphy [laughter]. He sometimes plays three, four, or five roles, so the movie studio gets five characters for the cost of one actor.

Do building regulations pose a challenge to this model?
Yes, of course [laughter]—but not all the time. If the client and I have the same desires that conflict with the code, then we always try to challenge it. However, if the client wants to play it safe, we will meet the building regulations. Sometimes clients initiate their own challenging requests, such as a desire for an unusual kind of glass. In this case, we would do all we can to assist them.

Speaking of glass, how you research materials for your projects?
I collect information from a variety of sources. I rely on the media, but I also seek information from personal contacts. For example, if you make a new material, I want to know about it. Meeting people becomes information, and I enjoy the process of discovering this information and putting it to use.

---

1 Japan's indigenous, polytheistic religion of Shinto seeks harmony with the natural world and emphasizes ritual purification.

Cell Brick

Crystal Brick, interior

The brain has millions of nerve cells. It is through the connections between these brain cells that consciousness emerges. I think about space in the same way. The part and the whole are interdependent and have the same value.

Your projects appear to celebrate this material information. In the Layers project, for example, you employ a variety of materials to address multiple surfaces in similar ways. The typical method is to address different surfaces in divergent ways—such as a ceiling, wall, or floor having different treatments.

The floor, wall, and ceiling are surfaces that people decided had different functions. These surfaces are each separate parts, but they are in fact the same surface. When I think of it this way, the surfaces have no weight and assume an abstract meaning. In terms of perception, light or wind might be kinds of "surface." People understand space by seeing it. Currently I am researching how people understand space.

The Lucky Drops house seems to adopt the strategy of light as surface, in the sense that it is clad in a thin, illuminated membrane.

Lucky Drops has an incredibly thin site, which is 30 meters [98 feet] long, and from 2.8 to 3.2 meters [9 to 10.5 feet] wide. In order to receive light, we had to design the building a certain way. The areas above and to the side were small, so I wanted light to enter from all sides. The walls and roof merged, so basically the exterior is all roof. We used fiber-reinforced plastic (FRP) panels for light transmission.

And the floor is metal.

Yes, in order to provide light to the lower level, the floor had to be expanded metal. As a result, light enters through the FRP material and "drops" everywhere through the expanded metal.

Light is clearly an important theme for your work.

Yes, it is a theme that happens naturally. Light, air, and greenery—these are all things necessary to humanity.

Gravity is another theme that influences your work. For the Magritte house, you attempted to design the concrete as if it were escaping gravity—as in Magritte's surrealist paintings.[2]

When Newton described an apple falling, he was probably generalizing about a force that was unknown. When I think of the law of gravity, it seems like the natural answer. Yet for him it was not natural—or at least not yet a "law." His was an important moment of insight and discovery. I want to do the same thing for antigravity.[3] I would like people to begin to feel that antigravity is natural.

You not only alter expectations regarding gravity, but also material properties. For example, you use heavy and light materials in opposing ways. In the Magritte house, the concrete has a quality of lightness. By comparison, the Aluminum House has a heavy quality—despite the fact that its aluminum is much lighter.

Yes, one expects concrete to be heavy, so we employ a sense of antigravity. Aluminum is very light and typically has a smooth surface, but we sandblast the texture and it looks heavier. When you see it, it looks really heavy and imparts a substantial feeling, but it's actually light.

The Aluminum House has a special structure.

Yes, it has a prestressed structure, which is the same as the Jyu-bako project. All of the walls and beams are made with one extrusion piece and one type of panel molding.

This kind of structure requires intensive research. Do you actively collaborate with universities and consultants?

Yes. The knowledge required to safely execute this kind of project is not readily available, so you have to collaborate—often with the manufacturer. For example, for the Crystal Brick project I collaborated with a glass brick manufacturer, a structural engineer, Tokyo University, a glass fabricator, and a contractor. Of course, you must collaborate with the client as well—making six groups in total. A group this size can actually make progress when one person could not. When you work collaboratively, a project can have greater success.

---

2 René Magritte's general approach toward dismantling a viewer's preconceptions in painting is a strategy that Yamashita often considers in architecture.

3 By this statement, we may interpret that Yamashita doesn't merely want to surprise; he wants us to become comfortable with the unexpected.

Layers

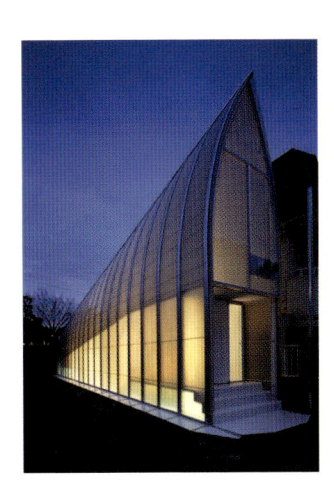

*Lucky Drops (left),
lower-level interior (bottom)*

The floor, wall, and ceiling are surfaces that people decided had different functions. These surfaces are each separate parts, but they are in fact the same surface. When I think of it this way, the surfaces have no weight and assume an abstract meaning.

Magritte, upper-level interior (left), lower-level interior (right)

Aluminum House

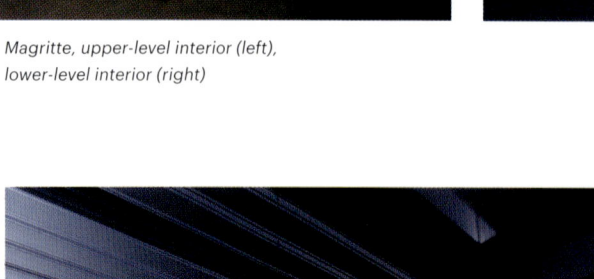

I would like people to begin to feel that antigravity is natural.

Jyu-bako

Is this a typical process for Japanese architecture?

No. Large projects merit this kind of collaboration in Japan, but small projects typically do not receive this kind of attention.

It is certainly rare in the U.S.

If you can do it, it's fun. If I have the opportunity, I gather the necessary people and collaborate. It is only natural. I myself am not a special person, and I can't do it alone. We work with talented engineers, as the standard of becoming a structural engineer in Japan is very high.

I imagine the Glucks Garten project required some innovative engineering.

Yes, the structure is strange. It is a concrete moment-resisting frame or wall structure. The beams become walls, and the walls become beams. It's good to have no border. The plan for the second- and third-level apartments is the same, but the shape of the cross section changes and the light quality varies as a result.

Does this structural idea occur in the Reflection of Mineral house?

No, the surfaces are merely changing in that project. We used the idea of the mineral to suggest that there could be different surfaces with varying opacity, just as light is reflected or transmitted through crystals at different angles. The quality of the interior space is enriched from this varied and multifaceted geometry.

You must work with some unusual clients.

Actually, they are pretty typical. Many clients want the design process to be interesting. If they are told that a particular design feature will be the first in the world, then they want to do it.

That's a good client!

Yes, it is a good kind of client.

Do your clients request more environmentally conscious design features? Sustainability has become a mainstream topic in Japan as well as in the U.S.

Ecology and sustainability are the most important words for twenty-first-century architecture. We need to reduce our CO_2 emissions, optimize material use, as well as reuse and recycle resources. The traditional *minka* residence in Japan was continually constructed and reconstructed over one hundred years ago.[4] This is the kind of project I am interested in.

We discussed using one element to accomplish multiple functions, which might be considered sustainable. Minimizing material use may also be considered a sustainable strategy. The steel skin of Penguin House, for example, is extremely narrow.

It is actually 3 millimeters [.12 inches] thick, with 1 millimeter [.04 inches] of insulating paint.

Unbelievable. Isn't this kind of paint expensive?

---

[4] Minka are traditional, private Japanese residences for artisans or farmers.

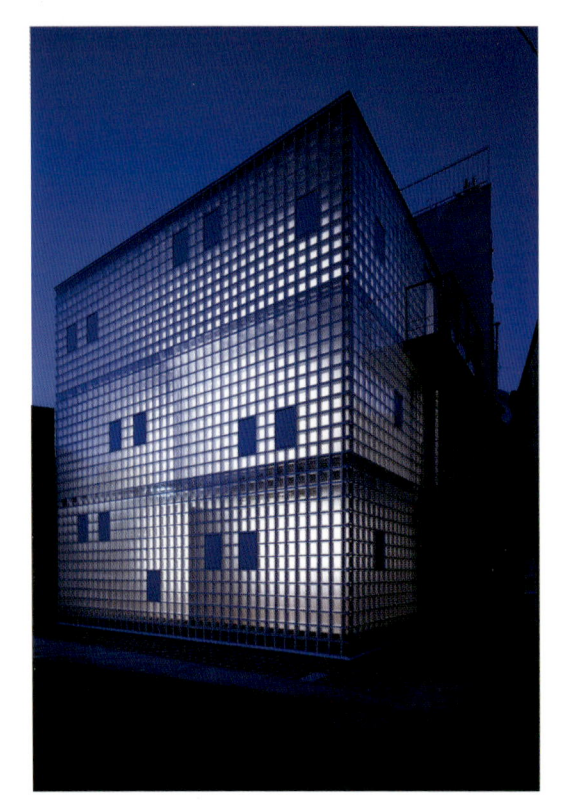

Crystal Brick

The beams become walls, and the walls become beams. It's good to have no border.

Glucks Garten

53 Weightless Surfaces Yasuhiro Yamashita

Reflection of Mineral (top),
interior (bottom)

Yes. It was originally developed by NASA to protect spacecraft from extreme temperatures. The kind we used was modified a little by Japanese scientists. The Penguin House marks the first time this paint was used on a residential surface in Japan.

Amazing.

It is a sustainable strategy to minimize materials, and it's a structural optimization strategy as well.

Making the most of residual land is also a sustainable strategy—such as with Lucky Drops.

Yes. Sites like this are considered trash. We are renewing these accumulating, forgotten, unwanted sites with our projects. Because the sites are undesirable, they are cheap, so young people buy the sites.

The Wafers project appears to float above its site. The construction process must have been challenging.

I like structure. I develop the structure and the conceptual idea at the same time.

Penguin House, window detail (top), interior (bottom)

I meet with the structural engineer, and the form and structure develop simultaneously.

What sustainable strategies have you applied in the design of the Nakdong Estuary Eco Center?

I mainly used local materials, such as Korean pine and ceramic tile. There are a lot of windows that illuminate the space, and we used solar-powered exterior lighting.

You are doing interesting work in other countries, such as in Ethiopia.

For the Ethiopian new year, we transported an old wooden Japanese house to Gondar, which is a UNESCO World Heritage site. The design effort for the so-called Millennium Pavilion involved adapting the structure to the new environment, and we are currently raising the necessary funds to incorporate solar panels and connect a wind turbine and pump for ground water. The house will be a training facility where local traditional crafts will be taught.

That must have been a rewarding experience and an interesting departure from practice in Japan. Do you have other sites in mind for this kind of work?

Yes. If you can, please call someone in the U.S. for me [laughter]. I would love to design projects in the U.S. as well as Europe. Since my design strategies are completely influenced by context, my work would probably be quite different in the West. This difference excites me.

Nakdong Estuary Eco Center

Wafers

A Small "!" Moment

A conversation with Oki Sato, Nendo

One of the youngest members of Japan's design vanguard, Oki Sato is a prolific inventor of objects and environments that disarm the casual observer. Despite their simplicity, Sato's works are imbued with multiple layers of meaning, and they systematically disrupt the viewer's initial preconceptions. Making use of a range of materials and technologies, Sato crafts these small, artfully choreographed elements of surprise not only to heighten our awareness of time and place, but also to engage broader themes in daily life.

Oki Sato was born in Toronto, Canada, in 1977. After obtaining a B.Arch and M.Arch from Waseda University, he founded design firm Nendo in 2002. Sato received critical acclaim for lighting and furniture designs in Tokyo, Milan, and Paris, and established a Milan office in 2005. Nendo has received many honors, including the Good Design Award (2004), the JCD Design Award (2005), the Design for Asia Award (2006), the Red Dot Design Award (2008), and the Furniture Design Award in Singapore (2008). Sato was nominated Designer of the Future by Design Miami in 2009 and was declared one of the "100 Most Respected Japanese" (2006) and "Top 100 Small Japanese Companies" (2007) in *Newsweek* magazine. He has taught at Showa Women's University in Tokyo (2006) and Kuwasawa Design School (2009).

Illoiha Ebisu (opposite)

You have an interesting background, having spent your childhood in Canada and then earning an architecture degree in Japan. Your design company is still fairly young but has accomplished a lot.

Nendo started in 2002, which is also the year I graduated from Waseda University. So I was twenty-two or twenty-three years old then. I had studied architecture for six years at school, and the environment was very strict there. After graduation, a rowing club friend of mine and I decided to attend a furniture fair. At the fair, everything was so free. Architects were designing teaspoons and teacups, and textile designers were designing cars. I'd never seen such a scene in Japan, so I thought I would like to do something like that. And we thought we would like to exhibit something in the fair someday. So that's how we made Nendo.

So you founded your company with several friends.

Yes, there were five or six of us. Now we have about thirty-six employees. The first year, we didn't have anything to do, so we exhibited at furniture fairs in Tokyo and entered design competitions.

That's impressive. Isn't it difficult for an unknown designer to be invited to a furniture fair?

It was quite easy to exhibit in Tokyo, and we won many awards in the first year. Then we had the idea to exhibit in Milan the next year—2003. So we exhibited at the satellite show for young designers and students.

Was your first product the disc-shaped light called Al(Pb)_lumi?

Yes, the one with electroluminescent film. It was a competition entry for students, and we won a medal—gold, I think [laughter].

And it uses yellow sheets of film?

Yes, the theme for the competition was about lighting for the twenty-first century. So I thought I would like to use electroluminescent film—very thin and light. It's only about 0.2 millimeters [0.008 inches] thick, and the entire light is 0.3 millimeters [0.012 inches] thick. We used lead for one-third of the disk,

Al(Pb)_lumi

and the rest was aluminum. The weight difference between the metals would cause the light to shift to one side. It's really like a disk floating in the air.

So that's how you developed your concept of a small moment of surprise?

Yes, a very small surprise.

And then you developed other light fixtures— like the plug-in Air Lamp that combines a fan with a light bulb.

Yes. I thought there were so many light fixtures in the world, but I couldn't find many fans. So I thought we could use light fixtures as fans that plug into the wall.

And you started to make various personal objects like the 365puchi calendar. It's such a simple thing but actually very clever—a tactile object that inspires us to interact with it. Did you have a plan at the beginning of Nendo? Did you set out to design small objects and scale up to larger ones, for example?

No, I didn't have any plans. First I made a few lamps, and in 2003 we decided to exhibit at the furniture fair. We thought we needed to make furniture pieces also—lighting fixtures

Canvas, interior

wouldn't be enough. That's how we started making furniture. Also we were designing Canvas at the time, which was a low-budget restaurant project.

How did you develop the idea for Canvas?
It was designed for my friend, who wanted to create a new restaurant. He told me that he bought a new building, so I thought, "Wow." I went to see it, however, and found a very old, two-story-high building. The first floor was an office and the second was a house. We didn't have a budget to remove the facade, so we thought about wrapping the whole building. So we went to a fabric store and bought 220 meters [722 linear feet] of canvas—a type of material typically used for tents. We wrapped the entire building and put lights inside, and we still had some fabric left so we wrapped the interior also. Still, we had more fabric left.

Let me guess—you wrapped the furniture?
Yes, that's right, the tablecloths and furniture [laughter]. We cut up the remaining fabric and used it to make printed business cards, matchboxes, and flyers. This was our first architectural project. It was quite awful, because we had to do many things by ourselves.

How did you treat the fabric that wraps the building?
First we wanted to make it very flat, but this was difficult to achieve. Instead, we thought about making wrinkles, in order to reveal geometric imperfections instead of hiding them.

So you made more wrinkles?
Yes, we had two pipes that would hold the fabric. So we cut excess fabric and gave the pipes a little twist. We wanted to do something that couldn't be done with solid architectural materials. Also we thought about exchanging the fabric over time, changing the colors or the wrinkle pattern every few years, for example. However, the owner likes the fabric just as it is. She likes the way it's getting dirty [laughter].

This approach is similar to Shigeru Ban's use of paper tubes—taking advantage of a cheap and easily replaceable material.
Yes, some people said that it's very Japanese, like shoji screens.

Were you working on the Drawer House at the same time?
Yes. Since land is so scarce in Japan, we decided to put all of the functional elements of the Drawer House in one wall. These elements can be pulled out like drawers into the main space as needed.

I'm impressed by the way this design translates the multipurpose nature of traditional Japanese architecture into a contemporary format. Would you say the house is a modern take on this idea?
Yes, something very similar—it embodies the flexibility of the Japanese living style. It is a very small house, and we couldn't place many windows, because there were so many neighboring houses. So we decided not to design any walls in the house. If we want to take a bath, for example, we simply pull out the bathtub "drawer" and the entire space becomes a big bathroom. If we open the kitchen drawer, however, the entire space becomes a dining room. The furniture may be easily moved around. When it's a sunny day, we can put a desk by the window, for example. It's very flexible.

The house has three floors, correct?
Yes—a basement, a ground floor, and the first floor.

If we want to take a bath, for example, we simply pull out the bathtub "drawer" and the entire space becomes a big bathroom. If we open the kitchen drawer, however, the entire space becomes a dining room.

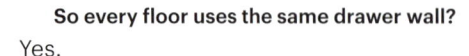

Drawer House, detail of stair

So every floor uses the same drawer wall?
Yes.

How exactly does the drawer mechanism work? Is the furniture on wheels or a track?
The television unit and bathtub are on tracks, because they are quite heavy. The rest of the furniture moves freely. We actually had a problem with the bathtub, because when it is full of water it has too much inertia. We can start to move it, but it doesn't want to stop [laughter]. So we made a large concrete block with silicone rubber to act as a wheel stop. The bathtub now acts like a bumper car.

That's remarkable. So do the clients actually put things away when they are not using them?
Not every day. They just move the furniture around, and when they have guests they put everything back inside the drawer wall.

Just like we do with closets.
So the people don't have to adjust to the house. The house adjusts to the way the people live.

This concept is expanded in the Book House to the scale of the community.
Right. The Book House is on a small island about three hours outside Tokyo. The island has only about three or four hundred inhabitants, and there is no library there for small children. The first idea was to design a private house with a library inside, but the client wanted to create an open library. So at first we planned to use glass to allow light and views into the library. At the same time, however, we had to consider the privacy of the house. We had difficulty creating the right balance between openness and closure. As the project developed, however, we thought about the house as a large bookshelf with a house inside it.

Is that when you had the idea to use fiber-reinforced plastic (FRP) panels behind the bookshelves?
Yes. The FRP is translucent, so it allows light to pass without allowing direct views. During the daytime, the house is filled with light, but the client has privacy. Also the shadows cast inside the house change every day, because people borrow books and return them to a different shelf location. At night the effect is reversed and the house becomes a kind of lantern.

So we might say that by using the library, the community becomes an active participant in the design. Library borrowers effectively transform the elevations of the house, as well as the overall light quality of the space inside.
And some people bring their own books and put them there. So the house is a very simple and fluid vehicle—not unlike the Drawer House.

This idea of fluidity is also present in Karaoke-Tub, perhaps in more of a metaphorical way.
Yes, this project is a kind of party room used for weddings. We designed a karaoke room

Drawer House with sliding furniture

Book House, interior (above), veranda with bookshelves (right)

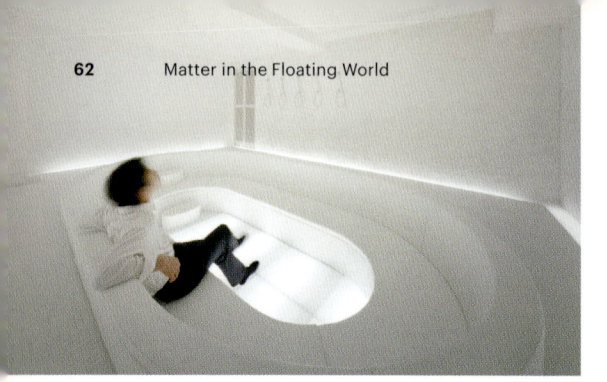

Karaoke-Tub

like a bathtub, so that everyone could sit together in the bathtub and sing. There are two colors of light, white and red, so people can balance the light like they're balancing the water temperature.

Another way you invoke surprise in a kind of "Aha!" moment is by harnessing the transformative qualities of particular materials, as seen in the Ukki Stool, for example.

Yes, we looked at many materials and finally found one that would work—a stretchable fabric with a good memory. The stool looks flat until you sit on it. We showed it in 2004 at our second furniture fair in Milan. A member of the jury would come almost every day and try it out. He was a very large person, so we were quite worried. He'd come and jump into it every day.

The Rakuyo-Bench employs a different kind of transformation, in this case related to duration and memory.

When someone first sits on the bench, lights begin to project subtle leaf patterns on the floor below. The color begins to change slowly—first green, yellow, orange, and finally red. So when someone sees the color of the leaves, they notice how long they've been sitting. Let's say there are two people sitting, and the first person hadn't noticed the leaf color changing. This one might be red whereas the next bench is green; so the first person would begin to understand the color relationship to duration.

What happens when you stand up?

The color fades away. That was the one thing I wanted to do—I didn't want it to just disappear. The leaf pattern fades over five minutes. So

Rakuyo-Bench

newcomers will notice if someone was sitting on the bench recently.

So how does it work—does it use LED lighting?

Yes, it uses equipment normally found in a planetarium, in addition to color filters that move. There is a sensor that detects when people sit down.

You also engage the sense of time passing with your dishware called Time. During the course of a meal, the dishes softly radiate changing colors underneath—is this your idea of a kind of synthesized diurnal cycle?

Yes, I want to convey a sense of time.

Why is this an important interest for you?

I think because I work here in Tokyo, in which there is no time. I can buy something I want twenty-four hours a day. Also, I can buy anything here.

Right—souvenirs from various Japanese destinations are all sold in Tokyo Station [laughing].

So you don't have to go to Hokkaido to buy something that's only sold there. There isn't anything new there because I can buy it here in Tokyo. That's quite sad, isn't it?

Time

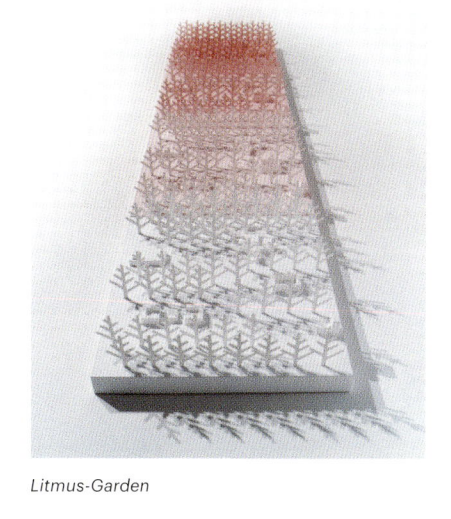

Litmus-Garden

Yes. So you are trying to reconnect people with a sense of local time and place. Sometimes you express such connections subversively, such as in the Tile-Plant and Crack-Vase. Plants grow within artificial grout joints or cracks in asphalt pavement—suggesting that natural forces don't always take the most convenient path.

I thought about small plants growing from cracks in the street, and I felt this was more natural than putting plants in a vase. This approach celebrates a strong, robust nature. This is the nature I want to show people.

Like the colloquial pairing of hothouse orchids and desert roses. The desert roses fight for life with scant resources, as opposed to the orchids that won't last a day outside the greenhouse. There's also an element of spontaneity in these objects—a sense of an unplanned event. Moreover, they relate aspects of our physical environment that are inconvenient or usually go unnoticed, as in your Litmus-Garden.

Yes, that piece was created for the magazine *Brutus*.[1] The theme was to make a miniature garden. I wanted to reveal the presence of acid rain, so we used litmus paper in the garden. When exposed to rain, the garden changes color over time. The color pink indicates the presence of acidity.

So it's a way to indicate water quality.

I wanted to show this aspect in a positive way, and I didn't want to shout the message—just to whisper it.

This creates a different kind of environmental awareness. If you yell the message at people, it doesn't work as well. However, once left to discover the meaning themselves, people may begin to take the message seriously.

That's right. It's a process of discovery. People have to experience it themselves.

You employ this process in different ways. The Hanabi light fixture transforms over time, for example.

Yes. I was thinking about the fact that incandescent lightbulbs give off a lot of heat. People regard this as a negative thing, which is one reason LEDs and electroluminescent film were developed. However, I thought about using this heat in a positive way.

So the lamp employs shape memory alloys to change the shape of the hood.[2] How long does the process take?

Let's turn it on [demonstrates].

Oh, it's fast! [laughing] That's amazing. What about when you turn it off? Wow, it's still pretty fast. The "leaves" of the light really respond to the heat of the bulb.

---

[1] *Brutus* is a popular Japanese magazine focused on lifestyles and pop culture.

[2] Shape memory alloys (SMAs) are metals that "remember" their original shapes, established after forging and cooling.

It also depends on the room temperature.

You also address time-based transformations in large-scale lighting installations, such as the Naoshima Standard 2 project, which employs a field of light cones.

We only had three or four days to design that project [laughing]. The student museum called us one day and asked us to visit Naoshima Island the next day. So we went, and we were told the exhibit would start in six or seven days, and there wasn't any signage for the art pieces. So we were designing on the bullet train [laughter]. We had a very low budget and the exhibit would last for six months, so the signs had to be durable. So we thought about using traffic cones. We found white ones, which we thought were very beautiful. When we put the light source inside, it gave a very soft glow. The effect was close to the Japanese lantern.

What a clever idea. So the lights are on a timer?

Yes. There are small signs all over the island. We had something like 725 cones at the main port, and each light was connected to a timer. Every hour, the lights would begin to move in a pattern related to the waves just offshore.

That sounds very complicated. Do you work with computer programmers?

Yes, we have programmers. We have to collaborate with many people, depending on project demands.

The shifting pattern is not only like waves—it also resembles the movement of clouds overhead.

Yes, some people were taking photos of the cones, because they thought the signs themselves were an art piece [laughing]. That was pretty funny.

That's the best kind of sign! Your work does seem to navigate seamlessly between the territories of graphic communication, product design, architecture, and other disciplines. Many of your projects seem to embody a kind of "identity crisis"—in a positive way. For example, Sorane is a light fixture and a speaker, correct?

Yes, it's a vibrating speaker. In the beginning, I wanted to design something like a plane of sky that would be translucent in the daytime and like stars at night. We discussed the concept with Pioneer, who had developed a technology to enhance the surface of acrylic to make it glow. There are lasers that illuminate the light from the side, and the acrylic catches the light. Pioneer also showed us this vibrating speaker, and we thought we should just combine the technologies. The speaker is located above the lamp and makes the acrylic vibrate.

Does it sound like a typical speaker?

You can hear most sounds, although bass is hard to replicate. We designed a lounge with eight or nine fixtures emitting different sounds, such as soft rain and thunder.

I would certainly love to experience that. On the topic of unexpected combinations, I've noticed other "identity crises" appear in projects like Rebondir.

Rebondir is a catalog-based retail company. When they contacted us, they didn't have a physical store. Since their reputation was based on the printed catalog, we thought we'd use the concept of printing in the first store. Also, Rebondir is known for their suggestions in coordinating different articles of clothing. So our idea was to print on physical materials. We thought about the heaviness and richness of stone, as well as the softness and warmth of wood, and we wanted to blend the materials in some way. We ultimately printed a wood-grain pattern on stone tiles, and a stone pattern on wood.

So you created a complete shift in material syntax. How did you "print" the materials on one another?

We scanned the actual materials, and the images were transferred to a kind of film. The stone and wood had this film applied in the factory—along with two or three layers of protective coating. Construction was quite difficult, because both sets of patterns had to align on site. If someone dropped a tile, the manufacturer had to make the same one again, with an identical printed pattern. In the end, each material is visually half wood and half stone.

A Small "!" Moment — Oki Sato

Naoshima Standard 2

I wanted to design something like a plane of sky that would be translucent in the daytime and like stars at night.

Sorane

Rebondir

Rebondir detail

Large surprises are quite easy, like saying "Boo!" I'd like to make the surprises as small as possible, in order to enhance the process of discovery.

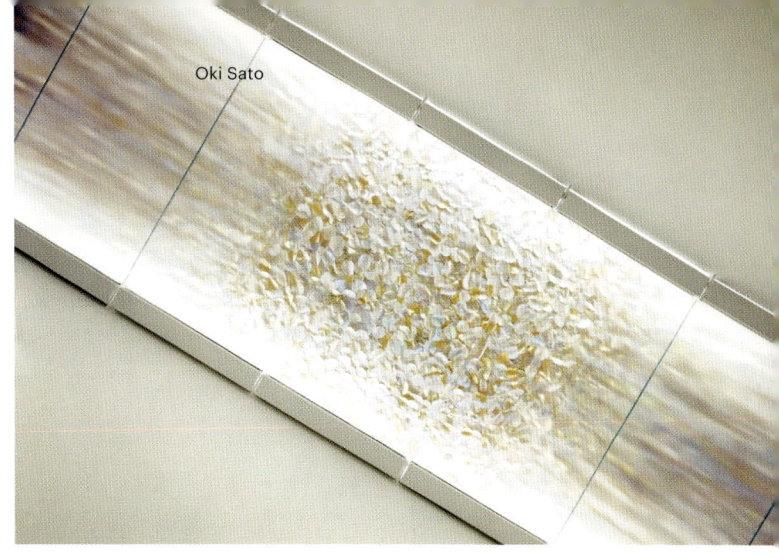

Illoiha Ebisu, ceiling detail

How do people react to the store?
Some people don't notice it's printed. They think there's a stone like that [laughing].

Others must think they've never seen those particular materials before. I imagine the ceiling treatment in Illoiha Ebisu elicits surprise as well.
Yes, it's a long textile layered with a film that is transparent from one viewing angle but translucent from another. As you walk down the corridor, you see the details of the textile within a limited view cone. In order to see more of the textile, you have to keep moving.

I see. So this is another kind of temporal transformation, which in this case relates to individual movement.
Yes, that's right.

You experiment with so many different materials and technologies. Do you test a lot of different materials yourself, or is it simply important to know the right people to ask?
Yes, we have found many people. We might see something new in an exhibit or a magazine, and then we ask many questions—what's going on, how much is the cost, can you change particular aspects, and so on.

And then you generate your own ideas for the new material. So your analytical process is inherently linked to synthesis. How do you simultaneously think about exhibition venues, business models for new product lines, and so on? Doesn't this work require a large investment in materials up front?
That's one of the problems I have [laughing]. Sometimes companies approach us with a brief for a new project, and other times we develop ideas on our own. We are actively involved in research and ideation all the time.

How does a typical client-driven process work?
We have an initial meeting and the client gives us a brief. We usually work for two weeks before our first presentation, in which we might present three or four ideas in small models and computer renderings. On the way home from the meeting, we might generate two or three more ideas. That's how we move the project along.

Are there any new "surprise moments" that you would like to create for people?
I always try to convey the surprising moments of my designs with a degree of subtlety. Large surprises are quite easy, like saying "Boo!" I'd like to make the surprises as small as possible, in order to enhance the process of discovery.

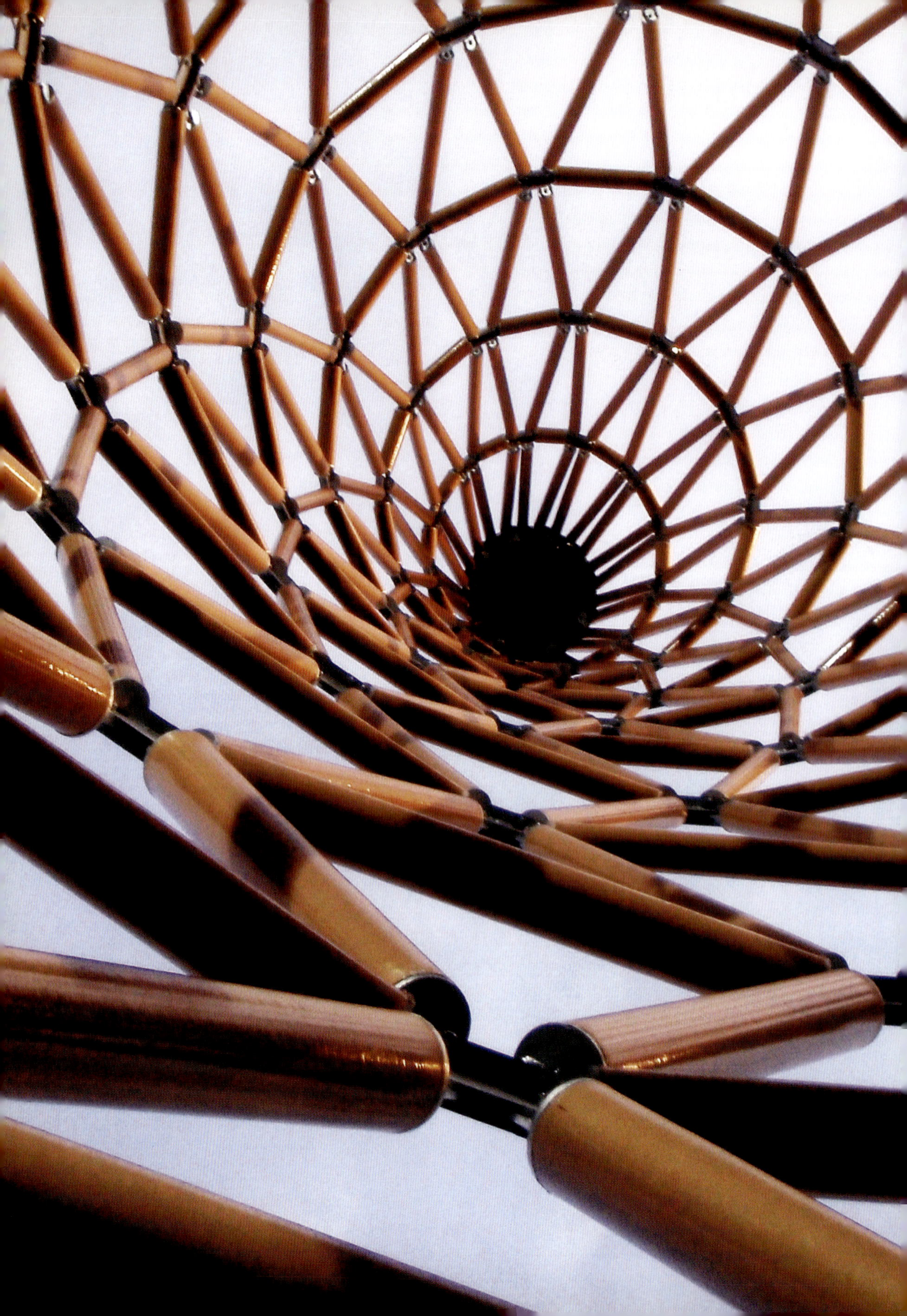

Strength in Weakness

A conversation with Shigeru Ban, Shigeru Ban Architects

In his meteoric rise to international prominence in the 1990s, architect Shigeru Ban shook up many common assumptions in architectural practice based on his post-disaster humanitarian efforts, his radically simple and clever design responses, and his development and utilization of alternative structural materials such as the paper tube. His work defines a broad spectrum of approaches—from stark white houses for the elite to beer crate–supported relief shelters—and defies easy categorization. Ban's ecological sensitivity and vigorous material-research campaign have resulted in surprising accomplishments, including a paper bridge, a shipping-container museum, and a vertical-garden retail tower.

Shigeru Ban, who was born in Tokyo in 1957, studied at the Cooper Union School of Architecture in New York. In 1985 he established Shigeru Ban Architects, a private practice in Tokyo. In 1995 he started working as a consultant for the United Nations High Commissioner for Refugees and at the same time established an NGO, Voluntary Architects' Network (VAN). Ban is best known for works such as the Curtain Wall House, the Japan Pavilion at Hannover Expo 2000, the Nicolas G. Hayek Center, and the Centre Pompidou-Metz. He has been awarded a number of prizes, including the Grande Medaille d'Or from the Académie d'Architecture (2004), the Arnold W. Brunner Memorial Prize in Architecture (2005), the Thomas Jefferson Foundation Medal in Architecture (2005), and the National Order of the Legion of Honor in France (2009). Ban was a professor at Keio University, Japan, from 2001 to 2008.

Paper Tower, London Design Festival, 2009 (opposite)

> I read Michael Kimmelman's article about you in the *New York Times*, in which he calls you "The Accidental Environmentalist."[1]

That is good, because I am always referred to as an environmentally friendly or sustainable architect, but I hate being called these things. I built paper tube structures back in 1986, before sustainability became popular.

> That was my first question, actually—before sustainability became de rigueur within architectural circles, you were creating structures that were not only environmentally and economically sustainable, but also addressed ideas about social sustainability.

I don't understand the meaning of sustainable or ecological architecture, because the act of building is in itself in defiance of the beauty of nature. Architecture is an inherently anti-environmental act.

> That's certainly a bold statement. Is sustainability always so problematic, then?

No, actually—because it is such an important vision, even if it is trendy, it is very good that people have become interested in sustainability. The only problem is the fact that people use the term without fully understanding it.

> Kimmelman wrote, "An heir to Buckminster Fuller and Oscar Niemeyer, to Japanese traditional architecture and to Alvar Aalto, he is an old-school Modernist with a poet's touch and an engineer's inventiveness."[2] You are an architect who can also think like an engineer, and the fact that your influences come from both the East and the West makes you hard to label. How would you define yourself?

I don't think it is necessary to define myself. I'll leave that to the journalists.

> I am interested in the nature of Japanese innovation, particularly in the context of a global practice such as your own. Would you say that there is some essence in your work that is inherently Japanese? Is it important to you to have some kind of Japanese sensibility in your projects?

Naturally, it's in my blood. Otherwise, I never studied architecture in Japan. Right now I'm mostly living in Paris. Also 90 to 95 percent of my projects are outside of Japan. Somehow I'm not very popular here.

> Is that right?

Yes, now I just have a few residential projects with Japanese clients. It's also interesting that if I check my name on Google, I get something like five hundred thousand hits using the English version, but only 10 percent of the hits with the Japanese version. Clearly I'm better known outside of Japan, a fact reinforced by the reality that I am only invited to participate in international competitions.

> Do you mind if I ask why?

I'd like to know why. Well, it's easy to say that I didn't study here. Also I only worked for Arata Isozaki for less than one year, and it was when I was still a student. Also I don't have a Japanese license, although both of my partners do. These things matter in a credential-conscious society like Japan.

> It is interesting for me, as a foreigner, to try to understand the different forces at work in this case. You have certainly gained notoriety in the West, and your use of materials is often a focus of this notoriety. I would therefore like to discuss your approach to materials. At the risk of oversimplifying your work, one cannot help but notice two distinct aesthetic tendencies: one is represented by the clinical precision of abstract, white structures, and the other is represented by the rawness of paper tube constructions.

I never saw that; this distinction just occurred naturally. I use white as a neutral texture in order to emphasize other natural materials, such as wood. When the main theme is not about a material, I just use white or light gray as the neutral texture in order to articulate it from others. And if the main theme is a picture window, for example, this is just a frame. So the frame has to be neutral, right? The frame for a portal is a white frame, so it has to be white. And in the Curtain Wall House, all of the furniture is wood in order to contrast better with the white frame. So it's not totally white,

---

[1] Michael Kimmelman, "The Accidental Environmentalist," the *New York Times*, May 20, 2007.
[2] Ibid.

Strength in Weakness

Shigeru Ban

Nicolas G. Hayek Center, street entrance

I don't understand the meaning of sustainable or ecological architecture, because the act of building is in itself in defiance of the beauty of nature. Architecture is an inherently anti-environmental act.

Hanegi Forest

Vasarely Pavilion, Aix-en-Provence

Nomadic Museum, Tokyo (top), shipping container detail (middle), entrance (bottom)

I believe the strength of a material has nothing to do with the strength of a building. Even a paper tube structure can be made to withstand an earthquake that a concrete building cannot outlive.

actually. I try to use concrete, steel, or anything available; it's just that I have to use the materials appropriately, and I don't think the paper tube is appropriate for every circumstance. It's a very particular material—good for particular opposites.

> How do you decide if a material should be abstract or neutral?

It depends on the theme.

> The Nomadic Museum, for example, is certainly not the white, undifferentiated box that most museums become.

Because the client told me right away he didn't like white walls. I thought it would be good to use a material that was aged. Even the containers are painted different colors. They have their own patina, because they have been traveling all over the world. This quality contrasts strongly with the paper tube, which is a very plain material.

> Speaking of unconventional materials, I am intrigued by your process of testing alternative materials in order to prove their viability to code officials, such as the wood-clad steel frame in Tazawako Station.[3] Do you feel that this kind of process is necessary for material innovation?

Actually I never invent anything new. I just use existing models differently. A long time ago, an inventor invented something totally new. But now if you want to invent something, you need a large amount of capital. It's very difficult these days for a single person to invent something original. I just use existing materials, giving them a different function or meaning, that's all.

> Even so, it takes additional money and effort to test alternative systems. Is this testing important for architecture today?

I don't know—I'm just doing what I'm interested in. Throughout the history of architecture, when someone invents a new material or structural system, a new architectural form results. Otherwise, people just follow the fashionable style, which is different depending on the time. I'm not interested in seeking trendy architecture. That is why I'd have to invent some new material or design an interesting structural system to make my own architecture without depending on trendy styles. So this is my main interest.

Also I'm not interested in so-called high-tech architecture, because high-tech is like a drug. If you take a drug, you simply want more and more. For example, I respect Richard Rogers, but his Channel 4 Television building in London, with its glass facade, stair, everything, is really a drug. It really goes too far, and the technology just becomes decoration. High-tech materials and special details are not really necessary. I'm interested in using normal materials, because I think this is a very original way of thinking.

People always want to develop stronger materials, but we can construct a building with weak materials so that it meets architectural regulations. I believe the strength of a material has nothing to do with the strength of a building. Even a paper tube structure can be made to withstand an earthquake that a concrete building cannot outlive.[4] The durability of a building has nothing to do with the durability of a material. It really depends on whether people love architecture or not. That's why if your building is built by a developer, it is only for making money and nobody will love it. So it will be easily dismantled and replaced with a new, trendy building. This temporary condition does not depend on what kind of material you use.

> This is interesting. Architects concentrate on the spatial program, but you also consider the temporal program of a building. A paper tube structure or mobile museum, for example, has a temporary quality; yet it is more durable in other

---

 3 Tazawako Station features steel plates clad in laminated timber. Ban was required to test this unusual system in order to demonstrate its fire resistance to building code officials.

 4 Earthquakes pose greater risks in Japan, both because of its significant seismic activity as well as its high density of building. Ban's comment loosely refers to the fact that wood frame buildings often outperform concrete structures during earthquakes due to better shear resistance, although this isn't always the case. See the data reported by the Nevada Seismological Laboratory, University of Nevada, Reno, http://crack.seismo.unr.edu/ftp/pub/louie/class/100/effects-kobe.html.

Vasarely Pavilion, structural detail

>**ways. How do you address the concept of time in your work, and how do you decide which materials to use?**

It really depends on the condition of the project. For the Nomadic Museum, the most difficult challenge was how to transport a fifty-thousand-square-foot building economically. I knew it had to be easy to assemble and disassemble. I actually had the idea to use the shipping container earlier, because it's an international standard. We can borrow containers from anywhere in the world. I also like the quality of the container, as I said earlier, because it is old and has a lot of history.

>**The idea of reusing something designed for a different purpose is quite interesting. One concern with reused or recycled materials has been progressive degradation, termed "downcycling."[5] However, new examples like this suggest that a common material or product may be "upcycled" in terms of its value to society.[6]**

I'm not the first one to use the container as a building material; there are many examples. Usually architects adapt the container as a space for living, but it's a terrible space to inhabit—small, too cold or too hot—I always see people living inside containers temporarily after a disaster. Shipping containers are made for things, not for people. I'm just interested in using the container as the bearing wall system, and I focus on the space between the containers instead.

>**This idea reminds me of your Furniture Houses, which use structural bookcases to support the roof and frame the spaces between. In fact, several of your earlier works are shaped by simple and direct ideas relating to the use of unadorned structure to frame space. Your recent commissions have become larger in size and more complex, however. Is it a challenge to implement simple ideas in projects like the Centre Pompidou-Metz, for example?**

---

[5] Downcycling is the recycling of a material into a substance of lesser quality. The term was popularized by William McDonough and Michael Braungart in *Cradle to Cradle: Remaking the Way We Make Things* (New York: North Point Press, 2002).

[6] Upcycling is the practice of taking something that is disposable and transforming it into something of greater use and value. See McDonough and Braungart, *Cradle to Cradle*.

Even this building is really an accumulation of my previous projects and experiments. For example, the idea for this roof came from a traditional Chinese bamboo hut. I have been really amazed by the architectonic quality of this hut, because woven bamboo is the structure, paper is used for waterproofing, and dried leaves are used for insulation. So it is really like the architecture of the roof. Since this discovery, I have been designing two different structures to develop this idea further. So it's not really new.

The facade is surrounded by glass shutters, which I have been using for some projects. Also the main gallery is a tube, and the end of the tube has a big window used to frame objects of the city, like a cathedral or a train station built by the Germans when the city was occupied. This is really a picture window used to connect the museum with the main city, because the site is a little far from the city center. So these are mainly ideas collected from my previous experience that undergo continuous development.

How do you see these ideas transforming in the future? What other commissions do you anticipate?

I will submit more large, institutional project proposals, and I still enjoy small, philanthropic projects—such as the recent rebuilding of an Islamic fishermen's village in Sri Lanka that was affected by the tsunami. It's not only important to work at different scales, but also for clients with different circumstances. The victims of a natural disaster need shelter, and this kind of work improves my mental balance after working for privileged clients. Privileged people can be very selfish. The power and money that politicians and other figures possess is invisible, so they hire architects to visualize their power through building. This has been the main role of architects historically. Even now, we work for big governments and corporations that seek to show their power and money with architecture. However, there are increasing numbers of underprivileged people and victims of natural disasters. You know, an earthquake by itself never kills people. The collapse of buildings kills people. Also flooding is becoming more of a problem because of deforestation, since increasing numbers of trees are cut for construction. This is the direct responsibility of architects. Then after a disaster, people need housing, and this is also the responsibility of architects. So architects in reality should have many things to do, but so far they are not really involved in disaster relief projects. I enjoy working in disaster sites, because I can utilize my ideas and knowledge, and the experience enhances my mental balance. Otherwise, there is no separation for me between project types.

Architecture for Humanity cofounder Cameron Sinclair once told me that he hoped to shift the conventional image of architects designing for wealthy clients to an image of philanthropists designing for the underprivileged. Do you view your disaster-relief work as an important opportunity for all architects to "restore mental balance?"

No, it's not something they should do necessarily; it's just more interesting because there are many opportunities. Normally architects are interested in making a monument. However, there are many architects doing this kind of work. In France, for example, there is an NGO called Emergency Architects. Perhaps the difference is that I do not limit myself to one type of work; there is no difference to me between designing a museum or a shelter.

How does your own Voluntary Architects' Network operate?

I don't have a proper membership; I always mobilize a team once a disaster occurs. Since I cannot afford to fly many members to a disaster site, I always try to build a team with local architects and students. Sometimes I send my students as well. I cannot answer all requests, however—after the tsunami I received requests from India, Sri Lanka, and Thailand. For the projects I can do, I always try to assist minority populations. After the Kobe earthquake, for example, I designed houses for Vietnamese refugees. I believe the

76 Matter in the Floating World Lightness

Centre Pompidou-Metz (top and middle left),
interior gallery (middle right)
roof detail (bottom)

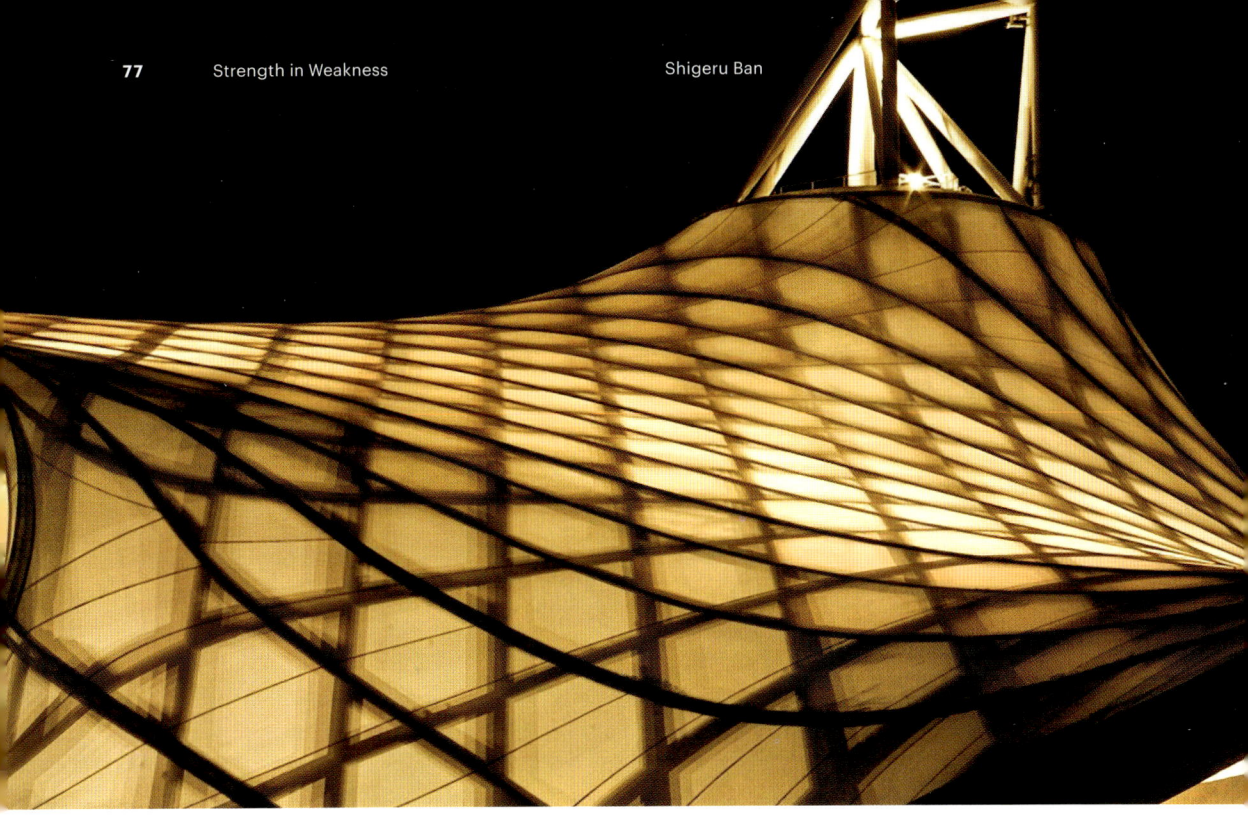

Centre Pompidou-Metz, roof detail

government has a responsibility to help by constructing shelters for all those affected, but there are always some minorities who are overlooked. In Kobe these Vietnamese refugees were not allowed to move into public housing, because of their particular employment arrangements, and their neighbors also tried to keep them out of the parks. I try to solve this problem by making healthier, more attractive dwellings so that the occupants may be accepted by their neighbors.

I am now working with students to design a simple partition system to be constructed in a gymnasium. As you know, after the first stage of a disaster when people lose their homes, they move into a big public space such as a gymnasium—as we saw with Hurricane Katrina. A few days are OK, but after a week or a few weeks people really suffer, because there is no privacy between families. So I have designed some very simple partition systems with students, and we are demonstrating this research to different cities.

So this partition system uses local materials?
Naturally. When I met the head of one disaster relief agency, he was very interested in my system, because he said that other systems are expensive and their manufacturers require him to buy one thousand or ten thousand units up front. However, no one knows how many units will be required until after a disaster, and usually cities don't have places to store these units in the meantime. So in my proposal, we work with local paper-honeycomb-board companies. Paper honeycomb board can be made immediately—in one or two days—so we don't have to stock anything.[7] We simply contact these companies immediately after a disaster, so local governments don't have to allocate special budgets for something unexpected. I proposed this method after seeing the same problems repeated in various disaster sites.

---

[7] Paper honeycomb board is a lightweight panel made of a paper honeycomb interior clad with various facing materials.

Kirinda Islamic Fishermen's Village, dwelling

> An earthquake by itself never kills people. The collapse of buildings kills people. Also flooding is becoming more of a problem because of deforestation, since increasing numbers of trees are cut for construction. This is the direct responsibility of architects.

In terms of disaster relief or conventional client-related projects, what do you think are some of architecture's greatest future challenges, and how would you address them?

If you look at any field—banking, medical, anything—the computer has really helped it to advance. But I think the architectural field is very rare, because the computer hasn't made architecture better. One hundred years ago, two hundred years ago, or more, we used to make better architecture. But now anybody can design it. Anybody can build it. The computer is a tool to simplify—to save time. We also try to build quickly. But to make better architecture, we have to spend more time designing and building. The computer helps people make iconic sculptures easily, and any shapes may be cut using digital fabrication. However, I don't think that is really the future of architecture. My professor John Hejduk was very lucky, because he passed away before the computer age.[8] Although the computer is really an important tool for us right now, I think the advance in technology won't make architecture better even after one hundred years. That is why I always bring my students to disaster sites to build by themselves, without the computer.

The mobility and flexibility of architecture is becoming very important. For example, if you go to Germany or England, you can see beautiful brick factories that aren't used anymore. Now all of the active factories are in China or Mexico, and maybe in a few years they will all move to North Korea or Laos. The buildings' life spans are becoming shorter. Also, because of the computer, people are really traveling all over the world to find good professions. So I think even commercial buildings' life spans are really short. This change is an important theme we have to face.

Yes, I read that Tokyo has the shortest building life span of any major city.[9]

One thing you have to know is that structural regulations related to earthquakes are changing, and that's why people are encouraged to dismantle buildings that do not meet current code. It's just the way of life. When you buy a so-called mansion, you have to know the year in which the building was built.[10] If it is older than 1980, its structure is out of date. Even in Kobe, none of the buildings built after 1980 with the new structural regulations were destroyed; they

---

8 John Hejduk was dean of the School of Architecture at the Cooper Union during the time that Ban studied there.

9 Thirty percent of Tokyo's building stock is transformed every year, and Japanese houses last a maximum of thirty years. See Stephen Taylor and Ryue Nishizawa, *Some Ideas on Living in London and Tokyo* (Baden, Switzerland: Lars Müller Publishers, 2008), 96.

only suffered minor problems. That is why the government is encouraging the dismantling of old structures. Also the city is not designed by urban planners or the government, but by developers. The projects are focused primarily on money, so that's why the life span of buildings is shorter.

> I once invited my former professor Yung Ho Chang to give a lecture, which he titled "Fast Slow Architecture." By fast architecture, he meant the rapid design services employed by most Chinese building firms today. By slow architecture, he was referring to his own practice! This challenge is a serious one. How can architects ensure a quality product when speed seems to be the primary driver?

But developers are not interested in that kind of aspect, right? I have received a few invitations to work in China, but I didn't want to do the projects, because they just wanted to buy the design, and they didn't want us involved in the construction document or construction administration phases. Chinese clients just want to get some unique designs created by foreign architects that they build themselves, and the result is totally different from the work you design. I'm not interested in participating in that type of process.

> I see. So it's important to stay in touch with all stages of the work.

Yes. That's why I limit the number of projects in the office, because I design everything myself. I once asked Renzo Piano about the number of employees he has. He said he hires as many people as he can remember by name. So I asked him, "How many people do you have then?" He said, "Two hundred." My memory is not good enough to remember two hundred names, so that's why my office is smaller.

> One of my friends worked for RPBW for many years, and he said that Piano is so deeply involved that he knows every centimeter of every project. I am sure you are the same way. How do you manage this level of hands-on involvement, especially with operations in Paris and New York, in addition to Tokyo?

Well, this number is limited. It's not two hundred people but rather thirty-five, and the number of projects is small enough that I can manage them myself.

> Regardless of office size, how do you think architects can respond to the significant resource challenges we face today?

I'm not so interested in so-called sustainable design. In Europe today, you can find very expensive curtain wall systems with double glazing and adjustable louvers, and the systems are always depicted with many arrows.

> [laughs] Yes, yes.

But the initial cost is much higher than for conventional systems. Also LEED and other similar regulations really make buildings more expensive. Even when I'm designing a summer house on Long Island, LEED requires us to make lots of environmental controls and to pay more for insulating materials, when the reality is that the house is only used during the summertime. This kind of regulation is good, but sometimes it's really too much. Do you know that in Japan we don't heat space twenty-four hours a day?

> Oh yes. I survived a Tokyo winter without central heat.[11]

We set the timer to go off after you sleep and turn on a half hour before you wake up. And traditionally, we heat with *kotatsu* or other devices.[12] This is a more sustainable way instead of using expensive materials and technologies to make buildings more sustainable with "many arrows."

That is why all of the facades in my new Swatch building open to receive natural

---

10 Japanese "mansions" are actually multifloor apartment buildings, typically constructed of reinforced concrete.

11 My family and I lived in a Tokyo apartment built in the 1970s, made of reinforced concrete with limited insulation. The strategy for enduring the winter in a typical Japanese residence is to focus on conditioning the body as opposed to the interior volume of air. This is true in modern as well as older dwellings.

12 Kotatsu are low tables with integrated blankets that insulate the user's legs.

Nicolas G. Hayek Center, customer service level

breezes, in order to reduce the use of air-conditioning. In old office buildings, the windows never open. So I try to harness natural ventilation as much as possible. It's a very simple thing. Also people enjoy the space in between the outside and the inside. However, office buildings today are well-controlled environments, totally separated from the outside. They are very expensive and are called sustainable buildings even though they use so many materials and complicated systems.

    Solar technology, for example, is something I believe we should embrace, but it does have a lot of embodied energy.[13]

The life cycle is probably twenty years, but the cost of the energy you save doesn't pay for the device. Still, we should develop solar power further and further. The technology is becoming sustainable. What is important is the definition of sustainability.

    Would you define sustainability differently?

No. I always say that I never think about it as the focus of the design. I started building paper tube structures in 1986 because I didn't want to waste material. I simply liked this kind of humble material the way it is. People have approached me after my lectures, saying, "We have a new kind of technology that will make the paper tube much stronger." But I'm not interested in making a stronger material. As I said, depending on the way you use them, even weak materials can be appropriate to make a strong building.

    There is certainly a direct approach to using materials in contemporary Japanese architecture, especially since the designs are not governed by the energy codes we have in the U.S.[14] When Westerners see Japanese building skins made only of plate steel, they criticize them for their lack of insulation. However, Westerners believe in conditioning every cubic centimeter of interior space, whereas Japanese just focus on conditioning the body. This is a deeply embedded cultural difference.

---

13 See Colin Bankier and Steve Gale, "Energy Payback of Roof Mounted Photovoltaic Cells," Energy Bulletin, http://www.energybulletin.net/node/17219.

14 Japan has three energy codes—one for commercial structures and two for residential buildings—but these codes are voluntary and there are no checks on construction. See M. Evans, B. Shui, and T. Takagi, "Country Report on Building Energy Codes in Japan" (Richland, WA: Pacific Northwest National Laboratory, April 2009).

Nicolas G. Hayek Center, planter detail

I'm not so interested in so-called sustainable design. In Europe today, you can find very expensive curtain wall systems with double glazing and adjustable louvers, and the systems are always depicted with many arrows.

Japanese architects are just spoiled. We are lucky, because Japanese people don't care about insulation or privacy so much. So we are taking advantage of these kinds of things in order to create something very unusual for Western people. Without having this kind of spoiled situation, this kind of architecture cannot be done. Also we get great technical support from the contractor and subcontractors. Even before we have a contract, they give us a lot of technical data in order to support us. So it's much easier to make a building in Japan, especially since we don't sue each other.

[laughs] Right!
That is why when famous Japanese architects win international competitions working with local firms, they cannot convince their teams. They're not used to being questioned, so they're not ready to answer logically. In Japan we think everyone shares the same feeling, but in other countries, everyone has different backgrounds—so we have to prepare the rationale for what we want to do very objectively. Also local firms are always on the client's side, because they don't want to do any risky experiments and because their relationship with the client is always more important than that with the architect. That is why I avoid this situation by partnering with local offices so that I can conduct the process myself. Otherwise, it's impossible to design what you really want, because the quality of the project gets reduced and there are many difficulties. Therefore, what you see Japanese architects doing here does not really apply to other countries.

Unlike many Japanese architects, you must be very flexible, because you've worked here and abroad.
Yes, because I was educated and trained in the U.S. I enjoy different contexts and conditions, and I'm ready to go anywhere.

ATMOSPHERE

> An empty space is marked off with plain wood and plain walls, so that the light drawn into it forms dim shadows within emptiness. There is nothing more. And yet, when we gaze into the darkness that gathers behind the crossbeam, around the flower vase, beneath the shelves, though we know perfectly well it is mere shadow, we are overcome with the feeling that in this small corner of the atmosphere there reigns complete and utter silence; that here in the darkness immutable tranquility holds sway.
> —Junichiro Tanizaki

The Japanese sensibility regarding atmosphere may be traced back to the origins of Shinto. The original sites of worship were not buildings, but rather natural features in the wild. A mountain or a stream would be considered the home of a deity, and a ritual site would be erected nearby for religious observances. This sacred enclosure would be minimally demarcated by the placement of four poles at the corners of a clearing or a rope stretched between two points. "Or to take an extreme example," claims Arata Isozaki, "the invisible *kehai*—or atmospheric indication of sacredness that the lay of the land itself might express—was deemed sufficient, such as when the locus of a spirit was discovered in a mountain fastness."[1]

The concept of atmosphere in Japanese architecture and design is intricately tied to the Japanese notion of emptiness, which is different than the Western notion of nothingness. Rather, emptiness is an indication of latent

21st Museum of Contemporary Art in Kanazawa, SANAA

energy and potential—a vessel waiting to be filled or a blank page awaiting the artist's brush. The sacred enclosure erected for Shinto worship is such a container, established to invite a potential visitation by a wandering *kamisamma*, or god. As Kenya Hara describes in his book *Shiro*, "Emptiness does not merely imply simplicity of form, logical sophistication, and the like. Rather, emptiness provides a space within which our imaginations can run free, vastly enriching our powers of perception and our mutual comprehension."[2]

In Hara's own work, he conjures devices and situations that stir the consciousness of the user. His products and graphic designs are the result of thoughtful consideration of multiple senses, and serve as empty containers anticipating uncertain fulfillment—offering questions rather than answers. According to Hara, "Creativity and 'questioning' are made of the same stuff. A creative question is a form of expression—it requires no definite answer. That is because it holds countless answers within itself."[3] With regard to architecture, this concept is embodied in the work of SANAA, whose stark and minimally detailed volumes liberate the creative ruminations of their inhabitants. SANAA architects Kazuyo Sejima and Ryue Nishizawa exemplify architect and historian Terunobu Fujimori's "white school," employing extreme precision in crafting empty containers devoid of unnecessary elements. According to critic Thomas Daniell, "These buildings seem intended as refuges from their surroundings, moments of provisional silence and stasis within a corrosive context of speed, confusion, and pollution."[4]

The movement to position architecture in sharp contrast with its surroundings became a way for contemporary Japanese architects to construct isolated spaces for reflection within the frenetic, splintered context of the modern Japanese city. In what Botond Bognar has termed an "architecture of resistance," introverted structures such as the early houses of Tadao Ando provided undisturbed sanctuaries for quiet self-reflection. In these tightly edited projects, "New relations between the space and the person were intended to engender new modes and meanings of existence."[5] Light is the most fundamental element for the realization of this kind of space, and Ando has always sought to utilize materials and construction techniques that enhance the visual drama conveyed by daylight. In her own effort to produce a numinous atmosphere, artist Eriko Horiki employs large swaths of handmade paper to capture and celebrate light. These *washi* surfaces change color and pattern throughout the day, circumscribing spaces that embody the Japanese concept of *utsuroi*, or the ability to perceive the gradual passage of time.

Influenced by the teachings of Shinto from his childhood, Fujimori seeks to construct contemporary "sacred enclosures," using raw, handcrafted materials. Primarily situated within rural settings, Fujimori's structures are not forced to contend with the turbulent urban context, and therefore they seek a more extroverted approach. Inspired by his study of various vernacular typologies, his architecture actively seeks a deeper connection with nature—including surfaces designed to propagate foliage. Fujimori's buildings are simultaneously contemporary and ancient, evoking the primal atmospheres of early Japanese ritual sites.

---

[1] Arata Isozaki, *Japan-ness in Architecture*, trans. Sabu Kohso (Cambridge: MIT Press, 2006), 151.

[2] Kenya Hara, *Shiro [White]*, trans. Jooyeon Rhee (Tokyo: Chuokoron-Shinsha, 2008), 45.

[3] Ibid.

[4] Thomas Daniell, *After the Crash: Architecture in Post-Bubble Japan* (New York: Princeton Architectural Press, 2008), 105.

[5] Botond Bognar, *The New Japanese Architecture* (New York: Rizzoli, 1990), 18.

↑
放射線科
中央処置室
検査科
内視鏡

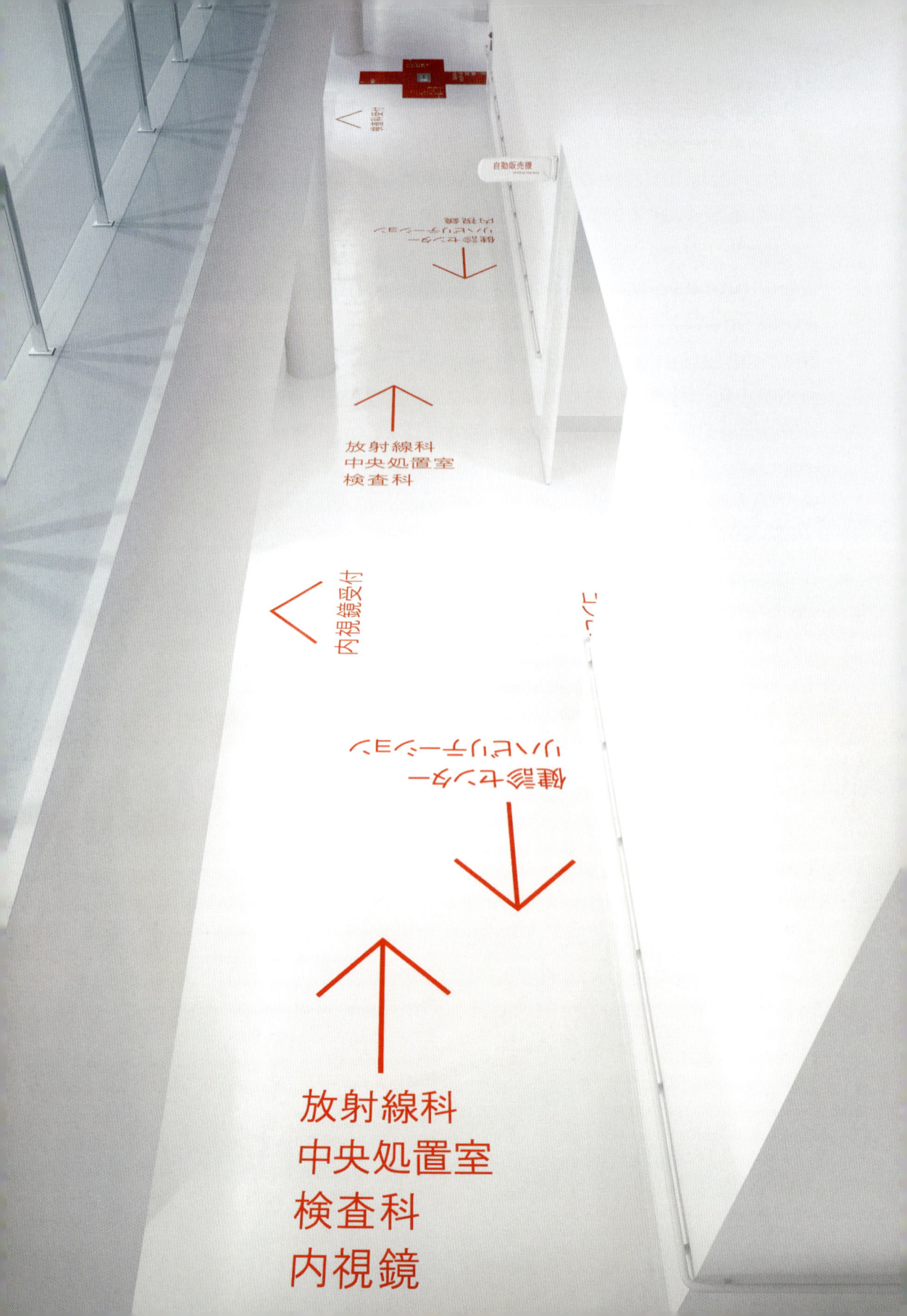

Information Architecture

A conversation with Kenya Hara, Nippon Design Center

In an age of increasing design specialization, Kenya Hara is a generalist extraordinaire. Hara's many talents and activities are infused with profound themes that are refreshing, maybe even necessary, in today's frenetic design culture. He is not only Japan's preeminent graphic design guru but also an accomplished industrial designer, art director, curator, and spokesperson for Japanese design—not to mention art director for Japanese retailer MUJI. Hara claims not to design products, but rather information. By studying innate human responses to materials, he is able to maximize the value of what he calls "senseware."[1]

[1] "Senseware" is Hara's term for technology that has a strong connection to tactility. Used as a theme for several exhibitions featuring Japanese fibers, senseware also relates to stone tools, paper, and other inventions that relate to human touch.

Born in 1958, Kenya Hara is a graphic designer, professor at the Musashino Art University, and, since 2002, the art director of MUJI. He is interested in designing circumstances or conditions rather than things. Hara has traveled the world widely in an attempt to investigate the meaning of design. These efforts were crystallized in the international touring exhibitions Re-Design, Haptic, and Senseware, each title representing a keyword that embraces the ever-changing value of existence. He incorporated traditional Japanese cultural features in his designs for the opening and closing ceremonies of the Nagano Winter Olympics, as well as in the promotion of the Aichi Expo. Hara has designed commercial products for many companies, including Ajinomoto General Foods, Japan Tobacco, and Kenzo; was involved in the renewal project of the Ginza branch of the Matsuya department store; and worked on the signage for Mori Building VI and Umeda Hospital. Hara has received numerous design awards, including the Japanese Cultural Design Award.

Sign design for Katta Civic Polyclinic (opposite)

Although your primary field is graphic design, you assume a variety of roles and are not so easily labeled.

I am a graphic designer, but my specialty is communication: instead of making things or products, I make concepts. My work is the identity people have with a product, what makes them gather at a place for a product. The product is not a physical object, but a language.

I also love the concept of design. Design is, of course, a twentieth-century concept, because design was easily compatible with the product economy that developed during that time. This relationship has been perfected for a twenty-first-century society, and design will play an interesting role in the future. I am interested in orienting design within this new role. Like mathematical and biological knowledge, design knowledge increases within a person's mind and he or she looks at the world differently, causing the world to change. Design knowledge thus broadens society's mental capacity for change, and I design with this capacity in mind.

I find it intriguing that you address this capacity beyond the visual realm and the standard two dimensions.

I am creating information architecture. I am making design directed toward the architecture of the mind—that is, information that enters the mind immediately through the senses of sight, smell, sound, touch, and taste. There is one other thing that accumulates within the mind as well: memory. These are the ingredients, and they enter from outside and through the existing senses. When a new sensation enters the mind, a memory is made. This is how information architecture is constructed.

You often discuss the way in which our senses are connected. For example, when I see a poster depicting food, I can imagine how it will taste. If I see an image of enlarged material texture, I can imagine how it would feel.

Yes—when individuals see something to eat that they recognize, they already know the taste. Thus, when we witness another person repeat an experience we have had—such as eating a particular kind of food—we share in the experience by way of our constructed memory. As children develop, they broaden the scope of this constructed memory.

Perhaps this is why young children put everything in their mouths! [laughs]

Young children are still developing their sight and hearing, so taste is an important sense.

It would seem that a multisensory design approach would be the ideal way to develop information architecture. In your work, you celebrate haptic as well as visually oriented design. You also engage projects assuming different roles—designer, writer, curator, and philosopher.

I edit information. I design form, decide on color, and so on. Of course, I don't do everything—I employ a sign maker to fabricate a sign or a photographer to take a picture. I ask many people to help collect the best information. I then edit this information to create one message.

The process of design must also be a close investigation. If I don't engage in a close investigation, information is disconnected and scattered. If I focus on things, however, my own creativity emerges. I work intuitively, writing the context that allows one message to develop.

I imagine this intense focus is critical to creating highly refined designs in which all extraneous elements are removed. This quality is evident in your work as well as in many Japanese arts and crafts—the simultaneous achievement of simplicity and a high level of creativity. Take your Tanpopo (dandelion wine) label or MUJI posters, for example—these works are simple, but they are not simplistic.

I know what you mean. *Kanso* means simple in Japanese.[2] It is an inoperative meaning, different from the English word *simple*. MUJI products are simple, but they have quality—one might say there is quality in something simple. For Japanese, this is a highly valued

---

[2] "Kanso" is defined as basic simplicity and the elimination of the ornate.

MUJI poster from 2003

Like mathematical and biological knowledge, design knowledge increases within a person's mind and he or she looks at the world differently, causing the world to change.

thing. Specifically, if something is simple, it can inspire. The capacity of the imagination is increased.

For example, imagine there is a table. When an eighteen-year-old man sees it, he thinks he can use it for his single lifestyle—that it would be perfect in his room. A fifty-year-old couple sees the same table and thinks it would look great in their bedroom. It may seem that this eighteen year old and the fifty-year-old couple are looking at two different tables, but the same table works in both cases. At MUJI we do not make two separate tables for an eighteen year old and a fifty-year-old couple. We only make one that satisfies multiple conditions. However, designing one table that satisfies a variety of demographics is extremely difficult. To be simple is to be empty. Through this emptiness, an ideal image can emerge—meaning that there is no image already existing, and you may insert your own image.

For example, the Japanese flag has a red circle, but it has no meaning. However, when this circle is surrounded by a white background, it has meaning. Some people say that it signifies the sun, and others think it represents rice with an *umeboshi* in the middle.[3] During World War II, the flag symbolized the sun rising over Japan, but this image became a negative one. Following the war people insisted that the red circle represents peace, which is how I view the flag. However, the red circle does not have meaning, because it is an empty sign. This emptiness allows for many meanings.

Japanese people have made use of this strategy in communication for a long time. For this reason, the Japanese do not say things clearly. For example, the phrase *yoroshiku onegai shimasu* is said all the time, yet it is unclear.[4] However, that does not mean it has a negative connotation. Depending on the context, the phrase can convey different meanings, and some have trouble with this. Similarly the Japanese word *ka* is an empty particle meant to encourage communication

---

[3] Umeboshi is a Japanese pickled plum.
[4] "Yoroshiku onegai shimasu" has no direct English translation, but one approximation is, "I hope you will take care of (someone or something) in a way that is convenient for both of us." Depending on the situation, it could mean "Please give someone my regards" or "Take care."

> To be simple is to be empty. Through this emptiness, an ideal image can emerge—meaning that there is no image already existing, and you may insert your own image.

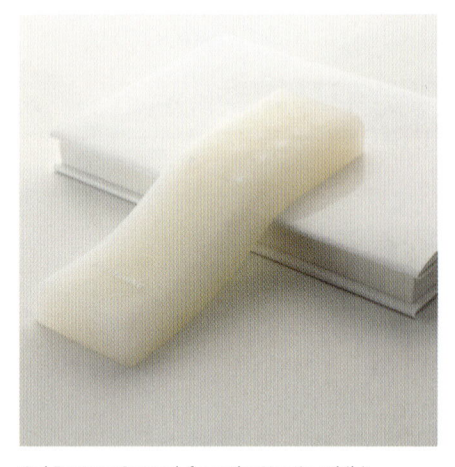

Naoto Fukasawa's Juice Skin, from the Haptic exhibit at the 2004 Takeo Paper Show

Gel Remote Control, from the Haptic exhibit, Panasonic Design Company

Kosuke Tsumura's Kami Tama, from the Haptic exhibit

Packaging for Hakkin, a Japanese sake

between people.[5] Thus, simple in this case means that many meanings are possible—the capacity of language becomes great.

The Japanese tearoom is very simple—it is small and contains nothing. The host invites a guest and makes tea. A vase filled with a few cherry blossoms evokes the meaning of the cherry blossom season, and this shared memory enhances the friends' conversation. Imagination is inspired in this way. We use the tearoom for its emptiness. Emptiness is part of Japanese consciousness.

Is this emptiness the same thing as ma?[6]
It's not just ma, although ma means "nothing." MUJI means "no brand," for example—it is simple, yet it is enticing because it carries many images. For some people, MUJI represents ecology. For others, it represents affordability. Yet another reading is sophistication. There are a lot of meanings, so the feeling of emptiness is not conveyed. For this reason, the brand is a simple icon like the red circle in the Japanese flag.

For Japanese people, how does the MUJI brand compare with that of a luxury retailer like Gucci? Can MUJI's popularity be explained by the fact that there is no logo—because people want to express their individuality?
People don't see MUJI or Gucci as a brand. When MUJI was first established, it was said to have no design, but that was not really the case. If it was just simple, we couldn't make a table or a chair. However, MUJI aspired to have a clear vision. Another trademark is its affordability. With other, more expensive brands, customers will part with a lot of money—a system is created in which customers feel like spending a lot of money. However, MUJI is a place where customers can find enjoyment in purchasing products for daily life.

I appreciate the notion of taking everyday products and transforming them via some small means. A number of designers and architects featured in your Haptic exhibition took this approach. One of my favorite examples is Naoto Fukasawa's juice box exhibit. By replacing the standard graphic label with a simulated fruit skin, he completely transformed the product—without changing the shape or size of the box.
Yes, we were not interested in creating eye-catching forms or flamboyant colors. The secret lies within the ordinary.

A conventional way to think about progress, for example, is in the pursuit of higher numbers. Eight, nine, and ten lead to eleven, twelve, and thirteen—and society will say that next comes fourteen. That is progress. However, what about 8.5 or 6.2? You realize that there is an infinite number of numbers in between the integers. The future is not fourteen or fifteen, but rather the limitless possibilities between eight and nine. Once you make this discovery, design changes completely. We consider the boring stuff of daily life and enhance it with a design that surprises. That is progress. My role is to awaken the power of design. That is to say, within the experience of daily life I want to make others think: can something be like this, or can a table look like this? It is crucial to make people realize something new about daily life that they thought they already understood.

For example, imagine a plate and a cup. A plate and a cup are clearly different from one another in shape, right? If the cup gradually becomes shallower and wider, however, it approaches the shape of the plate. Now imagine a subtle gradation from cup to plate. Try to establish a boundary between the two. At a certain point, we do not know if we are looking at a cup or a plate. This new form of ignorance actually results in a better understanding of what makes a cup a cup and a plate a plate. In daily life, we assume we know what a cup and plate are without a doubt. Yet, this little experiment surprises

---

5 Ka is a particle that indicates a question.

6 Ma is a concept that has many meanings and loosely describes an interval. Arata Isozaki defines nine aspects of ma in his book *Japan-ness in Architecture*. Some of the definitions are interstice, darkness, aperture, transience, and projection of the body. Arata Isozaki, *Japan-ness in Architecture*, trans. Sabu Kohso (Cambridge: MIT Press, 2006), 327–28.

people. Rather than making an amazing form for a cup, it's more effective to explore the gradient between a cup and a plate. In this way, people will realize how much they don't really know. This is beautiful design.

> This approach reminds me of your Matsuya Renewal Project, which is a kind of hybrid between minimal environmental graphics and architecture. One becomes aware of a dual condition in which signage represents a particular brand of products and is also the container for those products.

That's right.

> I wonder how we might expand this notion a bit? For example, with the exception of the paper on which it appears, graphic design is distanced from the material world. It is a decidedly nonhaptic enterprise—a realm of symbols and representation that relies upon our collected memories in order to communicate. Hence the phrase "The paper is only worth the information printed on it." However, you have demonstrated the vast potential that resides in "tweening" the territories of graphic design and product design, or between environmental graphics and architecture.

Recently I have become interested in the idea of senseware. Senseware is something that is close to humans and awakens human senses—it inspires our creativity. You mentioned paper as a medium. Paper's role as a medium was emphasized with the advent of electronic media. However, paper is not just a medium—I am realizing this right now—it is senseware. What is important about paper is its whiteness and its tensility. If paper were green, then it would more closely resemble a veneer. As a veneer, it would have reminded us of the tree from which it came, but people would not have been stimulated by it. The whiteness of paper, specifically, is extremely crucial. When paper was initially developed, there was nothing in the world as white. Although we consider bones, shells, and particular rocks to be white, they are really off-white or beige. When paper is put in water, crushed, and made into a rectangular shape, it becomes incredibly white when dried in the sun. The whiteness is extremely fragile and impressive. When we write on paper with black ink, we damage it. But this damage is a record. The emergence of black and white was a great turning point in human history. Thus, paper is not just a medium—its material qualities have inspired humanity.

During the Stone Age, our ancestors developed stone tools. Stone was also senseware. The weight and hardness of stone, as well as its coolness when touched, are special qualities of the material. The strength, mass, and durability of stone awoke humans. Stone inspired and drove humanity.

The exhibition Tokyo Fiber adopted the theme of senseware to investigate the power of materials to transcend media.

> What about digital media? The computer has made graphic design an even more ephemeral enterprise. How might the digital realm relate to the physical one? What do you think about electronic paper, for example?

Hmm, what would it be like? [laughter] Electronic paper is fine, but it can become boring. Even when humanity progresses, we do not depart our bodies. If you did not have your body, Mr. Brownell, and instead assumed a technologically sophisticated body, it would be compact and convenient, right? [laughter] But the human body does not really change. Our media may become more abstract, but our corporality does not change.

Electronic paper has its own beauty, but we should remember that the hapticity of this material does not inspire. Information operates in a relative way, not an absolute one. For example, if I were to say that I would eat five thousand eggs, I would not be happy. How could I obtain so many, where would I put them, and how would I digest them? However, if I were to see only one egg before my eyes, I would appreciate how I could eat it deliciously. I would boil it for exactly ten minutes, add some relish, and put it on a well-designed egg stand next to a spoon and saltshaker with good salt. I would eat the delicious egg.

Information is the same—if there's too much delivered at the same level, it's no good.

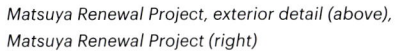

Matsuya Renewal Project, exterior detail (above),
Matsuya Renewal Project (right)

Paper is not just a medium—
I am realizing this right now—
it is senseware.

Program catalog for the Nagano Winter Olympics

94 Matter in the Floating World   Atmosphere

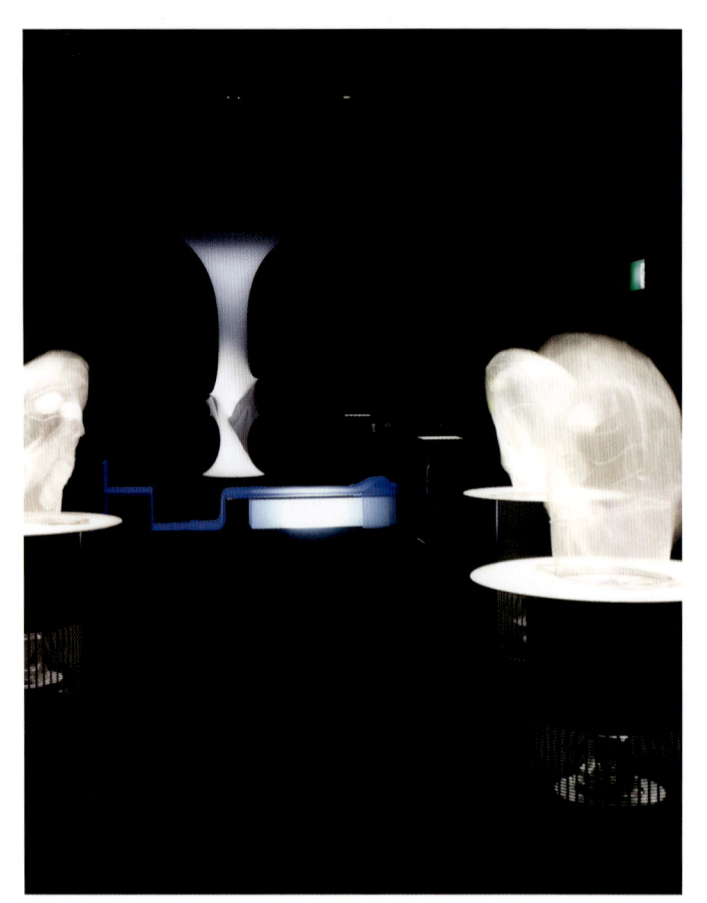

Tokyo Fiber exhibition space

Little TV That Rests in Your Hand, from the Tokyo Fiber exhibit, Sony

No Constraints Carpet—an electric blanket imparted with artificial animal qualities—from the Tokyo Fiber exhibit, Panasonic Design Company

Of course, there is actually an unconscionable amount of information in nature, but we are able to filter and decipher it in a meaningful way. However, information media are fragmented and not yet sophisticated enough to deliver content according to this filtered experience.

> In a conversation published in your exhibition catalog *Haptic*, you and Toyo Ito discussed the extent to which modern architecture has become obsessed with transparency and thin materials like glass and steel—despite the fact that the results can be sterile and uninviting.[7] It would seem that the recent surge and variety of new materials developed for architecture and design have transformed the collective consciousness about what is possible.

This could be the case. It certainly transpired in the Tokyo Fiber exhibition, in which designers worked with a collection of natural and synthetic fibers to create new objects and experiences. The human senses are capable of feeling a variety of things, but there is a whole world we still haven't felt. If you look at a simple map of the senses, we typically design for only a small portion. I am trying to find a way to expand the sensory reach of design.

When we design something, it's always about the outside—the color, shape and form, and texture. The exterior form is important, but how you engage something with multiple senses, in a previous experience, actually intensifies your impression. That is to say, "Until now I haven't tasted something like this," or "I haven't felt anything like this"—an experience not had until now. This discovery has to be experienced in a precise and conscious way. As a result, something new will broaden the world, whether it's natural or artificial. Material by itself is not interesting. The way of feeling it has to be well planned.

> Before modern times design used to convey meaning to more senses. For example, I recently met with a Japanese contractor who is reviving traditional Japanese construction technologies. He showed a kind of glue to me made entirely of rice, which has the strength of any common wood adhesive. He surprised me by putting his finger in the bottle and then sticking it in his mouth, demonstrating that the glue is entirely edible.[8] Of course, I'm not proposing a return to traditional construction methods, but I do think there is a lot of information about materials that we lost during the process of modernization.

That's true.

> Perhaps we could discuss your design for the Aichi Expo. How would you characterize your approach related to the material and ecological themes that were highlighted at that event?

The typical perspective is that the natural world and human world are in opposition to one another, but that's not the case. There is a difference between the artificial and the natural—but the more we develop technology, the boundary will blur. Currently this is the model of progress. If you consider making a really artificial table, for example, it will gradually emulate natural principles. As for sustainability, we must stop thinking about the human world as an artificial one that must return to a natural state. It is not about returning to nature, but moving forward. This is a more positive and perhaps political point of view, but I think Japanese people have arrived at this general idea. In modern history, of course, human activities have led to considerable environmental degradation—take the polluting Japanese steel industries or the atomic bombs dropped on Japan, for example—however, we have fortunately cleaned up our act in recent years.

> Water is a common symbol of purity in Japanese gardens, and you also employ water frequently in your work. I am thinking of the Humidifier and Water Pachinko installations, for example. It is interesting that you utilize a substance that most graphic designers would avoid, since it degrades paper.

I haven't really thought about it that deeply [laughter]. But I think it's good to think of

---

7 See Kenya Hara, *Haptic* (Tokyo: Takeo, 2004).

8 The contractor I mention is Kazuo Hayakumo with Kansai Construction Association Ltd., who is revitalizing traditional Japanese building materials and techniques for use by a broad audience.

water as beautiful, especially for the sense of touch. To the Japanese, water is extremely clean, and of course people rely upon it for the ritual Japanese bath.

I also employ other natural substances for their essential qualities. Colors, for example, carry fundamental meanings. White, black, red, blue—I use them a lot. They carry concepts. I just completed a book called *White*.[9] White is not a color but a concept. Black is the same—it's not a color but a concept, and has many forms. White is remarkable, black is dark, blue is ambiguous, and red is bright. Remarkable, dark, ambiguous, and bright are Japanese concepts of color. Physicists don't examine color for these kinds of specifications.

In the Heian period, people paid close attention to seasonal changes.[10] There were seventy-two recognized colors at that time. These seventy-two colors were derived from the five or six variations of color experienced during each seasonal change. Accomplished dye-makers were well respected for being able to attain the exact colors. People were attuned to the many color changes observed in each season.

Yes, I learned that the Japanese have many words for color combinations as well. *Sakura*, for example, symbolizes the red and white found in cherry blossoms.[11]

That's right. The two colors are both simultaneously present. The Japanese developed an extensive vocabulary to describe color. For this reason, color is conceived more like a value. Brightness, darkness, remarkable, and ambiguous are values. When I use black, white, or red, it's not an issue of color but of conceptual direction.

Speaking of conceptual directions, what future do you see for your work?

I want to create design that humans can understand. This is not about a large scale. I want to design a textbook for middle schoolers that is easy to understand. Math and philosophy textbook designs are stiff, and if I don't do them, it would be a shame. If there were a well-designed math textbook, it would be amazing.

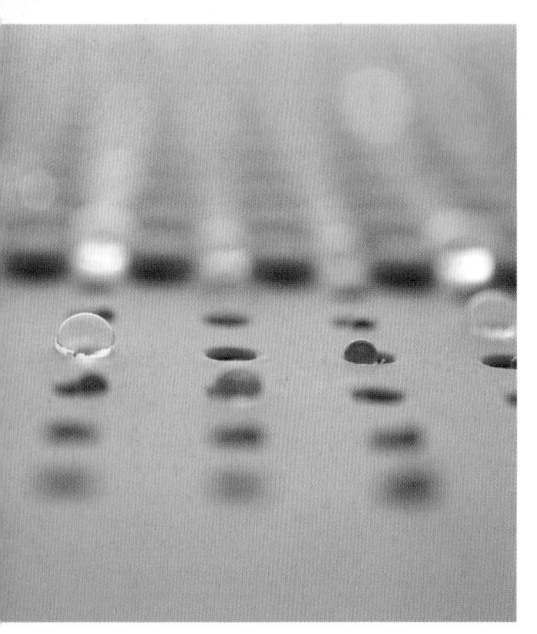

Humidifier, from the Haptic exhibit

[9] Kenya Hara, *White* (Baden, Switzerland: Lars Müller Publishers, 2009).

[10] The Heian period (794–1185 CE) is considered the last epoch of Japanese classical history. This period saw the development of a protocol for layering particular colors in court attire, called *kasane no irome*. The government actually dictated which color combinations could be worn by which classes.

[11] Sakura is the flower of a cherry tree.

There is a difference between the artificial and the natural—
but the more we develop technology, the boundary will blur.

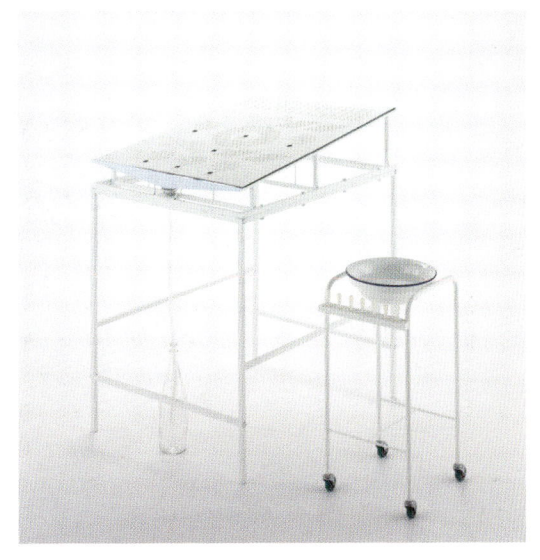

Water Pachinko, from the Haptic exhibit

Hara Design Institute + Atelier Omoya, Water Logo, from the Tokyo Fiber exhibit

Invisible Architecture

A conversation with Kazuyo Sejima, SANAA
with Florian Idenburg, SO-IL

Once an advocate of achieving lightness in architecture via skeletal frames and exposed tectonics, Kazuyo Sejima now seeks to create lightness via atmosphere. Her work with partner Ryue Nishizawa exemplifies the extreme minimalist ambitions of the so-called white school and has been accordingly dubbed "invisible architecture."[1] In a conversation held in SANAA's Tokyo office, Sejima and project architect Florian Idenburg discussed their multiple approaches to using materials in the service of undermining materiality.

---

1 D. J. Huppatz, "An Invisible Architecture: SANAA and the Art of 21st Century Museum Design," *Art & Australia* 47, no. 2 (Summer 2009), http://www.artaustralia.com/article.asp?issue_id=189&article_id=206.

Kazuyo Sejima was born in 1956 in Ibaraki Prefecture, Japan. She founded Kazuyo Sejima and Associates in 1987, after studying at Japan Women's University and practicing in the office of Toyo Ito. A partner with Ryue Nishizawa in the internationally acclaimed firm SANAA (Sejima and Nishizawa and Associates) since 1995, Sejima still runs her own independent office for small, local projects. SANAA is known for minimalist designs and an abstract approach to the investigation of space, with a portfolio that includes Dior Omotesando (2003), the 21st Century Museum of Contemporary Art in Kanazawa (2005), the Glass Pavilion at the Toledo Museum of Art (2006), and the New Museum of Contemporary Art in New York (2007). Sejima has taught at Keio University (2001–present), the Ecole Polytechnique Fédérale de Lausanne (2006), and Princeton University (2006–8). Sejima was appointed director of the architecture sector for the Venice Biennale, for which she curated the Twelfth Annual International Architecture Exhibition in 2010. In the same year, she and partner Nishizawa were awarded the Pritzker Architecture Prize.

Florian Idenburg was a project architect for SANAA in Tokyo until 2007 and is currently a partner at Solid Objectives-Idenburg Liu (SO-IL) in New York. He edited *The SANAA Studios 2006–2008: Learning from Japan: Single Story Urbanism* (2009).

Glass Pavilion at the Toledo Museum of Art (opposite)

Your first projects had simple programs yet were formally complex. However, there has been a kind of reversal over time—now your projects have complex programs and relatively simple forms.

Sejima: I also realize that I used a lot more materials when I started my practice than I do now.

Idenburg: And color.

Sejima: And color, yes. I learned how to design architecture at Toyo Ito's office, so there was that influence and also the influence of the so-called Bubble period.[2] I just tried to demonstrate how a building was made in a direct way. If it made sense to use steel for a ceiling, for example, I would specify and expose the steel. As the scale increased and the program became complex, however, I reconsidered how to make buildings.

Many architects use materials in explicit ways. Examples include Tadao Ando's studies in concrete or Kengo Kuma's experiments with stone and bamboo. What interests me about your work is the pursuit of dematerialization via abstraction—despite the fact that materials are required to make architecture. How do you achieve this quality?

Sejima: I agree that materials have their own character and good points. For example, if you make a table with steel or metal, it becomes very sharp, but at the same time cold. Wood looks a little bit warm and is also softer and more comfortable. I like to take advantage of these particular qualities, but at the same time I want to avoid conveying certain aspects of material meaning.

Material decisions are largely based on context and program. The environment surrounding the Toledo Glass Pavilion is so beautiful, for example, that the extensive use of glass on the exterior was not a problem. However, if the context had been different, we may have used a different material for the facade.

I'm interested in your desire for architecture to defy materiality. I'm also intrigued by your aspirations to take a material to its extreme limit. You apply this idea equally to the design of a

Glass Pavilion at the Toledo Museum of Art

building or a chair—how thin can a roof profile be, a column, or a seat, for example? Where did this pursuit of thinness originate?

Sejima: Sometimes this ambition originates from an aesthetic point of view. In Japan immediately after World War II, there was a scarcity of materials. In those days people had to make do with less and were therefore pressed to innovate. This physical reality influenced cultural attitudes regarding beauty.[3]

In the House in a Plum Grove, we set out to change the relationship between adjacent rooms. Although walls divide the spaces within the house, these partitions are made of thin steel plate. Therefore, they completely transform the conventional relationship between adjoining spaces, compared with rooms separated by conventional stud walls. House in a Plum Grove is perhaps an extreme case, but we typically pursue thinness in many building components.

---

2 The "economic bubble" in Japan describes a period from 1986 to 1990 in which stock prices and real estate were hugely inflated.

3 After World War II, Japanese cities faced serious housing shortages, and many design proposals were generated to optimize material resources and living space. See Thomas Daniell, *After the Crash: Architecture in Post-Bubble Japan* (New York: Princeton Architectural Press, 2008), 67.

Glass Pavilion, floor detail

Idenburg: It's not about trying to push a material to its extreme limit just for the sake of it. It's about trying to achieve a particular goal, and we need to push materials to the extreme to accomplish that goal.

In the actual process of design and construction, are you always pushing?

Sejima: Yes, especially with the structural engineer with whom we collaborate. We use the same engineer 95 percent of the time, and he also influences us. The contractors vary, however.

We can show a thin column or floor, but a thin roof is very difficult to achieve based on its many functional requirements, such as structure, slope, insulation, mechanical systems, and so on. In the New Museum, we were able to expose various systems, but other clients might not want this visual effect. In any case, we try to avoid creating a gigantic zone in which anything can happen, which is very unclear.

Since you are working a lot outside Japan, is it a very different process in other places? Is it a much bigger challenge to accomplish these feats?

Sejima: It depends.
Idenburg: I think, for instance, of the Essen project. We achieved something that was difficult to achieve here in Japan, right?[4]
Sejima: I think so.

Because of the geothermal system?
Sejima: Yes, this is one thing, so that we could avoid insulation.

That's amazing.
Idenburg: In Germany.
Sejima: And also the radiant-heat floor system—it's very popular in Germany, but in Japan nobody uses it.
Idenburg: So really it depends on the culture. Sometimes we can do things in other places.
Sejima: Also the New Museum. Normally a Japanese museum—even a contemporary museum—wouldn't allow us to expose the systems, but the New Museum is a very experimental museum, I think, and they expected us to take this direction. So it depends on the client, program, and site. It also depends on the team, because in the end buildings are made by people. We had many good subcontractors in Toledo, and the detail where the glass touches the floor is impossible to achieve in Japan.
Idenburg: Really?
Sejima: Yes, I think we would need more adjustment space for the grinding—it's so amazing.
Idenburg: I think every project is a story where we just try to see if we can do it.

Do you spend a lot of time in the construction administration phase ensuring the proper execution of the design?

Sejima: Yes, but this also depends. We often collaborate with a local architect. It is also very important that our staff be involved as much as possible. For foreign projects, we send our staff to monitor the work frequently.

That's impressive. Earlier you were speaking about materials and the notion to use them in unexpected ways. Let's take a material like glass, for example. It's very interesting how you use glass, because most architects think of glass with a limited sense of its potential. You use

---

4 SANAA's Zollverein School of Management and Design at Essen employs a geothermal heating system in lieu of insulation, allowing the exterior walls to be surprisingly thin and perforated with large apertures.

Matter in the Floating World   Atmosphere

Opaque Ginza, exterior detail

The most interesting example of a glass application is perhaps the Toledo museum. One thinks that glass is transparent, but many layers of glass make a completely different atmosphere.

Glass Pavilion at the Toledo Museum of Art, various optical effects (middle), ceiling detail (bottom)

curved glass, frameless glass, glass layered with other materials, glass with frits or patterns, stripes, big words, and so on. Why do you take a material that one usually expects to be simple and transparent and experiment so much with it?

Sejima: Originally I started using glass because I was interested in structure. I wanted to show the structural system, so I just used glass for the non-load-bearing parts.

Idenburg: To show that they're not structure.

Sejima: To show how the building was constructed. But then heat gain became a concern. Of course, the relationship between inside and outside is one thing I am very interested in. However, in order to mitigate heat gain, we have used frits and other shading applications. The most interesting example of a glass application is perhaps the Toledo museum. One thinks that glass is transparent, but many layers of glass make a completely different atmosphere. Sometimes glass appears to be a very hard and cold substance, but in Toledo the glass is softer. Although the Toledo glass is very transparent, when you view the curved panels obliquely the glass gradually changes.

Idenburg: But also at some point we were interested in old glass, no? The glass that would start to become physical, like a bottle.

Sejima: Not completely flat.

Idenburg: Yes, so then glass becomes more of a material instead of something transparent.

Sejima: Also glass is very interesting because the viewer's impression of it changes not simply because of his or her relationship to it, but in conjunction with other factors. Glass is heavily influenced in the planning process. For example, glass changes dramatically if it is positioned in front of a very bright surface or a dark surface, a shallow space or a very deep space. Exterior glass is also influenced by the sun's position. One can never completely control the impression, I think, but positioning glass must be carefully considered.

I understand. In your Novartis office building there is such a thin floor plate that there is an uncanny brightness. It's interesting to consider

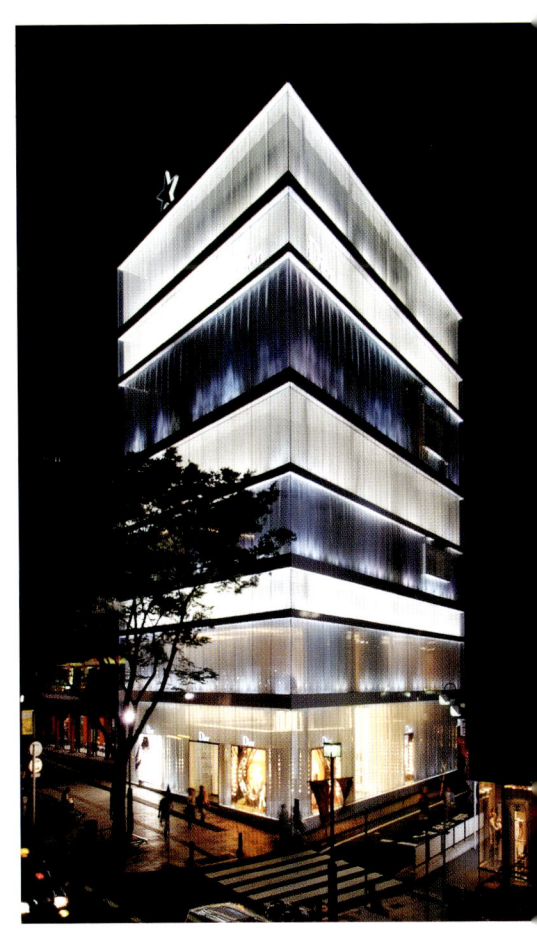

Dior Omotesando

this positioning strategy in light of architects' conventional considerations of glass. For example, when I was a young intern architect I was taught to represent glass as a dark field in drawings, because the architect I worked for always designed thick buildings [all laughing]. In terms of glass and other materials, you often achieve a sense of mystery inside and outside of a building—such as in Dior Omotesando or the IVAM extension in Valencia, Spain.[5] Of course, heat gain is a concern that leads to reduced transparency—but are there other sociological reasons that compel you to create this phenomenon of intrigue?

---

5 SANAA's design for an extension to the Valencian Institute of Modern Art is composed of a large enclosing volume that will create spaces between the original museum and its surrounding site.

Sejima: We developed the scheme for Valencia because there is very good weather. In the spring we had a meeting in northern Europe, and afterwards we traveled to Valencia, and at the airport suddenly we had to take off our coats. Valencia is a very comfortable place, and even when there are hot days in the summer one can find comfort under a tree. One program requirement was to make a public space, but a space enclosed by glass would require a lot of air-conditioning. So we decided to make a "between" space—not an image, but an actual space. We collaborated with Arup engineers, and they generated a lot of simulations. According to their calculations, this semiexterior space would be a little colder than the outside without any added energy. The exterior shading panels would actually be structural and self-supporting. Arup's simulation has helped us determine the number and angle of the perforations.

Idenburg: The sun angle, the wind, and the view.

Sejima: So because the panel thickness is 12.5 centimeters [5 inches], it is able to span 33 meters [108 feet]. Because it is a structural panel, its design is being determined from both structural and mechanical points of view.

> That's amazing. That's a very different application than, say, the Ogasawara Museum, where you're dealing with a relatively small expanse of patterned glass.

Sejima: In Valencia we wanted to create an actual half-outside/half-inside space devoid of high technology. Of course, Arup's simulation is very high technology, but the resulting form is simple.

> There's another technique you use that I like to call the "push-pull effect." The Police Box at Chofu Station has a smooth skin that reflects the local surroundings, while a circular void in the surface seems to pull the background forward.

Sejima: You know, it comes from the function.

Idenburg: You always explain everything by function.

Sejima: It's a very small building but should be a kind of landmark. People suddenly notice it's a police station, so we thought a lot about

Police Box at Chofu Station

the surface of concrete. This was the most difficult thing. On the site the contractor was very careful, and the concrete is very smooth to the touch, but not completely smooth. We thought the building should be a landmark, yet melt into its surroundings—so we tried to use a reflective surface with the hole as structure.

The hole is structural?

Idenburg: For shear.[6]

Oh!

Sejima: The front facade and back facades are both important, and these two concrete walls are connected by a tube. There is also a glass window, because the policeman will remain inside a very small space for twenty-four hours a day. Normally a police box is just a box that operates as a landmark. Although the facade is very important to the city, it's also a space for people.

> I'm also interested in the Naoshima Ferry Terminal, where you used stainless steel–clad shear walls. It seems that one can see all the way through the structure.

Sejima: At Naoshima we wanted to achieve a very smooth, reflective roof surface. Since visitors all approach by a large ferry, the roof becomes the main elevation for the building. So we really wanted to make a very beautiful roof that would reflect the sky and natural surroundings, but this effect was not completely achieved, because of its inherent difficulty.

---

[6] The "hole" is defined by a steel cylinder that adds rigidity against lateral loads.

The U Building appears to accomplish a similar effect, but the grain is quite small, so the glass reflects the sky, while human activity remains visible.

Sejima: It is a typical office building, but it is situated in front of a new train station and public plaza, so the client asked for a kind of landmark. Normally in Japan office buildings are clad with fixed-glass curtain walls, but I thought it would be better if people could open the windows. We first designed sliding glass doors to have a very human scale, and the louvers are effective for sun control. The building reflects the sky, becoming some huge screen and thus a kind of landmark.

How does the building act at nighttime? Does it become completely transparent?

Sejima: It becomes completely transparent.
Idenburg: Is there some special film on the glass?
Sejima: Not film, but a very soft, reflective glass.

Although you primarily use materials to reinforce abstract forms, you occasionally use them to add a kind of tactile warmth. For example, the Y House has a very abstract white tile, but also dark stone. Or the Weekend House in Gunmai, which has a lot of glass and a reflective ceiling, but also wood columns and floor. Is it important that your work have both abstract and concrete qualities?

Sejima: Not necessarily. Spatial considerations are critical, and creating spaces that are comfortable and not too cold is important. Sometimes the proportion of the space can achieve this comfort; other times a material choice can serve this purpose.

You work a lot with physical models. Is it critical for every project that you study how it feels to be inside a space?

Sejima: Gradually I try to bring not only materials, but also other things. A good balance may be achieved by modifying thickness, size, or other qualities of elements. The scale of architecture is larger than that of the body, but I think about how to make a closer relationship.

Idenburg: To bridge the gap.

Naoshima Ferry Terminal

Sejima: Yes. Even if we use thin steel plate, it is very heavy compared with our body's weight.

Do you consciously try to use new materials in projects?

Sejima: Not always.
Idenburg: Sometimes I think you get fascinated by some material and try to see a new way to use it.

Like with the expanded metal in the New Museum.

Sejima: Yes, it was very difficult. It is a very high building that can be seen from far away and also up close from below. Also the galleries required no windows, but offices need windows, so we had to have some integration.

Idenburg: By continuing the mesh over the windows, we maintained the idea of the boxes as one piece.

Sejima: We didn't have such a large budget, but we didn't want to use a very cheap material. From far away the building becomes a kind of wall, but gradually there is a different feeling as you get close to the building. Depending on the sun angle, the exterior looks like a very thin mesh or an opaque wall.

New Museum of Contemporary Art, cladding detail (top), front facade (bottom)

Spatial considerations are critical, and creating spaces that are comfortable and not too cold is important. Sometimes the proportion of the space can achieve this comfort; other times a material choice can serve this purpose.

Idenburg: I was always curious, because suddenly, you found this material. We were struggling to find a way to make a flat box, and we asked "How about mesh?" I don't know where it came from, but suddenly it was there.
Sejima: I also don't remember.
Idenburg: We tested the biggest diamond dimension. We made a special order, and we still have it somewhere.

Which size did you choose—the biggest one?
Sejima: No, twenty-five centimeters [ten inches].
Idenburg: The skin was exciting for the mesh-maker to work on. They now have a picture where they have the biggest mesh hanging in their showroom—they are very proud. Actually, that's one thing—to go back to an earlier question—that you can push people in the United States if it's a really important project to be part of, so then contractors can be innovative. It's about trying to get people enthusiastic to try and push a material, and I think with the mesh we definitely found people who wanted to push it.
Sejima: We first contacted a Japanese company.
Idenburg: There were two companies competing in the end. The Japanese company really wanted the job, but the bid went to the English company.
Sejima: Maybe now the Japanese company could win, based on the exchange rate between the yen and the pound [laughter].

The New Museum has a distinctive texture, but many of your projects are quite smooth and abstract. Your partner Nishizawa's N Museum proposal for Naoshima, for example, has a completely featureless ceiling. Do you ever reach a point where you've gone too far? If so, do you have to pull back and introduce something else?
Idenburg: When I visited the 21st Century Museum of Contemporary Art in Kanazawa during construction, I thought, "Ah, this is too cold, too white, too much abstraction" [laughter]. But then, when we came to the opening, all the art was installed and many people were there. It had become a building for people. I think architects forget that people will come as well as art, and those things will soften the texture.
Sejima: And especially Kanazawa, great artists came and changed the space dramatically. So it's very amazing—sometimes it looks very big, sometimes one can see the edges, but sometimes they're blurry; so it depends on the art.

Kanazawa and your other buildings create a particular atmosphere—a kind of floating sensation. I'm reminded of childhood memories when I used to stare at clouds, and to me you're capturing a similar experience in your buildings. Where does this phenomenon come from? Do you want to create a kind of ethereal, ungrounded space? Is it because the Japanese city is so visually chaotic that you want to make architecture a retreat from the confusion?
Sejima: On the one hand, a space should be independent, but on the other, it should have a good relationship to its inhabitants. It's difficult to explain.
Idenburg: Do you mean that a space should not have too much influence on how people use it? It's more like an atmosphere.
Sejima: Without people, a space should be something. But at the same time, a space should have a capacity to communicate with people. The space should influence its occupants, but not necessarily by touch.
Idenburg: A sense of protection.

Is the word *funiki* something you often consider?[7]
Sejima: I'm very interested in funiki. One could design a space with all white walls, but there must be balance. For example, a wall made of brick painted white evokes a different feeling than a concrete wall painted white. The concept of balance is critical in achieving a particular atmosphere.

Perhaps the goal is for occupants to have an unburdened lifestyle.
Sejima: Or just to spend the time freely.

---

[7] "Funiki" means atmosphere or mood.

108 Matter in the Floating World   Atmosphere

*21st Century Museum of Contemporary Art,
corridor (above), ceiling detail (top right),
east entrance (right), exterior gallery (below)*

Invisible Architecture — Kazuyo Sejima

A space should have a capacity to communicate with people.

21st Century Museum of Contemporary Art, west entrance (top), HHStyle Casa (bottom)

Substance and Abstraction

A conversation with Tadao Ando, Tadao Ando Architects & Associates

No survey of material-focused architecture in Japan would be complete without Tadao Ando. For my generation, Ando's work provided the most compelling example of a Japanese modernism—with buildings crafted from contemporary materials embodying essential qualities of Japanese space. The relentless precision of construction in Ando's architecture is world-renowned; yet somehow his work is able to establish a balance between physicality and ephemerality. For this conversation, I ventured to Ando's vertiginous office in Osaka to ascertain his architectural secrets.

Tadao Ando is one of the most renowned contemporary Japanese architects. His work is characterized by large expanses of unadorned architectural concrete and other raw materials. He has designed many notable buildings, including Row House in Sumiyoshi, Osaka (1976), which gave him the annual Prize of the Architectural Institute of Japan in 1979; Church of the Light, Osaka (1989); the Pulitzer Foundation for the Arts, St. Louis (2001); Teatro Armani, Milan (2001); the Modern Art Museum of Fort Worth (2002); and 21_21 Design Sight in Tokyo (2007). Among the many awards he has received are the Grande Medaille d'Or from the Académie d'Architecture (1989), the Pritzker Architecture Prize (1995), the Gold Medal of the American Institute of Architects (2002), and the Gold Medal of the International Union of Architects (2005). Ando is an honorary member of the American Institute of Architects and the American Academy of Arts and Letters, as well as the Royal Academy of Arts in London. He has been a visiting professor at the University of California, Berkeley, Yale, Columbia, and Harvard.

Chichu Art Museum, courtyard (opposite)

If Western architects were asked to describe a significant material innovation in modern Japanese architecture, most would likely refer to your perfection of reinforced concrete. Your name is practically synonymous with the material in its most beautiful form—indeed, what architect has not sought to achieve "Ando concrete"? How did you first become interested in concrete as a building material?

I did not invent reinforced concrete, of course. It was a fundamental twentieth-century construction material, along with glass and steel. Before I began working as an architect, there were already great works of exposed concrete designed by architects such as Le Corbusier and Kenzo Tange. However, as a young person starting my architectural career, I felt that it would be possible to achieve a more beautiful expression in concrete.

You certainly had high aspirations. How did you pursue this goal?

The most commonly used cement is portland cement. The name actually comes from the high-quality gravel used for its manufacture.[1] I assumed that portland cement was invented to realize a concrete with the same color, texture, and beauty of Portland stone—the stone used to construct Buckingham Palace in England. However, the actual results were not what I expected. So I developed my own personal goal to achieve a concrete that would be as beautiful as this Portland stone. After all, the material promised a synergy of aesthetics and constructibility—or, put another way, the potential for stonelike beauty without the geometric limitations of stone itself.

Of course, the composition of the concrete is one thing, but making beautiful exposed architectural concrete depends upon the quality of the formwork as well as the quality of the steel reinforcement within the concrete. Since the level of skill exhibited by Japanese carpenters is quite high, I was confident from the beginning that I could achieve uniquely beautiful exposed concrete. Also I wanted to elevate the perception of contemporary architecture and its use of modern materials, so it was important for me to use concrete specifically for this purpose. Thus, while concrete has become a universal, international material for the twentieth and twenty-first centuries, it has been especially well suited to the strong carpentry skills developed during prior centuries in Japan.

You express concrete and other materials with direct, raw honesty in your architecture. Yet at the same time, your work conveys abstract, atmospheric qualities related to the play of light against simple, taut geometries. How is it possible for architecture to be simultaneously palpable and abstract? How do you achieve this duality?

Architecture is naturally composed of substance. The function of human contact is essential to architecture, and architects should not avoid the tactile dimension. Abstraction, on the other hand, did not develop as a concept within architecture or art until the end of the nineteenth century—it's an expression of the twentieth century. Abstraction relates to a modern way of life and a modern way of thinking. Thus, from the beginning of my career, I always believed that architecture should exhibit both qualities of substance and abstraction simultaneously. This is a goal I have pursued from the start.

Is this one outcome of material innovation—that materials might transcend their original reading? How do you approach the subject of innovation in materials?

---

[1] In 1824 English mason John Aspdin invented portland cement, which was a stronger and more consistent cement mix than other versions. Aspdin named the cement based on its similar visual appearance to limestone from nearby Portland, England, that was used in Buckingham Palace and other landmark buildings. Ando's initial disappointment may be attributed to the difference between his and Aspdin's aesthetic expectations for the cement. For more information about the origins of portland cement, see Pieter A. VanderWerf, Ivan S. Panushev, Mark Nicholson, and Daniel Kokonowski (Portland Cement Association and Inc. Building Works), *Concrete Systems for Homes and Low-Rise Construction* (New York: McGraw-Hill, 2005), 28.

Awaji Yumebutai, chapel ceiling

Hyogo Prefectural Museum of Art

I developed my
own personal goal
to achieve a concrete
that would be
as beautiful as this
Portland stone.

Water Temple, approach

Church of the Light

I always believed that architecture should exhibit both qualities of substance and abstraction simultaneously.

Church on the Water, interior wall detail

There is no architecture without materials, so achieving innovation in materials is completely connected to achieving innovation in architecture. Without a doubt, researching and developing better materials is essential. In terms of concrete in particular, I don't believe it has been perfected yet—I'm still making efforts to improve concrete.

> It is well known that successful material execution is paramount in your work. Between the directness of material expression and refinement in detailing, however, it would appear that there is little or no tolerance for mistakes. In fact, it would seem that just a few construction errors in one of your projects would require a complete rebuild. Given the fact that architects don't typically control the construction process, how have you been able to guarantee that contractors achieve such a high level of error-free quality in all of your projects?

Completed works are almost never rejected outright. In order to avoid problematic situations as well as control the quality in the final project, I insist on open and thorough communication. I frequently engage the contractor, who contributes his knowledge to the design of the project. In Japan it is typical for contractors to come regularly to the architect's office. I ask them all the questions I have and try to ensure that all parties understand each situation clearly. For example, the concrete subcontractor who makes all the reinforcing steel must have a clear comprehension of the task at hand and must have all the inputs required to coordinate the whole project.

> Aside from frequent and clear communication, are there any special methods you employ?

What is critical is to show the reference or target that has to be achieved. The beginning of my career was the most difficult time, because there was no reference point for the construction quality I desired for my first small houses. Now when I receive a new commission, I take the client and contractor to completed buildings so they can see my expectations firsthand. During construction I always ask for mock-up walls so that the contractor has to train and understand the target. Earlier in the design process, I also ask contractors to build models of critical components of the project so that they can address any surprises or questions then, in addition to understanding general design expectations.

Once the target is clear, I believe that people anywhere in the world can raise their capacity to meet it. Quality control issues and "misses" arise when expectations are unclear.

> I am interested in the junctions between materials. As you know well, common construction practices include strategies for hiding imperfections at these junctions. Devices such as wood molding or a rubber base disguise ragged edges between a wall and floor, for example. Avoiding the use of such strategies generally requires much more care and time-consuming detailing. Do you spend more time on every project to achieve perfect material transitions—or have you now amassed a basic library of details that you use for reference?

Well, it's both. Of course, there are some details that I decide upon from the beginning, but there are many details that require more thought and development over time. I don't believe that my office takes more time to develop these details than other architecture offices would. However, I think the contractor who works on my projects does invest more time than he would on a conventional building. In Japan the general contractor is involved with the entire design development phase. When I work abroad, the architect of record typically has more to investigate than if he or she uses standard details.

> There are many new materials and technologies available to architects and designers, and some common materials are being redefined—such as light-transmitting concrete or foamed aluminum. What do you think about these new kinds of materials and the way in which material expectations are being transformed? Is this trend a worthwhile exploration or a fad?

Awaji Yumebutai, promenade (above), courtyard with fountain (below)

> The singular obsession with form in architecture schools today must change, and architects will need to lead active roles in solving global environmental problems.

This is a difficult question to answer in general terms. However, in my conception, a building should last for 150 years. One cannot afford to be fashionable. When you build something, you have to make it meaningful. It does not mean that recent experimentation is not meaningful; however, each material must be analyzed individually to determine if it is really worthy of use and is capable of lasting over time—not only in terms of fashion, but also in terms of physical durability.

Your work has quite a recognizable signature. However, I am intrigued by some of your more recent projects in which it appears that you are experimenting beyond this signature. For example, the HHStyle Casa building is composed of steel plate and corrugated-metal interior cladding as opposed to reinforced concrete.

The change you imply does not relate to a desire to alter a style or experiment with materials as a primary goal. Each project is a response to its own particular situation and given conditions. HHStyle is built on a small street that will eventually be widened according to the proposed master plan, so the building is temporary in nature. The client is renting the site for ten years, so we could not

Chichu Art Museum, Walter de Maria exhibition space

21_21 Design Sight, interior gallery

design any major excavation nor specify heavy construction materials. Steel seemed like a natural choice in this case, and I decided to treat exposed steel the same way I normally treat exposed concrete. For HHStyle I became fascinated with the connection between folded sheet metal and cloth. Since the client here was Issey Miyake, I pursued this connection more deeply for the interior surface treatment.

Every project is treated on its own terms, and the material choices relate directly to specific project needs. It's important to note that while I've earned a reputation for using reinforced concrete, I've also explored many other materials, such as wood, brick, steel, glass, and so on.

Yes, I agree that it's important to consider the diverse material choices you have made throughout your career, despite the predominant interest in concrete. On this topic, are there particular materials with which you would like to experiment more in the future?

Well, I cannot say for certain. However, I know that I would only use materials that I am comfortable with and that I enjoy working with. Steel, for example, is a material that I have worked with for a long time. However,

HHStyle Casa (above), entrance (right)

in the next phase of my career I may shift back to wood, given the huge global demand for steel today. In a world where every Chinese and Indian citizen desires a comfortable Western-style home, there will not be enough concrete or steel to accommodate this desire. Given such a scenario, I predict we will return to the widespread use of wood.[2]

> Interesting. I can also imagine a more localized model of renewable-resource harvesting in this scenario, as opposed to the way we ship large quantities of materials around the world today. Of course, other resources like water are in increasing demand.

This is a big problem. In Tokyo people have based a lifestyle on the free consumption of fresh water, but perhaps they will have to employ gray-water strategies instead. Food is also a challenge, and the current population is unsustainable. We will have to find balance. It is important to consider the environment at the scale of the globe. Architecture will continue to find opportunities, but the singular obsession with form in architecture schools today must change, and architects will need to lead active roles in solving global environmental problems. These roles should obviously consider material issues, such as recycling and so on.

> You're right. There's a growing interest in diverting materials from the waste stream in order to maximize material efficiency and minimize pollution. I agree that there are many opportunities for applying sustainable thinking to materials.

I wonder about plastic, for example. Plastic is made from petroleum, but given the increasing scarcity of oil, perhaps the cycle can be reversed and fuel can be made from plastic. The profession of architecture needs to refocus its energies on these kinds of issues, rather than simply making fetish objects. Otherwise, architects won't be needed anymore.

---

[2] In addition to resource and transportation considerations, wood construction may be on the rise based on new developments in hybrid construction—meaning that new fire-resistant compositions of wood may be now used in combination with other materials for commercial and institutional programs. See Korky Koroluk, "Hybrid Building Systems Could Mean a Return for Wood in ICI projects," *Daily Commercial News and Construction Record*, Oct. 20, 2009.

Substance / Abstraction — Tadao Ando

Water Temple

Omotesando Hills (left, above)

A Canvas for Light

A conversation with Eriko Horiki, Eriko Horiki & Associates

As concerns mount about the fading of Japan's great artistic and cultural traditions in the wake of globalization, Eriko Horiki offers an inspiring example. She seized an opportunity to save a dying Japanese washi paper manufacturer in Kyoto and has since transformed the handmade paper industry. Horiki has been able to preserve washi by making it contemporary—pushing its technical limits to achieve new artistic possibilities. Although her medium is two-dimensional, Horiki uses washi to define spaces that convey Japanese notions of ephemerality.

Eriko Horiki was born in Kyoto, Japan, in 1962. Determined to reinvigorate the fading tradition of Japanese washi papermaking, she founded the washi company Shimus in 1987 and the design firm Eriko Horiki & Associates in 2000. Horiki creates original interior artwork based on innovations in washi fabrication, which she calls "washi as architecture." Her work has been featured in numerous locations, shown in venues including the Tokyo Midtown Galleria, the Sogo flagship store in Shinsaibashi, the arrival lobby of Narita International Airport, and the Carnegie Hall stage for Yo-Yo Ma. Horiki's awards include the Japan Association Award of Artists, Craftsmen and Architects (2001), "Woman of the Year" by Nikkei Woman (2003), and the Joie de Vivre Award by the Bureau du Champagne Japon (2009).

Okuaga Furusato Hall (opposite)

How did you become interested in washi paper?[1]
I originally worked at a bank and entered the field indirectly. Around the time I quit my job at the bank, I was asked by a paper company to be part of the office management department—not the design department. I quit my job at the bank and began working at the paper company. The paper was made by hand, not by a machine. Even though I was in the office management area, I would sometimes assist in the production of paper, but I didn't design. However, I was always surrounded by designers. I would watch them, and I thought their work looked like so much fun. The designers went to Echizen in Fukui-ken, where there was a papermaking factory.[2] I asked if I could come even though I didn't know anything about it, so I could see it. When I saw the craftsmen working there, I realized how long it took and how hard the work was to make paper by hand, and I was very moved. I thought this traditional world of crafts was amazing, and I thought the traditional knowledge of these people was inspiring—both the thought process as well as the art. Beyond just the management of the business, there was a great pride in the work.

However, two years later the company went under. This was because the paper was made by hand and no matter what kind of design they developed, a machine could produce cheaper paper faster. It was not handmade paper, but it had a similar design made by machine, so consumers bought the cheaper version. As a result, the price competition was the reason the company did poorly. At that time I wondered how a company with such a high level of art and technique could fail simply because of economics. It was a profound problem that concerned me deeply. I believed the technique and artistry of our traditional crafts needed to be maintained, but who could do it? There was no one to do it, so I thought I had to act. At twenty-four years of age, however, I had not studied design, had no work experience in the field, and didn't have any money. I met with the head of the company for advice. He told me to meet with the president of Gofukudonya, a company that sells kimonos and supports artists in Kyoto, where the traditional arts are fostered.[3] I went there and told the head I wanted to make washi paper and asked him if there was a way I could learn. So at twenty-four I established the Shimus brand. That's how I started.

What an amazing story—the washi-making experience must have affected you deeply.
I entered the field knowing nothing—I couldn't read a drawing, didn't know how the field worked, and I had no experience. So I learned as I went—I am self-taught and didn't go to school for papermaking. Traditional craftsmen are very fixed in their methods and can't really do new things, which is problematic. Since I didn't know anything, I didn't know what I could or couldn't do and therefore thought I could do anything. In this sense, I was a person that did what I didn't know I couldn't do.

When I first entered the field, I decided that I must accomplish three things. First I had to differentiate washi by demonstrating its value. People didn't buy the more expensive handmade paper because they didn't know why it was expensive. However, handmade paper lasts longer than machine-made paper, and it doesn't degrade like the latter. Consumer products like wrapping paper or stationery are used once and discarded. Handmade paper serves long-lasting functions, but we can't take advantage of it if it's used as a disposable item. So I developed a product that could be used for long periods of time. When I thought about

---

1 Washi is a light, strong traditional Japanese paper made by hand from the inner-bark fibers of three plants. The name "washi" literally means "Japanese paper." The Institute of Paper Science and Technology at Georgia Tech, Atlanta has a good description of washi-making: http://www.ipst.gatech.edu/amp/collection/washi/index.htm.

2 Echizen washi dates back to 774 CE, and from the fourteenth century onward, Echizen washi was officially used by court nobles and samurai.

3 Gofukudonya means a wholesale store that sells kimonos (traditional Japanese clothing).

A Canvas for Light — Eriko Horiki

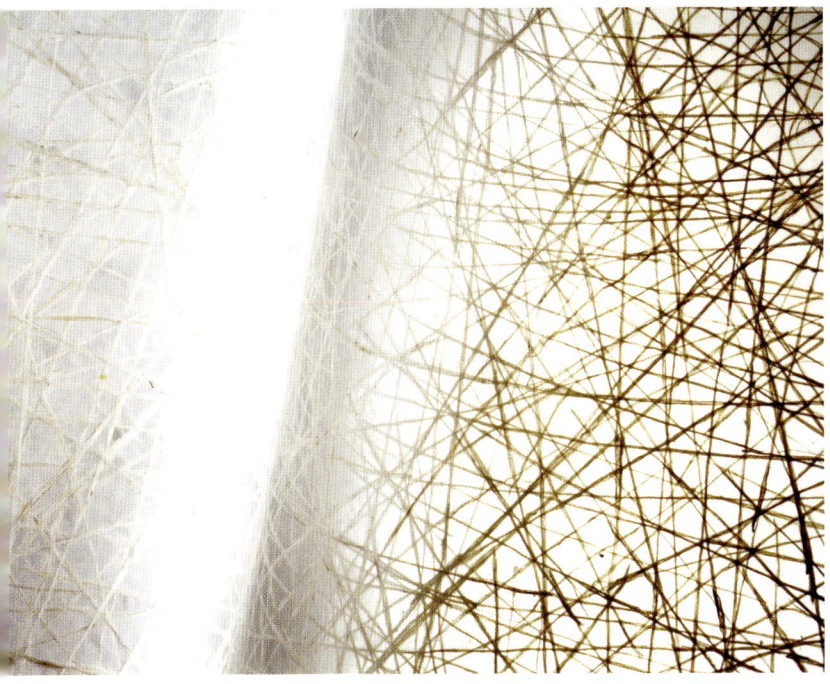

I was a person that did what I didn't know I couldn't do.

Shimus Material B (top), Shimus Material D (right)

I thought I had to make paper that would change the atmospheric feeling of a space.

how it could be used, I thought of interior architecture. In this setting, paper is not just used once and thrown away the next day. It lasts for three, five, or ten years. Washi can last for ten to twenty years as an interior wall. Thus, I was able to differentiate washi paper in the marketplace. Moreover, washi can span larger areas than glass, acrylic, and metal. That is why I directed my work toward interior design from the beginning.

> **If you had no experience in papermaking, how did you know that handmade paper would last so long?**

I knew this fact from going with the designers to see the craftsmen making paper. In seeing the papermaking process and talking to the craftsmen, I realized the strength of paper. I saw the craftsmen's technique and effort, and became committed to continuing this technique for the next generation. When I decided on the application of interior architecture, I had to figure out what kind of washi paper I needed. This was about twenty years ago, and at that time paper was available in 60- to 90-centimeter [24- to 35-inch] widths for individual use and 90- to 180-centimeter [35- to 71-inch] widths for *fusuma* and shoji doors.[4] One of these pieces would cover one door. In a traditional Japanese house, this amount of paper is enough for a fusuma, a shoji screen, or a door. However, in modern architecture, dining and living spaces are all combined. Everything has become larger, the ceilings have become higher—even businesses use more space, so I knew that one piece of washi paper would not be large enough.

So I thought, could a bigger piece of washi paper be made? The ceilings in today's home are about 2.4 meters high, with ceilings of large spaces around 2.7 to 3 meters [8 feet 10 inches to 9 feet 10 inches] high. I thought if the paper were hung vertically within a modern architectural space, it could add a dynamic quality. So I asked a craftsman if we could make bigger sizes of paper, and he said he had heard that sheets of paper three times bigger than one tatami module were made in the past, and this technique and tools were still available. Then we decided to make 2.1 x 2.7-meter [6-feet-11-inch x 8-feet-10-inch] paper using those techniques and tools. Once we decided upon a size, we next had to determine the contents.

I asked why washi had been used for the past fifteen hundred years—why had it been admired? In thinking about the traditional house, paper was used for shoji screens. Vertical and horizontal pieces would be used to create beautiful forms. The sun would illuminate the shoji screen, and the horizontal and vertical pieces of wood would cast beautiful shadows. This pattern would change during the day, depending on the sun— becoming long and short, dark and light. In Japanese this is called *utsuroi*—the ability to feel time changing.[5] This is one of the Japanese senses. Based on this concept, I thought I had to make paper that would change the atmospheric feeling of a space. This is because there are a lot of constructed spaces without access to daylight—for example, a basement has no natural sunlight. I wanted to mimic shoji and show shadows that you couldn't see in that kind of space. For this type of application, we make one piece of washi with three to seven thin layers. Only the first front layer can be seen through light that enters from the front. However, the remaining layers appear when light penetrates the back of the paper. This leads to a changing atmospheric feeling. So in places like basements, it is possible to create an environment with this feeling.

> **This work was first shown in an exhibition, right?**

Yes, in Tokyo. Until then there was no paper of this size used for interior design.

> **Where did you make this size of paper first?**

Takefu City in Echizen—the area of paper production I had mentioned previously. In order to justify making such a large piece of paper for interior design for the first time,

---

[4] Fusuma and shoji are sliding doors used to separate rooms.

[5] "Utsuroi" describes moments of delicate transition and is related to various time scales from seasons to ages.

Sleek Screen exhibition (left)
The Art of Japanese Paper and Light exhibition (below)

we wanted to exhibit it and make a presentation. I chose a gallery in Tokyo that was popular in the press and asked four famous designers to produce their own work using the large pieces of paper. So I was the producer of the exhibition [both laughing]. I didn't know anything but I was the producer [smiling]. As a result, I was able to work with these amazing designers and I was able to learn, so the exhibition was a success.

Who were the designers?
Shigeru Uchida, Takashi Kanome, Toshiyuki Kita, and Yo Shouei—the exhibit was at the AXIS Gallery in Tokyo.

Because light is so important to your work, did you hire a lighting designer?
At that time, although I was focused on making a large piece of paper, I had asked a lighting designer to do the floor formation. For the next exhibition I collaborated with Toyo Ito, Sei Takeyama, and Takashi Sugimoto, and a lighting plan was integrated as a part of the work. This is because I make paper, and although I employ light, what I really have to achieve is air and atmosphere. Making space through collaboration with people is really fun.

Please explain the difference between your two ventures—Shimus and Eriko Horiki & Associates.
Shimus is a company that I started when I first went into business. I founded Eriko Horiki & Associates in April 2000, after leaving Gofukudonya. I officially bought out the rights to the Shimus brand and started this company. In the future I would like to subdivide it into another company that makes screen partitions and other design elements.

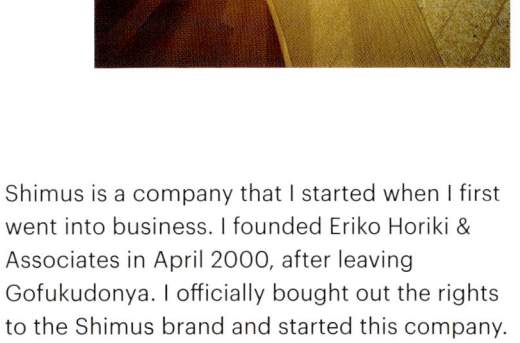

What insights have you gained from your papermaking process?
My clients have really influenced the process. When they tell me they want a certain type of paper, I listen. For example, a customer asked me to make an egg once. To make an egg by a typical method, I would have to use bamboo for the structure and apply paper to it with glue. However, an egg doesn't have bones, so then it wouldn't end up really looking like an egg—so I tried to make the form of an egg without any bones or glue. This is how I developed three-dimensional paper sculptures.

Three-dimensional paper?

Shimus's Light Object collection

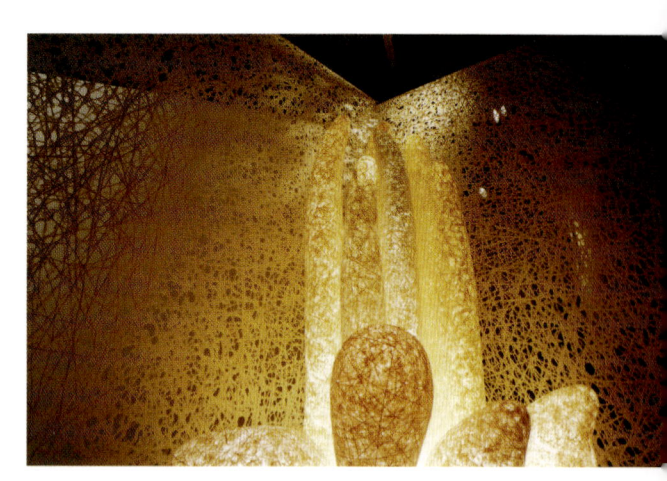

Sleek Screen exhibition, showing paper sculptures

Yes, first I make a form, and then I wrap paper around it. When the paper has dried, I remove or detach the form through a small hole in the paper. This hole is used for the insertion of a light source.

What about large-scale sheets of paper?
The architect Masayuki Kurokawa wanted me to make a tearoom out of white and black washi using two large pieces of paper. Mr. Kurokawa asked me if I could make two pieces each that were eight meters [twenty-six feet three inches] long. After seeing the drawings and listening to him, I saw that the tearoom was located in between white washi and black washi that were individually hung. On the floor of this tearoom, there was a plate with water in it. The white washi in the foreground was expressing the light, and the black washi in the back was expressing the darkness, and the ceramic dish holding the water represented the sea. I realized that the tearoom was a small universe. There is no seam in the universe. Thus, I thought I shouldn't make any seam joint using glue. I had to make one seamless piece of both black and white washi in order to express a small universe. That was the catalyst for me to make larger pieces of paper. After that we started responding to what designers and architects were thinking on an individual basis.

Despite the fact that washi is a traditional art form, you have repurposed it as a modern medium.
First of all, one of the most important things about paper is that it can burn, smear, tear, and discolor—which is a big problem when it is used for architecture. In order to overcome these problems, we have developed papermaking techniques with secondary processing methods utilized by other industries. With something like a secondary process or integration with other materials, the possibilities for washi are expanded. You are saying that washi is traditional, but washi was quite innovative when it was developed fifteen hundred years ago. In Japanese the words "tradition" and "innovation" seem to be opposed, but tradition is actually the way innovation evolves and is carried forward. If you say "tradition" now, it refers to the technique of craftsmen. We received knowledge from over a millennium of technique. How did these craftsmen innovate in their time?

A Canvas for Light — Eriko Horiki

Prayers Through Washi exhibition

Prayers Through Washi exhibition, entrance

So in order to make large-scale pieces of paper, we have to develop the technology. In one way, we are practicing a traditional art; but in another way, we are pushing the technology into a new territory. We are doing things like laminating washi with glass and pasting washi on acrylic panels. We have also developed a special glass coating on the surface of washi—the same coating used for cars. It's really interesting that these kinds of things can be applied to washi paper. As we continue collaborating with architects and engineers, the possibilities broaden.

How much time do you spend actively researching these kinds of material treatments?
By now I have been in business for over twenty years. In the first ten years, I tested the paper mostly by my own hand. But now my staff is increasing and I spend time researching and challenging my staff with new ideas. I am in the papermaking area about a fifth of the time; the rest of the time I am in meetings or monitoring installation work on project sites, in addition to working as a president. I also give lectures about washi. Although I only spend about 20 percent of my time researching, I am always thinking about the material research [smiling].

Is that right?
Yes, I am always thinking about making washi—I draw designs while I am on the train and I think about what technology is necessary to achieve the designs. I think about lighting techniques as well.

Do you test lighting often?
I do a partial testing, but not on the entire piece of washi. This is because one doesn't know how the light will work until the paper is installed in its actual space. There are so many ways for light to enter, right? So it's all imagined—it's an experience [both laughing]. However, I am always trying to imagine the light and how it will affect the piece. I really take the time to think about it clearly. We dim and brighten the lights in the installation space so that the work can be shown in any situation.

It's similar to cooking, isn't it? There are known ingredients and methods, but the outcome isn't completely predictable.
That's true [smiling], and depending on each ingredient and seasoning, the taste also can differ—it can be sweet or spicy, so you have to

Lisn Aoyama store and gallery

keep testing. The capacity to imagine is very important, as is managing the paper. This means considering if the washi form will remain intact without changing.

For example, when using washi pasted on an acrylic panel as a wall, the middle part can fall out—almost like its own stomach falling out, and that's not beautiful. To avoid this problem, we process acrylic into a boxlike shape. Because the box is installed by hanging, its own heaviness will not be an issue; it stabilizes the washi paper. You don't see this box just by looking at the design; a complex structure is hidden. If you don't do this kind of thing, you can't use washi for any type of architecture.

With our changing technologies and lifestyles, what kind of spatial atmosphere is most appropriate today?

What is the most important is utsuroi, and creating an atmosphere that makes it possible to sense the passage of time. In Japan there is a distinct sense of the seasons as well as the different times of day. I think it's really important to feel a sense of time using light and washi as the medium. I want to create that kind of utsuroi space—I don't think there are enough spaces like that.

Your Jomon no Mori Pavilion seems to embody the concept of utsuroi.

Yes, it is a gate structure within a museum that exhibits dolls and tools from the Jomon period.[6] The gate is intended to resemble a pit dwelling from this period.[7]

---

[6] Jomon was Japan's Neolithic period, dating from 10,500 to 300 BCE.

[7] Jomon-period pit-type dwellings consisted of a shallow pit with an earthen floor, and they were covered with a thatched roof.

In order to make large-scale pieces of paper, we have to develop the technology. In one way, we are practicing a traditional art; but in another way, we are pushing the technology into a new territory.

Campus Plaza Kyoto

Mino Washi no Sato Kaikan museum

It's important to lead as well as to follow; this is in fact the role of the creator. It's no good if you are moved and don't do anything about it, right? You have to connect your own creativity to others.

Jomon no Mori Pavilion (top), detail (bottom)

I know this is not an actual building, but wouldn't it be remarkable if you could design an autonomous work of architecture entirely of washi?

Yes, absolutely [smiling].

With regard to other ambitions, how does your work relate to growing environmental concerns?

Washi-making has been an ecologically sensitive craft since fifteen hundred years ago, so it's really simple [laughing]. In developing this material for architectural applications, my goal is ecological thinking. With such a natural product and water, we can connect humanity.

What about the other materials you are incorporating?

I am consciously developing various metals and resins to be easily disassembled and recycled in the future. This is an important consideration—a kind of waste management. Washi is an ecologically friendly product, and I want people to see its beauty.

You have certainly created many interesting opportunities for washi—such as designing a stage set with Yo-Yo Ma.

Yo-Yo Ma wanted me to design something with a Silk Road theme. In developing a concept, we discussed the role of the creator. Culture was influenced from person to person, era to era, place to place through the Silk Road. We thought the individual had this type of influential creative role—when you go somewhere and present something, people listen to you, see your work, and you influence them. These people then participate and broaden their own world. This is the idea of the Silk Road itself—making connections.

I created washi based on this concept. "Shimus" actually means to connect—*shi* equals paper and *mus* equals connect, referring to connections made with other materials as well as with people. Thus, Yo-Yo Ma and I thought the same way. Our instruments were different—music and paper—but the experience was an interesting collaboration [smiling]. It's important to lead as well as to follow; this is in fact the role of the creator. It's no good if you are moved and don't do anything about it, right? You have to connect your own creativity to others.

Yo-Yo Ma stage art

Evoking the Primal

**A conversation with Terunobu Fujimori, the University of Tokyo
with Dana Buntrock, University of California, Berkeley**

In a profession frequently obsessed with style and pedigree, Terunobu Fujimori is a refreshing anomaly. Although most ambitious architects fashion their reputations practicing for the biggest names in the field, Fujimori defined his early career as an architectural historian, traveling and researching traditional building techniques in many parts of the globe. Now an accomplished architect himself, Fujimori crafts structures in a manner he calls "international vernacular." These are buildings that conjure history while preserving the present, and that command our respect while injecting an occasional bit of humor.

Terunobu Fujimori was born in Nagano, Japan, in 1946. He received his PhD from the University of Tokyo in 1980 and was appointed a professor there in 1998. An eminent historian of Japanese architecture, Fujimori has published several books, including the recent titles *The Contemporary Japanese Tea House* (2007), *Ground Tour* (2008), and *A Tour of Architectural Materials* (2009). In addition to teaching architectural history, Fujimori has also designed a collection of notable houses and museums in his international vernacular tradition, including the Jinchokan Moriya Historical Museum (1991), the Tanpopo (Dandelion) House (1995), the Takasugi-an (Too High Teahouse) (2004), the Lamune Onsen (Soda Pop Spa) (2005), the Yakisugi (Charred Cedar) House (2007), and the Coal House (2008).

Dana Buntrock is an associate professor of architecture at the University of California, Berkeley. She has written widely on all aspects of Japanese architecture, specializing in the period after 1900. Her book *Materials and Meaning in Contemporary Japanese Architecture: Tradition and Today* was published in 2010.

Shin-ken (Firewood Tearoom) (opposite)

One of the most recognized characteristics of your work is the inclusion of plants within the building envelope—a strategy you have described as a kind of parasitic assimilation of nature in architecture, as opposed to the kind of harmonious integration seen in typical green roof installations.[1] How do you integrate living materials with "dead" ones? How do you traverse the fine line between architecture and landscape architecture?

Fujimori: This is a very difficult problem. At a basic level, architecture is what people make. Plants, of course, are part of the natural world. I have a great interest in the relationship between the natural world and the built world, and I have sought to encourage this relationship from the beginning. There are various aspects that I have cared about, and when I first had the chance to design a building, this is a relationship that I thought I would exploit in the context of my work. Fundamentally, though, I did not have the confidence to say that I could reflect this relationship successfully. After all, aesthetics are part of the human world, and plants are part of an older world. Plants don't align with the aesthetic control of people—trees, grasses, and so on do not fit our systems. They win in this match.

Are there particular architects that have managed this relationship successfully?

Fujimori: I don't think there are really any architects who have successfully linked the two systems. One exception is Le Corbusier, who talked about the roof garden. If you look at his work, you'll see that Le Corbusier's first influence was the *piloti*, and his second influence was the roof garden. The very first roof garden he made was on a house, and in that case it was completely covered with a lawn.[2] After that, however, Le Corbusier experimented with the roof garden in small, less conspicuous ways.

I visited Le Corbusier's Unité d'Habitation in Marseille, for example, and went up to the roof garden to look—despite the fact that most visitors don't seek it out. There were four trees there, but I had to search for them.

When Le Corbusier designed the National Museum of Western Art in Tokyo, the client asked him to design a garden on the roof. When the roof garden dried up and died, the client contacted Le Corbusier and asked, "What should we do?" His answer was noncommittal. The garden was in an odd place that wasn't really conducive for growing plants. Plants need to have a successful place to develop in order to make the relationship between plants and architecture effective.

You can look at the roof of Rockefeller Center in New York and see that there's no relationship between the architecture and the plants. In this case, the lack of relationship is fine—the beauty of the architecture is distinct from the beauty of the landscaping. Creating a shared beauty, however, is quite a difficult proposition.

You have pursued the goal of a shared beauty in your own work, however.

Fujimori: I have tried different approaches to create a shared sense of beauty, and the only time I feel I have been really successful is with the Leek House. The client said that during the first two years, the leeks bloomed quite beautifully there, but it wasn't the same afterwards.

Another good example is on Oshima—an island near Tokyo—on which I designed the Tsubaki Chateau. The project is a *shochu* brewery for which I designed a grass-covered roof topped with a tree.[3]

Buntrock: The client puts an unbelievable amount of effort into caring for the building. The Leek House also requires serious annual maintenance.

---

[1] See Fujimori's description of the Tanpopo House in Terunobu Fujimori, *Y'Avant-Garde Architecture* (Tokyo: Toto Shuppan, 1998), 28. "In the natural world, small man-made things are parasitic, whereas nature acts as a parasite on the large man-made things of city and architecture."

[2] Le Corbusier's 1923 Villa La Roche had a roof terrace, and by his 1928 Villa Savoye, Le Corbusier had fully incorporated the roof garden as articulated in his five points of architecture.

[3] Shochu is a clear, distilled alcoholic beverage similar to vodka.

Tanpopo (Dandelion) House

Ku-an (Right Angle Teahouse)

Aesthetics are part of the human world, and plants are part of an older world. Plants don't align with the aesthetic control of people—trees, grasses, and so on do not fit our systems.

Matter in the Floating World · Atmosphere

Nira (Leek) House (bottom), roof detail (top),

Tsubaki (Camelia) Chateau

Fujimori: Yes, the maintenance is very tough, because weeds keep growing on the roof. However, the project may also be successful because the design embraces a variety of growing things [laughter].

There seem to be more examples of foliage-covered buildings in Japan than in the West. Why is this?

Fujimori: Because Japanese people really like plants [all laughing]. Especially people from the working-class neighborhoods of Edo, who liked plants like morning glories and possessed the skills required for serious gardening.[4] Today people in these neighborhoods live in townhouses, so there are no gardens. However, people cultivate potted plants there. If you visit these neighborhoods, you will see lots of plants placed out along the road. Despite the fact that these messy pots are located within the public way, nobody complains.

Did the tradition of grass-roofed *shibamune* dwellings influence the modern Japanese cultivation of plants in urban settings?[5]

Fujimori: People in the city did not have grass on the roof. They grew bonsai plants. Have you seen a good bonsai—a truly wonderful one?

Yes…well, at least it seemed good to me [all laughing].

Buntrock: You should elaborate on what makes a wonderful specimen.

Fujimori: Really good bonsai plants look like full-sized trees despite their tiny scale. The cultivation of bonsai is part of the tradition in old working-class Tokyo neighborhoods. People also grow morning glories and lantern plants.

Buntrock: Yes—there are lantern plant festivals where you can purchase the plants and take them home.

Is an urban setting a requirement for the integration of architecture and foliage? Is this relationship less important in your Lone Pine House, for example, because it is located in the countryside?

Fujimori: Yes, in the country there are many existing plants, so you do not need more [laughter]. I have incorporated plants there, but they are not conspicuous.

Buntrock: Oshima is also in the country, though.

Fujimori: It is—however, the Tsubaki Chateau client really understands my work, so he's willing to do the necessary maintenance. Normal clients, however, probably wouldn't forgive me for the level of upkeep required.

Buntrock: Is the Pine Tree House client a "normal client?"

Fujimori: Yes.

So we might consider maintenance as an important contextual factor. I'm curious about how the necessity of ongoing maintenance relates to some of your favorite precedents. The Potala Palace in Tibet, for example, is an edifice that seems as if it occurred without people—a "structure built by heaven," as you have written.

---

4 "Edo" is the name for premodern Tokyo.
5 "Shibamune" is the name for a traditional thatched-roof Japanese dwelling on which plants grew.

Ipponmatsu (Lone Pine) House

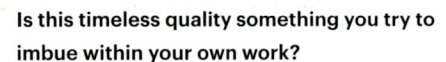

Potala Palace, Lhasa, Tibet

Is this timeless quality something you try to imbue within your own work?

Fujimori: Unfortunately, what you're suggesting is impossible. Although I might feel that an ideal architecture is seemingly absent of human influence, it's impossible to create architecture like that today. Therefore, you have to think about what you can accomplish with the human hand.

However, if someone finds one of my buildings five hundred years from now and thinks it was made by a god rather than a human being, I would be very happy! [all laughing]

Buntrock: Five hundred years for a building of wood construction? Perhaps you should work with stone [laughter].

The vernacular, material-rich architecture you have categorized as the so-called red school best approximates this condition, but it is, of course, dependent on human influence. The minimalist white school architecture, however, is clearly associated with a modern approach to building—yet this work is often highly abstract and seemingly devoid of the human hand.[6] Your Akino Fuku Museum fascinates me in the way that it employs both approaches. The white gallery is a particularly striking minimalist space, for example.

Fujimori: I didn't think that I was making a minimalist room when I designed that gallery. The goal was to make a space in which to showcase art, and I didn't want to see all the various materials that comprise the building. Therefore, I designed all the surfaces to be white in order to prevent a visitor's attention from being drawn away from the artwork. In most museums you see various commercial products, including floor finish materials, light fixtures, and many other things on the ceiling. I find this visual noise to be unpleasant, so I endeavored to make everything white. The floor is white marble, and visitors are required to remove their shoes before entering the room.

When Toyo Ito visited the museum, he was really surprised. As you know, he works in what is a typical minimalist vein. So when he saw this gallery, he said, "You did it all in the same material—that's really minimal!" I had not been thinking in this way, but now I think this example could be defined as "minimalism's minimalism."

You have a small room in the Tanpopo House that is clad in white plaster.

Fujimori: Ito was also surprised by the same kind of technique at Tanpopo House. As you know, there is a room lined entirely with wood, and the material makes a very strong impression. I know someone who constructed his own office space entirely out of Oya stone.[7] The floor, the walls, the ceiling—they are all the same material. There are no mortar joints, and the room conveys a very powerful feeling.

---

6 See p. 14 for a description of Fujimori's red and white schools.

7 Oya is an igneous rock that may be easily carved.

> Although I might feel that an ideal architecture is seemingly absent of human influence, it's impossible to create architecture like that today. Therefore, you have to think about what you can accomplish with the human hand.

Akino Fuku Museum, gallery

I thought, "I have to do something like this—this is great!" So I attached wood to the surfaces in the Tanpopo House. Because I used wood planks, however, I revealed the joints. I wanted to do something more sophisticated with the joints, but this was as far as I could go.

> So you modified the Oya stone approach based on the material?

Fujimori: It looks similar, but it's not an imitation of the other project. You have this impression of being immersed in the material. There is a window in the room at the Tanpopo House, but rather than sensing that the space is thrust beyond the window, you are conscious of the space that is enclosed by the material.

> We have been discussing material readings, but I am also curious about your construction approaches. You use a combination of old and new techniques, for example.

Fujimori: Yes.
Buntrock: They're all old, aren't they? What new materials do you use?
Fujimori: I don't use any new materials on the surface. There are new materials underneath, however. The parts that perform—the insulation and waterproofing—are all new materials. The finishes are all older materials.
Buntrock: You use cement, but it is usually mixed with soil, so it's hard to call it new.

> What about technique? I met with a Japanese contractor, for example, who is investigating dying Japanese construction techniques—such as *shikkui* plaster in traditional Japanese castles—and trying to make them new again.[8] Do you attempt to update old construction techniques?

Fujimori: I don't have any interest in tradition for tradition's sake, and I have no special place in my heart for Japanese tradition—other nations' traditions are just as important to me. For example, if you think about earth walls, African earthen construction is the most interesting example, and far more interesting than Japan's. If you think about wood, on the other hand, the place where it was really used was in the British Tudor era—this construction

---

8   The contractor I mention is Kazuo Hayakumo with Sumaito Inc., who is revitalizing traditional Japanese building materials and techniques for use by a broad audience.

Tanpopo (Dandelion) House, interior, detail (below)

I don't have any interest in tradition for tradition's sake, and I have no special place in my heart for Japanese tradition— other nations' traditions are just as important to me.

process employed lots of small pieces of wood to make a wall. I am interested in what I call "international vernacular," and I am intrigued by common methods of material usage that are shared by a variety of nations.

What are some of your favorite construction techniques that you have developed? How are they old or new—or both?

Buntrock: The use of a chainsaw? [all laughing] That has always looked incredibly fun to me.

Fujimori: I like everything, but lately I'm getting tired of plaster. I feel I understand it well, and I don't want to use it anymore. The materials and techniques that interest me are the ones I haven't used yet and the ones I'm still trying to think about. One example is *shinkabe*, which is a post-and-beam construction with an infill wall system, the only real examples of which are found in Japan and Tudor England.[9] I'm not really sure why this is, but I'm very curious about it.

I want to try new things, and I'm always interested in methods I haven't seen before. I would like to do something with earthen construction, for example, which does not perform very well in Japan because of freeze-thaw cycles, moisture, and so on. I'd love to build someplace like Africa or California where these concerns would be minimized.

Your work has a particular "cultivated rawness." In the Tanpopo House, for example, you went to great lengths to instruct the contractor to make the materials look raw and unpolished, despite his reluctance to do so.

Fujimori: When I was a child, I loved to make things with raw materials, as all children do—with no interest in special techniques and technologies.

Buntrock: But if the Jinchokan Moriya Historical Museum hadn't been your first building, do you think you would have done that? You responded strongly to the program of that building and to the nature of the community.

Fujimori: Well, I'm sure I would not have ended up a contemporary architect. Steel, glass, and concrete are not pleasant matches with the riches of the natural world. Also the village in which I was raised had particularly strong ties to Shinto.[10] As an adult I have begun to understand this fact, but you cannot really recognize that sort of influence on yourself. However, when I speak with other people about my childhood, they claim that my experience was unusual. So maybe there's a relationship between the influence of Shintoism and my preference for raw materials, but I'm not deliberately trying to emphasize that relationship in my work.

Your discussion of Shintoism and the riches of the natural world—in addition to the way in which you incorporate natural and living materials in your buildings—might lead us to consider you an ecologically minded architect. Yet we know you are not so easily labeled. What is your opinion of sustainable design, which has gathered much momentum recently?

Fujimori: I care about the environment, of course, and I've studied ecological approaches in architecture. My work is different than what others try to do with sustainability, however. I find that when you look at conventional architectural expressions of ecology, they're not really interesting. They don't really have an architectural character, nor are they really important as buildings. They are not making any substantive change beyond normal modernism.

Simply put, I'm interested in nature and people, and in the creative capacity of humanity that can flourish within the rules of nature. It's the expression of this relationship that holds power for me, rather than something like energy usage.

How do you feel about Japan's considerable dependence on other nations for material and energy resources? Many Japanese people are becoming increasingly concerned about this issue.

---

9 Shinkabe is a traditional Japanese plaster-wall construction technique in which the wood structure is exposed.

10 Japan's indigenous religion of Shinto seeks harmony with the natural world and emphasizes ritual purification.

Jinchokan Moriya Historical Museum

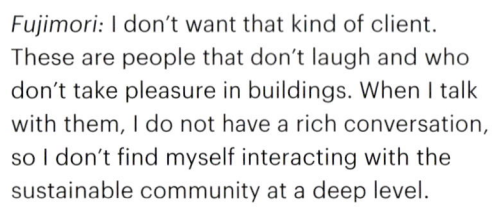

Tan-ken (Charcoal Tearoom)

Fujimori: I don't want that kind of client. These are people that don't laugh and who don't take pleasure in buildings. When I talk with them, I do not have a rich conversation, so I don't find myself interacting with the sustainable community at a deep level.

That's too bad, considering your important contributions.

Fujimori: Yes, it is. However, it's simply not interesting for me. I once designed a master plan for an ecological community called Sprout of the Earth, and there were many academic environmental advisors involved in the project. I designed a kind of termite mound that was to be twenty meters [sixty-five feet seven inches] tall and covered with grass. I worked with a German consultant to ensure the viability of the idea, and a company we talked to confirmed its potential. With this good news, we shared our proposal for the tower with the other academics, but they were vehemently opposed to the idea.

Why?

Fujimori: They didn't understand the purpose. The client asked the advisors to think beyond a typical conservative attitude and to come to the project with an open mind. However, the group couldn't agree on a direction, so the project was not built in its original planned location.

That's a real pity.

Fujimori: The good news is that the client funded a 1/5-scale model of the design with special grasses growing on it. He felt that an audience outside this conservative ecological advisory board would appreciate what we are trying to do.

In addition to this project, what other future endeavors do you have in mind?

Fujimori: I'm still excited by what I'm doing now. I started designing at the age of forty-five, so I'm still a newbie.

I find your *kengai-zukuri* research to be particularly compelling.[11] The notion of architecture connected to mountains—such as the Nunobiki Kannon—must be one of the most profound integrations of buildings and nature. If you had your chance, would you want to build your own example of kengai-zukuri?

Fujimori: Yes, yes. At a large scale, it would be deeply inspiring—but that kind of thing is not desired in Japan, and it would be quite difficult to achieve here today. Perhaps it could be done in America.

---

[11] Fujimori describes kengai-zukuri (the so-called cascade style) as a method of assimilating architecture within the sides of mountains or cliffs. In his book, Fujimori explains that kengai-zukuri "would mean that the temple was built hanging onto the side of a cliff on a rocky mountain in the way that hawks build their nests." Fujimori, *Y'Avant-Garde Architecture*, 13.

Evoking the Primal — Terunobu Fujimori

Takasugi-an (Too High Teahouse)

Sprout of the Earth

Nunobiki Kannon, Nagano

I'm interested in nature and people, and in the creative capacity of humanity that can flourish within the rules of nature. It's the expression of this relationship that holds power for me.

FLOW

Japanese culture is characterized by an acute awareness of flows. Seasonal changes and the passage of time, mobility and transit, and material and spatial transitions are all acknowledged and incorporated seamlessly into daily existence. As landscape architect Barrie B. Greenbie notes, "Japanese culture, which puts so much emphasis on the ephemeral (symbolized by the briefly blooming cherry tree) and consequently on life in the moment, is peculiarly aware of time."[1] In fact, the collective Japanese consciousness approaches the concepts of space and time differently than Westerners do, integrating them into a singular entity, ma, or time-space.[2]

The physical environment in Japan is not considered a fixed entity, but rather a transitional context—a notion literally reinforced by frequently recurring seismic tremors, the visual predominance of transportation-scapes, and the unrelenting presence of building construction and maintenance. The average life span of buildings in Japan is among the shortest in the world, and fast-moving cities like Tokyo exude a palpable sense of transformation.[3] This increasingly unstable condition has simultaneously inspired and frustrated Japanese architects, who conceive new structures as fluid sequences of interconnected spaces that are at once attached to—and set apart from—the volatile urban milieu. Toyo Ito's investigations into nimble, ultralight structures designed to house "urban nomads" are both celebrations and critiques of the contemporary urban condition. Conceived as transitional objects, the mobile

Shiki Community Hall, Atelier Hitoshi Abe

fabrications of Ito and his contemporaries exhibited a heightened sense of ephemerality. According to Botond Bognar, "The intricate, thin and semi-transparent layers of the new urban fabric woven by these architects, allude to an invisible depth and unexplainable void, reminiscent of the goal of Buddhist philosophy, which frustrates rationality and causes knowledge or the subject to vacillate."[4]

Recent works of Japanese architecture incorporate the quality of transience in layered surfaces and blurred spatial transitions. In his designs for several boutique stores in prominent urban neighborhoods, Jun Aoki has experimented with a variety of sophisticated, light-transmitting envelopes that simultaneously permit and deny views to the inside. These surfaces feature coatings and interstitial materials that create visual oscillations for passersby, thus thwarting easy comprehension.

Hitoshi Abe has also experimented with the concept of flow in the form of layered, perforated surfaces—as well as interlinked, topological spaces or "ribbons" that facilitate smooth physical transitions. His Shirasagi Bridge and Shiki Community Hall projects pay homage to the time-lapse visualizations of Eadweard Muybridge and Marcel Duchamp, revealing structural "slices" as a kind of frozen movement. Related to Abe's ribbon approach, architect Shuhei Endo conceives buildings not as isolated entities, but as spatial episodes within an urban continuum. Inspired by the traditional calligraphic technique *renmentai,* in which the brush remains in contact with the page, Endo inscribes architecture with seamless material surfaces that intertwine and blur interior and exterior environments.

Designer Reiko Sudo creates textiles that serve a variety of scales and applications—from personal accessories to building interiors. Using a variety of advanced as well as old-world techniques, Sudo produces fabrics conceived as continually transformable, fluid substances. Similarly captivated by the notion of flow, artist and physicist Sachiko Kodama creates dynamic sculptures that react to a variety of environmental stimuli. Made of ferrofluid triggered by electromagnetic impulses, Kodama's continually transforming pieces allude to a fluid, responsive existence that has been characterized as "liquid architecture."

---

1 Barrie B. Greenbie, *Space and Spirit in Modern Japan* (New Haven, CT: Yale University Press, 1988), 43.

2 Ibid. There are actually nine different definitions for "ma," all of which relate to some quality of time, space, or their combination. See Arata Isozaki, *Japan-ness in Architecture*, trans. Sabu Kohso (Cambridge: MIT Press, 2006), 327–28, note 16.

3 According to the 1988 and 1993 editions of the Japan Housing and Land Survey, the average life span of a building in Japan is twenty-six years—compared with forty-four years in the United States and seventy-five years in the United Kingdom. See http://www.stat.go.jp/english/data/jyutaku/index.htm.

4 Botond Bognar, *The New Japanese Architecture* (New York: Rizzoli, 1990), 30–31.

Recoding Materiality

A conversation with Jun Aoki, Jun Aoki & Associates

Jun Aoki's work is defined by its materiality. Although his designs are driven by sophisticated formal, theoretical, and technological ideas, his architecture must be confronted at the material level in order to be fully appreciated. Aoki demonstrates the phenomenological power of delicately wrought, multivalent surfaces to reshape conventional material assumptions and ultimately affect space itself. These surfaces should be considered experiential fields, acting as visually oscillating membranes that effect a perceptual recoding of physical substance.

Jun Aoki was born in Yokohama in 1956. He received his Bachelor of Engineering and Master of Engineering degrees in Architecture from the University of Tokyo by 1982 and then worked for Arata Isozaki & Associates until 1990. Recognized for his design of a series of stores for Louis Vuitton as well as private houses and exhibitions, Aoki has received many awards, including the Architectural Institute of Japan Annual Award (1999), the Aichi Townscape Award (2004), the Minister of Education's Art Encouragement Prize (2005), and the Good Design Gold Award (2008).

Louis Vuitton Roppongi, facade detail (opposite)

Your architecture possesses a strong material identity, which is evident in the careful development of layered, veiled, and cellular surfaces that predominate in your buildings. When we reflect upon your debut project—the Behemoth installation at the Spiral in Tokyo in 1991—we see an early interest in materiality.[1] Since then, materiality seems to have become the primary focus in your work. Do you believe that materials make your architecture?

As an architect, first I ask, "What do I want to do?" The answer often relates to the quality of the atmosphere within the space I wish to create. When most people encounter architecture from within, they feel the architecture rather than seeing it. So this means that the atmospheric quality of space is very important for architecture. If you change the feeling of the space, it will be different architecture even if the architecture has the same diagram or composition.

In my first projects, I concentrated on the manipulation of the internal space of architecture. But in our age, sometimes we cannot design internal space at all. For example, if a client asks you to design an office building, the office space must be very flexible, so it will be a very neutral space and you cannot touch the design of the internal space. However, when I started to design for Louis Vuitton in 1998, I had the opportunity to design not only the internal space but also my first building facade.

That was in Nagoya?

Yes, Nagoya—the Sakae project. If we consider the flexibility of the retail space, we must acknowledge the fact that it will change every five years. So I thought the best solution for the space was just a black box. Thus, the major goal was in fact the facade, or the design of the exterior surface. For the architect such a design effort has a pejorative feeling because it is a very superficial thing. It also changes a lot according to fashion trends and so on. So although at first we considered developing some new material, we were concerned that after five years it might become very common. Since the character of the building would have to hold up over a long time, we decided to take a phenomenal approach and create a feeling of dematerialization instead. So we didn't develop any new material for this project, but only used transparent glass with some transparent film printed with the checkerboard pattern. It's very low-tech [laughter].

But that's good, isn't it? Sometimes low-tech solutions are the best ones.

Yes. With this low-tech method, we can extract a new feeling from the very common material of glass. So for me this was very interesting, and my general approach to materials is to create a dematerialized feeling. In the Louis Vuitton Roppongi project, I proposed to use a fiber-optic system, which is not a very new idea. If you use fiber optics, it is very simple to transmit an image. But if the ends of the fiber optics are inserted into the perforations of limestone, something changes. The surface looks just like limestone without a projected image, but once an image appears on the surface of the stone, for me it is very exciting.

Yes, very exciting.

But this was also very low-tech, because at the time this usage of the fiber optics was not so new, and I think it was more fashionable to use plasma or liquid crystal displays. So in this case I wanted to make some transition between the stone and the image. So you might be held in suspense by the question of whether it is a stone or an image; however, it is actually not a stone, nor an image. It is just a transition.

That's certainly a kind of dematerialization.

Yes, that's one kind of dematerialization.

What about the stone in the Ginza Namiki store?

Because I designed two stores in Ginza, I knew these two must be very different. The former project—Ginza Matsuya—has a very

---

1 Designed by Fumihiko Maki, Spiral is a high-profile venue for design exhibitions in Tokyo's Aoyama neighborhood. It was commissioned by the Wacoal company and built in 1985.

151   Recoding Materiality   Jun Aoki

You might be held in suspense by the question of whether it is a stone or an image; however, it is actually not a stone, nor an image. It is just a transition.

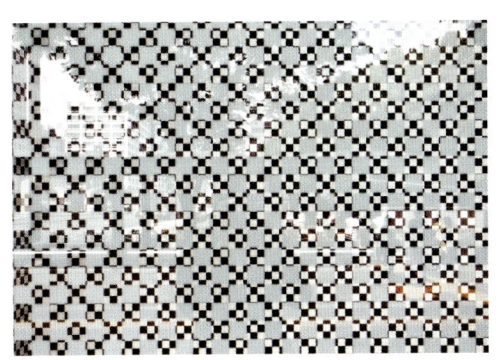

Louis Vuitton Sakae, Nagoya, storefront detail

Louis Vuitton Roppongi, entrance

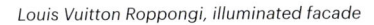

Louis Vuitton Roppongi, illuminated facade

Louis Vuitton Ginza Namiki

open feeling, so to make some contrast with this project, I designed the Namiki store to have a very closed, thick feeling. My first idea was to use stone, but people have a presumption about stone. Stone has a very heavy, thick, rigid feeling. But we wanted to add some new nuance, which was not in the end a kind of dematerialization, but rather a way to reveal something else about the existing material. Essentially, we were looking for some idea about how we could make this heavy limestone feel light. And I was reminded of our experience in the Omotesando project on the seventh floor: there is a large hall, and this three-story-high hall is enveloped by white linen. On the floor we used terrazzo, which was a special terrazzo with a resin cement base. It has no joints and is a homogeneous white floor. We also used a lot of white circular stone, which created a subtle pattern within the floor. But you know, since terrazzo is like fake marble, I thought it would be very hard to persuade the Louis Vuitton people to use it, because it is not real marble. By accident we learned that the president of Louis Vuitton has terrazzo in his bathroom and likes it—so it was OK [laughter].

How did you extrapolate the Omotesando floor idea to the Namiki facade?

After seeing the effect of the Omotesando floor, we thought if the inset stone were translucent, it would feel really light. In Namiki we used a glass fiber–reinforced concrete panel. It was difficult to develop our idea because the material is very delicate, so we tried more than one hundred patterns. We selected the pattern after checking the one-to-one scale in the drawings, and then we developed details. The GRC panel had to be more than 15 millimeters [9/16 inch] thick; otherwise it would be too weak.[2] However, if we used 15-millimeter-thick marble, it would not transmit enough light—the maximum thickness for translucent marble is 10 millimeters [3/8 inch]. Therefore, we reinforced the thinner panel with glass using silicone caulking and sealant. It was quite a challenge, but in the end the glass holds the panel.

---

2 Glass-reinforced concrete (GRC) is a thin concrete section that uses glass fibers for reinforcement instead of conventional steel.

Louis Vuitton Ginza Namiki, corner detail (top), cladding detail (bottom)

If you apply extremely high-quality makeup to your face, you realize it's a real face, because the best cosmetics are not intended to hide the real face but rather reveal its essence. Thus, the superficial can create reality.

Louis Vuitton Omotesando (top), main entrance (bottom)

That's amazing—a truly authentic kind of dematerialization. There are other types of dematerialization in your work as well, such as the use of very thin applied materials in the c House or U bis exhibition. This kind of application seems to challenge solidity.

After some of the Louis Vuitton projects, we reached the point where we were using superthin materials. We thought of these like paper, and also a paper for wrapping. And because the surface of architecture is more important for me, this treatment may be compared to a woman's cosmetics. Suddenly this analogy became very interesting, because if you paint your face very white, it becomes quite fake and you recognize this is not real. However, if you apply extremely high-quality makeup to your face, you realize it's a real face, because the best cosmetics are not intended to hide the real face but rather reveal its essence. Thus, the superficial can create reality [laughter].

I also read Roland Barthes's book *Empire of Signs*, which is all about Japanese culture.[3] In one chapter Barthes discusses the Japanese tradition of wrapping with *furoshiki*.[4] He writes how he received a present from a Japanese friend that was beautifully wrapped. Once Barthes opened the package, he found a new package inside, and once he opened this box, he found more wrapping—endless wrapping—and in the end, he found a very cheap thing inside [laughter]. This is a very interesting insight about Japanese notions of reality. In this case reality is an insubstantial object. The wrapping method itself becomes the reality of the present. And so I have a very similar feeling about cosmetics. In Louis Vuitton Namiki, by using the very thin material of GRC, we wanted to create a reality of internal space with only a surface. The surface can thus make a virtual reality for people. For example, from the outside you cannot say how many floors or what kind of spaces are inside, but you can get a sense of the volume of the store by just this wrapping. So even a very thin surface can communicate with people and also create some reality.

I remember *White Walls, Designer Dresses* by Mark Wigley—a very interesting book about ornament or this kind of surface.[5] For example, he reminds us of Le Corbusier's statement that today's decoration is no decoration. Thus, a plain white wall means nothing, but the white wall is a kind of dress for the architecture. Namiki uses a kind of abstract yet sophisticated decoration for the architecture—we can use not only the white dress but also any dress. In this way, we can develop decoration for architecture in a positive rather than a negative sense.

I would like to relate your earlier description about the real face and the made-up face to Terunobu Fujimori's theory that Japanese architects today are divided among two camps: the red school and the white school.[6] If the red conveys a kind of raw, primitive materiality and the white represents refined abstraction, could one posit that both schools coexist in your work? For example, the Aomori Museum and several of your house projects are composed of strikingly different material sensibilities within the same project—perhaps like a plain face juxtaposed with a cosmetically altered face?

Well, like a cosmetic idea, I don't want to hide the material reality. Let's take reinforced concrete, for example. Our challenge is how we can change a very solid material by deriving an ephemeral material value from it. We don't care to reveal the surface of reinforced concrete, but instead try to add some new feeling with a particular treatment, or by combining it with other materials. This combination creates a certain feeling for people. For example, concrete and glass would be a very common combination, but if you have concrete with some wallpaper

---

3 Roland Barthes, *Empire of Signs*, trans. Richard Howard (New York: Hill and Wang, 1983).
4 Furoshiki are traditional Japanese cloths used to wrap and carry gifts, clothes, or other items.
5 Mark Wigley, *White Walls, Designer Dresses: The Fashioning of Modern Architecture* (Cambridge: MIT Press, 2001).
6 See my reference to Fujimori's red and white schools on p. 14.

patterns and the glass, it's a very different combination. The combination of different colors of materials is, of course, very important in Japanese culture. Our ancestors had many names for color combinations. For example, the word for cherry blossom—*sakura*—means a combination of white and red, not pink. There are not only names for two-color combinations, but up to twelve-color combinations![7] I have a dictionary of these colors—it's very interesting to me.

> It's like a kind of word painting. A word can conjure up an entire color palette in the mind's eye.

Yes, yes. Of course, we can talk about just one material, but our ordinary experience is actually an amalgam of various qualities and feelings, so it is not so bizarre to concentrate on the combination of materials.

> Speaking of materials, I am interested in your use of particular motifs at multiple scales. Let's take the circle, for example. You use the circle as a spatial, form-making device in projects like the Mitsue Primary School or Mitsubishi Motors, and you also use it to generate details, as in the Farm exhibition or Louis Vuitton Roppongi.

I have a phobia of the right angle [laughter]. The circle and spiral have a contradictory character. They are closed, but also have a very open feeling. The Mitsue Primary School looks like just a circle, but it is really the mixture of several curved lines. It's like a typhoon, so it's a kind of spiral shape. Using this gap created by the curved lines, we could insert vertical circulation elements, such as stairs or slopes. Thus, this became not a closed space, but rather a space that radiates from inside to outside. This configuration also reveals movement, because while it is centralized, it also has a kind of centrifugal force. So we never use the circle to create only enclosed space, but through penetrations we try to show contradictions between openness and closure, or enable a transformation between a closed feeling and an open feeling.

At the scale of the detail, material elements have strong identities, and linear elements may be coursed and extended into lines.

However, a circle has a strong geometric disposition and its scale can be transformed. If a circle's only parameter is scale, the size of tubes or rings becomes very important for us. The circle is a very simple element, and it can infill any space.

> It's like a cellular network. Just as there is ambiguity between openness and closure in your radially constructed spaces, an ambiguity exists with the circle at the detail level as well. The cells are closed yet they connect to make a larger whole.

Another interesting quality about the circle emerges when we draw it. When circles are arrayed in a pattern, we get two kinds of spaces—the space inside the circle, and the space in between circles. This indefinite condition is like that of camouflage, which is a very special pattern for me, because while almost every pattern has a figure and a ground, it is hard to say which elements are figure and which are ground in a camouflage pattern. With the circles, sometimes we can place more importance on the interstices between circles rather than the space inside the circles. In the O House, for example, there is an interstitial zone that becomes the most important interior space—so this concept relates to the scale of the detail and the uncertainty between figure and ground.

> I think your details are becoming increasingly sophisticated, and the materials increasingly refined and delicate, such as in the White Chapel. Does this trend indicate a future direction for your work?

Each project decides the direction, but I am generally obstinate about the joint [laughter]. It means I don't like the ceiling poking itself, for example, because I'm pure. Materials must be connected directly to each other, so we want to hide or eliminate the feeling of the

---

[7] The Japanese Heian period (794–1185 CE) saw the development of a protocol for layering particular colors in court attire, called *kasane no irome*. The government actually dictated which color combinations could be worn by which classes. See http://www.sengokudaimyo.com/garb/garb.ch14.html.

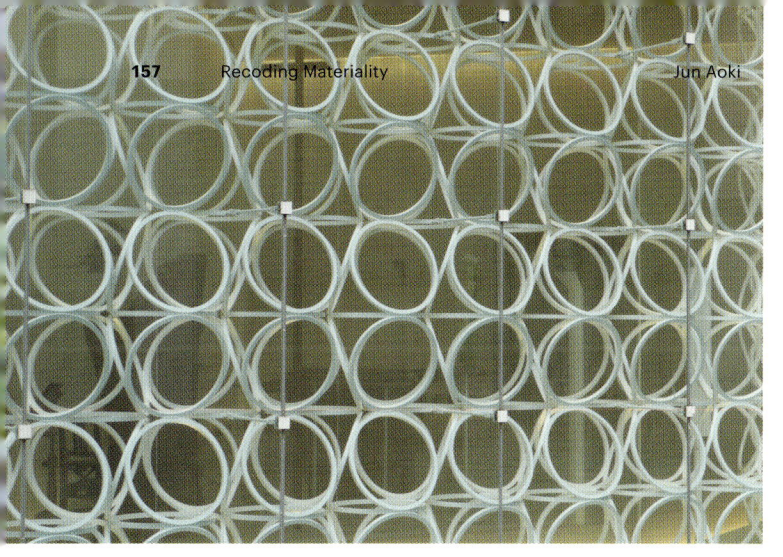

White Chapel, detail

> I have a phobia of the right angle.

joint. However, this indicates a sophisticated detail, which is also a very expensive detail [laughter]. Modern aesthetics thus pose an economic challenge because they are predisposed toward abstraction—a contradiction in the sense that dematerialization is created with real materials. Sometimes I will show panel joints, for example, but typically we want to control the joint in pursuit of a feeling of atmosphere.

> It's interesting that you mention modern architecture, because although you have designed projects with a kind of "zero detailing" in the modern spirit, you have also used decoration in a way that modernism did not espouse. The designer Karim Rashid advocates an acceptance of ornament, saying that it is human. You seem to use ornament in the service of constructing atmosphere. It's an elemental kind of ingredient for your work.

Yes, and there are many possibilities in this field, because modern architecture did not care about abundant textures or spatial ambience.

> How might you relate this idea to your approach to nature? Take your Farm exhibition, for example, in which you show plants intersecting with this kind of constructed geometry. Are you expressing an attitude about the natural versus the artificial?

Maybe the differentiation between the natural and artificial does not make a lot of sense.

When we go to the countryside to look at a rice farm, for example, we say that it conveys a very natural feeling, but it is in fact extremely artificial [laughter]. Agriculture is not nature. We have the spectrum from the very natural to the very artificial, and we can divide it into two halves and plot points within a range, or we can add a little bit from each side and make a combination.

> We see new building materials being crafted in increasingly sophisticated ways in pursuit of environmental sustainability. As Japan and the rest of the world become more concerned about dwindling material and energy resources, how do you see materials changing?

I cannot make a forecast, but my personal feeling is that every material will be changeable. It will be like a part in a large puzzle. In terms of building renovation, the most difficult thing is to pull down the exterior wall, but on the other hand, we cannot create a truly permanent material. Every material must decay and so we must examine the feasibility of replacement. This idea likely means that a building's structure must be kept for a very long time, but its surface will be more changeable. Thus, architecture will be divided between long-term elements and short-term elements.

> What about in Tokyo, where the buildings have short life spans because of high land values?[8]

Land is very permanent [laughter].

Sekka-tei Teahouse, Kyoto, Entry Vestibule

Kinkakuji, Kyoto, veranda detail

That must be a challenge for your work, which is about refinement and permanence.
Permanence is related to people's love of the building. For example, Louis Vuitton stores are intended to change every five years. However, the client wants to keep my designs for a longer time. So they are very sustainable [laughter].

An interesting point.
Demolition or the scrap-and-build idea is very antisustainable. So we feel that if we design very good architecture and people love it, it will be sustainable in that sense.

Speaking of Louis Vuitton, do you think the Japanese attitude toward luxury is changing?
It is changing. Modern architecture has a relationship with *sukiya*, which is a very minimalist form of Japanese design.[9] The "less is more" idea is almost the same for us. Sukiya is a paradox in that it is intended to look inexpensive and humble, but it is in fact the most luxurious kind of design.

Like *wabi sabi*.[10]
Wabi sabi is also the same. This is one of our basic attitudes toward materials, objects, and architecture. Sukiya is also a very basic origin for our modern architecture. Contemporary aesthetics of luxury are more direct and contradict this Sukiya mentality. And so we are now transcending from these aesthetics to other aesthetics. Sukiya aesthetics were born in the Edo period, and at that time we had another very different culture called Kano Ha, which was represented by very rich paintings and ornamentation.[11] *Kinkakuji*, an older example of a teahouse covered in gold, also represents a different aesthetic sensibility.[12] Thus, Japanese have had dual feelings about beauty.

How are these feelings changing?
It's currently more direct—a kind of straight luxury. But I think there's a kind of spiral development, and it will transform to a more wabi sabi kind of luxury.

But you still see combinations, correct? Take the Aomori Museum, where you contrast white-painted brick with earthy stucco, for example.
Yes, but this humble material can give a very new feeling, and this material feeling is not in the material itself. A material is perceived according to a code—a social code. And so we can manipulate the code itself. This is a very interesting idea for us. If we make a new kind of code through the realization of our architecture, the people's code will transform accordingly. The material will therefore be recoded.

---

8 Thirty percent of Tokyo's building stock is transformed every year, and Japanese houses last a maximum of thirty years. See Stephen Taylor and Ryue Nishizawa, *Some Ideas on Living in London and Tokyo* (Baden, Switzerland: Lars Müller Publishers, 2008), 96.

9 Sukiya is a Japanese architectural style used for teahouses and private residences in the Azuchi-Momoyama (1574–1600) and Tokugawa (1603–1867) periods. The style is characterized by a rustic simplicity intended to blend with natural surroundings.

10 Wabi sabi is a uniquely Japanese concept with complex meaning. In general terms, it refers to the appreciation of ephemerality as expressed in imperfect, unadorned natural materials, objects, and spaces.

11 Edo was a previous name for Tokyo, and the Edo Jidai was the premodern period in Japan from 1603 to 1868. The Kano school was made up of official painters for the shogunate and flourished for four centuries, between the Muromachi and Edo periods.

12 Kinkakuji, or "Temple of the Golden Pavilion," is a temple covered entirely in gold leaf built in Kyoto, Japan, in 1397.

Aomori Museum, exterior brick detail (above), exterior courtyard (left)

Aomori Museum, temporary exhibition space (left), Aleko Hall (bottom)

Pattern and Movement

A conversation with Hitoshi Abe, Atelier Hitoshi Abe

To experience a building designed by Hitoshi Abe is to encounter a meticulously crafted performance. Abe's architecture is choreographed to the subtle movement of the body in space—it always seems to anticipate one's position as well as one's possible fields of view. His work articulates this dance with highly operative patterns, and he encodes surfaces with the inscribed memories of their construction or local context. This conversation in Abe's Sendai office reveals his passion for invention and enabling of dynamic experience.

Hitoshi Abe was born in Sendai, Japan, in 1962. He earned an M.Arch at the Southern California Institute of Architecture in 1989 and worked for Coop Himmelb(l)au in Los Angeles from 1988 to 1992. He returned to Japan and established Atelier Hitoshi Abe in Sendai in 1992. In 1993 Abe earned a Doctorate in Engineering at Tohoku University and taught there until 2007, after which time he became chair of the department of architecture and urban design at the University of California, Los Angeles. Abe's atelier has won several awards, including the Chicago Athenaeum International Architecture Award (2007), the SIA-Getz Architecture Prize (2008), and an Architectural Design Commendation from the Architectural Institute of Japan (2009).

Rainbow exhibition at the Kanno Museum (opposite)

I'd like to discuss your background as an architect and your interest in materials.

I remember clearly that I wanted to be an architect when I was ten years old. I don't know the reason, but I know I always wanted to be an architect. I also adored Thomas Edison and was always fascinated by the inventions he created with common materials—like burning bamboo to make a filament for a lamp.[1] I viewed him as a magician that could completely transform simple substances into different things. So this idea of invention was there since the time I decided to be an architect. That's probably why I'm interested in transforming materials, structural systems, and even programs. I believe that architecture is closely related to the notion of invention.

Perhaps this is why you conduct university-based research and collaborate with engineers and fabricators. Like Edison, you must see importance in a research-intensive practice.

Working and teaching at the university gives me more freedom to do experimental projects. If I were to remain completely in the professional world, it would be difficult to develop new ideas. Take the Kanno Museum, for example. There's no way to relate that project to any standardized structural system. So we had to conduct physical tests to determine the strength of the material. We made samples and asked a professor who specializes in steel structural engineering at Tohoku University to test them. Without this testing, we couldn't have realized this project. This is one of the advantages of teaching at a university.[2]

That's a compelling example. In the Kanno Museum and other projects, I appreciate the way in which you celebrate materiality by revealing particular material textures or exploiting a material's potential to create immersive patterns. The Aoba-tei restaurant, for example, captures the experience of standing beneath the shade of zelkova trees using backlit, perforated steel plates.

I never see a material as a neutral, invisible entity. If I look at a stone, for example, I am fascinated by its shape, texture, and weight. I'm also interested in its transformative power. We would not have assumed that bamboo could be used to generate light—yet Edison transformed the material by using it as a filament. Thus, when using materials one should not try to erase their character, but rather look for their hidden potential to create something new.

The story of the Aoba-tei project is actually really funny. We were working with two floors within an existing building that had some sort of ugly balcony. We wanted to connect the floors, so we needed a device to mediate the space. Our solution was a kind of tubelike steel shell that negotiated the space between the floors. This shell became a kind of inhabitable, telescopic device. We realized that the connection between the floors was not enough, and that we should establish some sort of visual connection with the trees in front of the building. That's why we developed a kind of dot pattern that mimics the passage of light through a tree canopy. As a result, the material becomes something more than itself. One typically focuses on the surface of materials, but these holes create a visual depth that reveals hints of the illuminated

---

1 Edison experimented with bamboo filament lamps as well as paper-carbon type lamps at Menlo Park. See Frank Lewis Dyer and Thomas Commerford Martin, *Edison: His Life and Inventions* (Teddington, UK: Echo Library, 2008), 161.

2 As in the West, many prominent architects and designers in Japan teach as well as practice. The academic structures are notably different, however. In the United States, for example, students are typically taught by different professors each semester, and research is either student-driven or an extracurricular activity dictated by custom arrangements between students and faculty. In Japan, however, a design studio is run like an atelier, and students remain with the same studio professor for much of their academic curriculum (similar to the sciences). As a result, Japanese architects and designers fortunate enough to teach studio essentially have two offices—one that is business driven and one that is research driven. Because intellectual protocol is more loosely regulated in Japan than in the West, and because a professor teaches the same students for multiple semesters in Japan, pedagogical work there can tackle more robust research problems that benefit from knowledge sharing and that require longer schedules.

Aoba-tei restaurant, interior facing street (left), view to second level (right)

soffit behind the steel. As a result, the surface appears much deeper than it is, and it creates a kind of visual vibration. So not only do you experience the tree pattern, but also this visual vibration. This effect is something I could not have calculated before.[3]

> It is definitely a striking effect—something a photograph cannot capture. I certainly became aware of this vibration in the space. Like Aoba-tei, you have experimented a lot with steel in your work. How did you decide on the particular lozenge shape for the Kanno Museum panels, for example?

We had conceived of the spaces in the museum like soap bubbles separated by thin membranes. When we talked with the structural engineer, he suggested that we use steel framing with drywall to cover the wall. However, I really didn't like that idea; I thought the structure of the building should be strongly related to the original concept. So I called the steel fabricator who worked on the Aoba-tei restaurant and suggested that we meet with the structural engineer. At first we feared the structure would be too heavy because we needed three layers of steel. But we found a way to reduce the number to two layers, which was good, since steel is priced by weight. Then the structural engineer suggested we emboss the steel, and I loved the idea. The steel fabricator also confirmed this could be done. We decided upon the elongated lozenge shape because it greatly increased the potential surface area of the weld points between panels. The embossed shapes alternate so that a horizontal one matches with a vertical one and vice versa.

3 Visual vibration is a consequence of the movement of the eye in front of layered, porous surfaces. This phenomenon may be seen in traditional Japanese architecture, where multiple layers of light-transmitting screens are used to create a visual separation between public and private domains.

When using materials one should not try to erase their character, but rather look for their hidden potential to create something new.

Kanno Museum (top), interior (middle), exterior detail (left)

This way, we thought it would be hard for the shapes to be misaligned during construction.

I see. The concept is like a slotted bolt connection.[4]

Right, so it's easy to create. We had to design and build a mold for the panel in such a way that the thickness could be consistent. We tried a few earlier patterns, but there were always cracks in the panels. We found that this particular shape performed much better. So this process demonstrates how a conceptual idea can lead to a very practical issue.

It's unusual to see this pattern on the walls of a gallery space. Museum curators usually demand spaces composed by sterile, unadorned surfaces. Since museum architects usually want to make bold statements, the exterior and interior conditions are usually separated as a result.

That's right.

There is also a kind of playfulness expressed here. Because the embossing has a functional rationale, we might call it a performative pattern.[5] This is a strategy that you employ in a wide variety of ways.

It's funny—I believe my interest in pattern-making originated during the design of the Miyagi Stadium. When we drew sections through the stadium, we realized that they were like stills in a movie. The sequential layering of sectional transformations became a kind of moving pattern.

That phenomenon is present in your Shirasagi Bridge.

Yes, exactly. That's how the idea came about. The bridge was a renovation project and we couldn't add much weight, so we had to use lightweight elements. I was fascinated by this kind of series of layers showing the transformation of a shape. The series of sections is actually a kind of repeating pattern. I also created an experimental object similar to the bridge, but that could be transformed into many different shapes. It consisted of sixteen frames and was connected with various pipes so that each frame could move independently. So in a way, it was a kind of architectural toy—a system that could describe various forces or the condition of the field. It was also a kind of rule, implying measurement.

We then tried another project based on that idea—the Yomiuri Guest House. In this house, the rule was a ribbon. We attempted to fold the ribbon in order to delineate the spaces of the house. It's a simple rule that allows for the precise control of different angles. By folding this ribbon on the side, we could transform the condition of the topology into interior space. So the building mediates between the interior and exterior.

In recent years this idea has turned into various patterns. If you look at the facade of the Sasaki-Gishi Office and Factory, for example, there is a simple staggered pattern used for the openings. However, the pattern changes where the structure carries especially strong loads, so the pattern shifts and generates a slightly different pattern. In this way, I am very happy when I see design resulting from the special conditions of a project—like the way the unique pattern on a butterfly's wings relates to the specificities of its environment, including flower nectar, soil composition, and so on. Pattern can express the special conditions of a project as a kind of design.

I see these patterns as a method to map flows. When I first saw the Shirasagi Bridge, for example, it reminded me of the futurists' infatuation with stop-motion time sequences or Duchamp's *Nude Descending a Staircase*.[6]

Right.

---

[4] A slotted bolt connection is one in which two structural plates are perforated for a mechanical connection by a bolt, and one or more of the perforations is elongated in order to provide a more generous construction tolerance.

[5] Simply put, a performative pattern is one that addresses a particular function—as opposed to ornament, which is purely for decoration purposes.

[6] Duchamp actually claimed that he saw no connection between *Nude Descending a Staircase* and futurism, but I mention both based on the shared influence of stop-motion photography. See Elmer Peterson and Michel Sanouillet, eds., *The Writings of Marcel Duchamp* (Cambridge: Da Capo Press, 1989), 124.

166 Matter in the Floating World   Flow

Shirasagi Bridge

Yomiuri Guest House

Pattern can express the special conditions of a project as a kind of design.

Sasaki-Gishi Office and Factory (top)
Shiki Community Hall (bottom)

In this case, the bridge encapsulates a kind of frozen movement, as well as a representation of multiple structural possibilities. As for the other projects, one might say that the ribbon in the Yomiuri Guest House maps spatial flows, and the Sasaki-Gishi Office and Factory pattern maps structural flows. The Shiki Community Hall seems to anticipate human movement in its undulating structure.

Right—it's a boundary line, basically—a kind of invisible field of possible activity.

There are other boundary strategies that you employ, such as your concept of "architectural pleats" used to create a visual distance between your Sekii Ladies Clinic and its site.[7]

I should also mention the Bouno House collective housing project, which we conceived as different parts of a body carved to make various dishes. The massing of the building conformed to the allowable building height and shape by code. Before we designed anything, we generated a kind of landscape by creating a geometrical order. Normally housing projects are designed with units that are entirely equal, but due to the particular site geometries and constraints, we carved up the buildable volume into a variety of different unit types—some tall, some short, and so on. This conceptual carving led us to conceive of the building as a cow; in order to create a good meal, you have to divide the body into different kinds of meat.

So this unusual strategy also allowed you to maximize the design potential of the units, expanding their height and so on.

Yes. Also different users want different things—people who want high ceilings but not much window, people who are more interested in looking outside than having high ceilings, and so on.

Speaking of windows—what about your attitude toward light? How does this affect your material choices?

We use different kinds of white materials, like tile with a diagonal scratch pattern or aluminum spandrels painted white. I have always been interested in the kind of material quality that light can create on white surfaces. So for the little residential projects around here, I tried to use white materials in different ways.

How about your Rainbow exhibition? It appears that you were utilizing the Kanno Museum as a kind of prism or multicolored light box.

When we were working on the Kanno Museum project, I was aware that we would probably have to use different types of white finishes for different surfaces because of their varying qualities. So we applied a very shiny white to the floor. The interior surface of the exterior walls is painted in matte white. And the other interior walls are painted with a ceramic powder—I like the texture, which is rough like sandpaper. I specified this finish for the interior walls in order to hide inevitable surface defects, and to distinguish these walls from other surfaces. The result is a complex yet subtle strategy of different surface treatments.

After the construction was complete, we were asked to do an installation. We didn't want to do a model exhibit, so we suggested that we play with light. We started to put different kinds of colored film over different openings, and then we realized that this experience actually told a lot about this project—things we didn't know, like which light sources were affecting which spaces. Under normal circumstances, the daylight entering the windows is the same color—but when each aperture is colored differently, the source of each light becomes apparent. Suddenly, applying different colors to different light sources started to reveal a kind of competition of the light. So I was fascinated because this was the best way to describe the nature of the building in terms of the light positions.

I can't help but think of artists like Dan Flavin and James Turrell and their carefully detailed light installations, which are typically constructed within anonymous spaces.

---

7 Abe discusses the concept of architectural pleats in *Hitoshi Flicker* (Tokyo: Toto Publishers, 2005).

Bouno House, model

Ftown Building

I'd like to create some sort of landscape where people can find the clues to create their own interesting lifestyle.

Rainbow exhibition at the Kanno Museum

In this case, however, the Kanno Museum became the installation itself. That's highly unusual, isn't it?

Yes, I'm happy the client likes it, which means it works.

This use was made possible based on the way you conceived the spaces and executed the surface treatments—the ceramic paint, for example, makes the steel feel very soft, almost like a pillow.

I was really concerned about the patterned room as a background for the sculpture. I feared it could be quite irritating to the eye. So that's also why that finish treatment works—it's actually better than a big, flat wall. It gives some sort of depth and helps you really understand the sculptures as three-dimensional objects.

Your description of visual depth makes me think of some of your other work. The Miyagi Water Tower, for example, employs depth in an unusual way, based on the use of several layers of structure. How does a heavy building like this achieve this kind of visual lightness?

This project type tends to be quite heavy, doesn't it? You have to support one hundred tons of water at the top with heavy structure underneath. Since we didn't want to do that, we made it as simple as possible. So we decided to wrap the tower in a layer of thin structural elements—a delicate, continuous framing that would create an invigorating spatial experience for people. By treating these frames as a kind of continuous phenomenon, you can generate a special quality of space. I think the architecture is about how you can actually create a relationship between these frames.

So it's a type of performative form, in this case.[8]

Yes, a performing form or something like that. It's the same as a bridge, actually.

Are you taking a similar approach in your design for an electric utility tower?

Yes, since utility towers are not very popular, the client wants a tower that essentially disappears in the landscape. However, they don't want to pay more for a new kind of tower. The program calls for a tall tower, which is like a huge column. So we conducted our own study to invent a new column. Our current proposal employs military camouflage. We studied various camouflage patterns, and then we took photographs of the area and transformed them into a kind of pattern. If the tower is painted with this color, it will begin to blend into its surroundings. However, if you come close, you will see a really weird pattern on the south facade. I've been quite fascinated by the idea.

What is it like to work on a museum one day and an infrastructural project the next?[9]

It's interesting to experiment in a different field and see opportunities to apply architectural methods of thinking.

Knowledge transfer must work the other way as well. Perhaps your architecture is influenced by engineering approaches toward optimizing structure? Could work on utility towers influence the design of houses, for example?

We designed a tall house based on a prototype built by architect Makoto Masuzawa in 1952. Masuzawa's residence was designed to optimize resources during a period of dwindling supplies that occurred after World War II.[10] It was meant to be a kind of minimal dwelling that anyone could construct. However, Masuzawa didn't just try to create a building; more likely, he tried to create a typical modern lifestyle through the design of his house. So there's a kitchen, bathroom, tatami room, possible kid's room, and so on, all in a tight space—and residents would basically have to live the way he designed.

But the question today is not like that anymore. There is not only one way to live our

---

[8] Performative form is derived from function that also achieves a particular visual effect. It is like performative pattern, but has spatial implications.

[9] Generally speaking, Japanese design firms tend to seek and accept a wider range of clients and program types than their Western counterparts.

[10] After World War II, Japanese cities faced serious housing shortages, and many design proposals were generated to optimize material resources and living space. See Thomas Daniell, *After the Crash: Architecture in Post-Bubble Japan* (New York: Princeton Architectural Press, 2008), 67.

9tsubohouse Tall

Whopper house, second-level interior

contemporary life. So the task now is not to show how one lives, but to provide more possibilities so one can find the best way to live. The 9tsubohouse Tall maximizes these possibilities by providing more volume, so people can add a third floor if they want. Also we distributed the bathroom, kitchen, and toilets that were all in one corner in the original house. By loosening the structure of the spaces, the inhabitant has more freedom—for example, whether to sleep downstairs or upstairs. Also I tried to remove the sense of direction in the original house by spreading windows equally around the wall surfaces. Now you can open your house in any direction. It removes the tension from the modernist agenda.[11]

> Did this house influence the design of your Whopper house? Given the placement of retail or office on the ground floor and living quarters above, it is actually one of the oldest dwelling typologies.

Yes, it probably did. I try to make space loose—a little undefined. What is important about that project is the second-floor space, the outside terrace. The project is surrounded by nasty buildings and a busy road, and the client had little children at home. So my idea was to create some sort of buffer zone within this busy environment so the kids could feel comfortable there. In that way, this house also has no direction, and sunlight enters through the skylight and the three-story volume reflects this light around. So the second floor is actually a pleasant place to stay.

> It seems that your work is simultaneously flexible and suggestive, meaning that it allows for multiple possibilities of living and also encourages creative uses of space. Architecture should give people freedom without becoming generic.[12]

Yes, I'd like to create some sort of landscape where people can find the clues to create their own interesting lifestyle. These clues are important, because they impart a special character to the landscape, which leads to a sense of place. And you need that sense of place to live. That's what I'm trying to create—a sense of place, and that's why I'm so interested in capturing the special qualities of the site and program in architecture. This is more important than forcing the program to fit. So we need to loosen the program and the plan, and we need to use materials in the service of creating these clues.

---

11 Abe is referring in this case to design that dictates a particular living style, as opposed to his more flexible proposal.

12 As architecture approaches maximum flexibility, it also becomes increasingly banal (think of endless open office spaces). The goal is to provide flexibility as articulated by particular design cues, rather than diminishing the role of design.

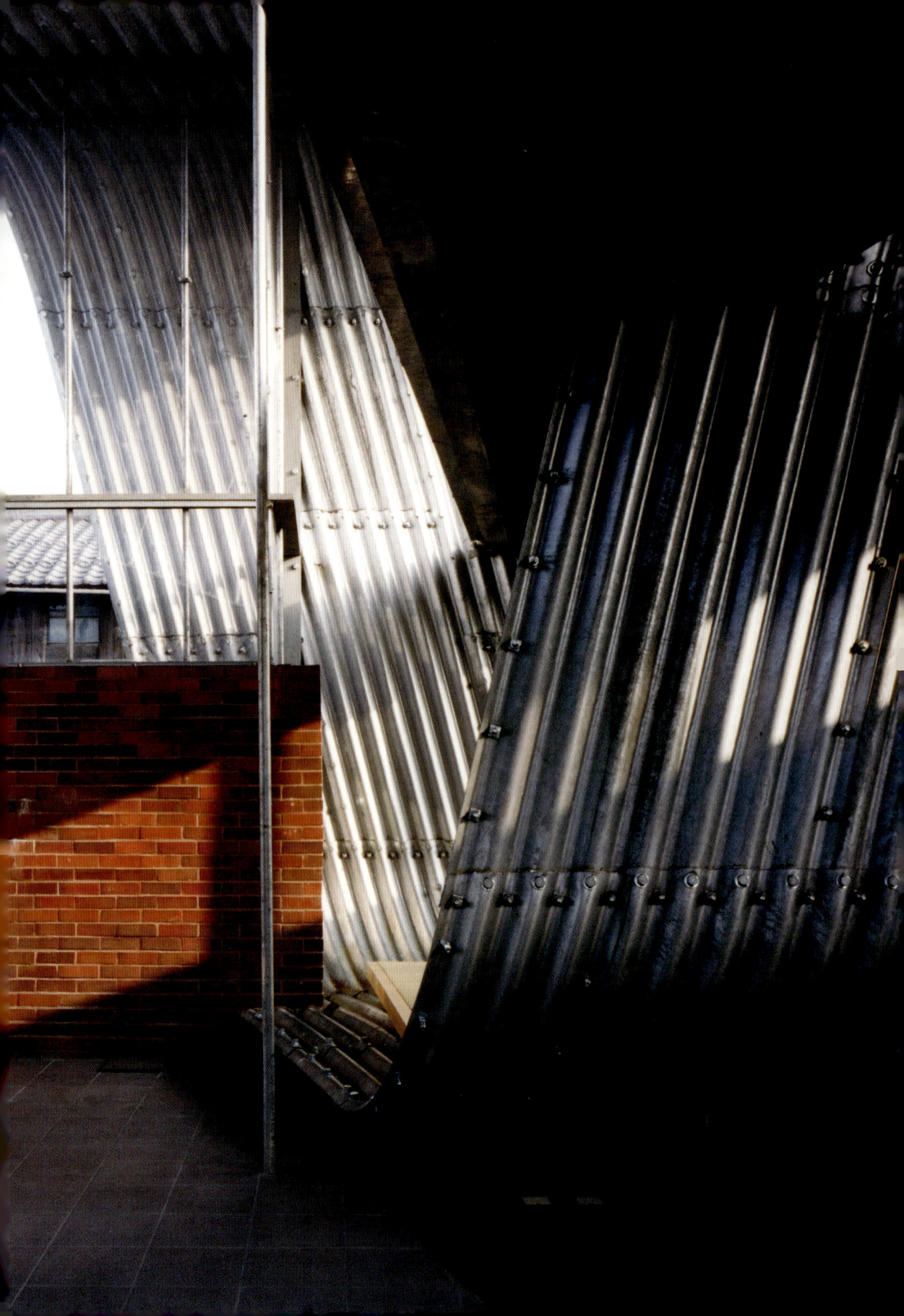

Connective Tissue

A conversation with Shuhei Endo, Shuhei Endo Architect Institute

For Shuhei Endo, continuity is everything. In his architecture, he strives to make connections between inside and outside, large and small, space and material, and gesture and form. Inspired by the traditional Japanese calligraphy technique called *renmentai*, in which the brush doesn't leave the paper, Endo treats material as a fluid gesture and folds space in upon itself. Inscribed by humble industrial materials like corrugated steel, rooms, entrances, and apertures seem to emerge effortlessly out of the landscape and form a completely interconnected experience.

Shuhei Endo was born in Japan in 1960. He obtained an M.Arch from the Kyoto City University of Arts in 1986 and worked for Osamu Ishii & Biken Associates for two years. Endo established the Shuhei Endo Architect Institute in Osaka in 1988 and gained notoriety for works in corrugated metal such as Springtecture H and Slowtecture S. He has won several awards, including the AIJ Annual Architectural Design Commendation (2006, 2008), the Osaka Governor's Prize (2007, 2008), the Good Design Award (2005), and the Kenneth F. Brown Asia Pacific Architecture Design Award (1998). In 2004 Endo was a professor at the Salzburg Summer Academy, and he has taught at the graduate school of Kobe University from 2007 to the present.

Springtecture H (opposite)

I am intrigued by your invention of the word "paramodernism." How do you define this term?

That is an extremely difficult question. Because paramodernism is a new concept, I cannot explain it easily. *Para* comes from parallel and is used as a prefix to indicate the possibility for another type of modernism. Could there be another modernism? Could the two terms be used in concomitance? If so, let's call this new term "paramodern." For me, modernism is like the Japanese term *kangen-shugi*, which means atomism, or rather, Platonism.[1] If you look at it this way, it has the same meaning—things are divided, small ideas are discovered, parts are divided again, and new ideas are formulated.

In creating architecture, however, this kind of atomism is not present. Architecture is not a composition. Architecture without composition is when there is a thread, there is a needle, and there is a mountain. It is not composed of small parts, but rather a collection of related ideas. This is where space and architecture can emerge. This is what I strive for. This is paramodernism. My architecture is connected, or rather, the outside and inside are connected, and the private and the public areas are connected. There is no break. I am thinking of the possibility for an architecture that is not composed of smaller pieces.

Do you feel it is necessary to create a new vocabulary to describe your work—terms like Springtecture, Bubbletecture, and so on?

First, paramodernism is a *gainen*, or concept. Architecture is not a concept; rather, it is a thing, an object. As a result, when I think of one project or another, the place, client, and function each differ—they all vary. In these situations the single concept of paramodernism is not a sufficient descriptor. Springtecture emerged, for example, when I designed a set of projects with a springlike feeling. The springlike framework and the building methods central to these works warranted a merger of the words "spring" and "architecture" to make "Springtecture." Similarly, I coined the term "Bubbletecture" for projects conceived around the structure of a bubble.

Therefore, as a basic concept, paramodernism describes the architectural approach in general terms. However, there are distinctions within this application. I think of architecture in this context of combined levels.

It is interesting that these new terms embody dynamic structural concepts. For example, "spring" describes a structure locked in a permanent state of outward thrust, while "bubble" indicates a delicate shell of minimal substance enclosing a maximum volume. These different material-related themes connect structure to program, and also result in a highly varied collection of work that lacks a singular identity. When clients request a Frank Gehry building, for example, they have a particular image in mind, based on the fact that Gehry's work is so recognizable. In your case, however, the projects are highly diverse and do not conform to one kind of approach.

Architecture is an extremely diverse thing. Clients and sites vary. Therefore, each building should yield many ideas.

Once you begin working on a project, when do you decide what type of approach you will devise? When, for example, do you realize "Oh, this is Springtecture"?

I usually decide after I have seen the site. Then I think about what would be best after learning the functional program.

One interest I have is the strategy of material programming—the process of conceptualizing, selecting, and deploying materials in the physical environment. Given your structural- and material-related design approaches, I would say that your process incorporates a kind of site-inspired material program. When you look at a building site, what forces do you consider? Does your work seek a particular relationship with nature, for example?

Gravity is related to the idea of nature. Wind increases, waves get larger, and trees

---

1 "Kangen-shugi" also means reductionism.

Springtecture H (top and bottom)

Architecture without composition is when there is a thread, there is a needle, and there is a mountain. It is not composed of small parts, but rather a collection of related ideas.

Bubbletecture H

> It is through the consideration of gravity that I get closer to understanding the natural condition.

Slowtecture M

grow due to gravity. Gravity affects the state of nature. Therefore, although architecture is specifically made for human beings, it is always affected by natural forces. It is through the consideration of gravity that I get closer to understanding the natural condition.

Modernism is human-centered but does not consider gravity in terms of recognizing larger environmental forces. However, paramodernism seeks to create a relationship with gravity. Thus, it is a type of modernism that has a relationship with nature. My intent is not to make something close to nature, but the result is close to nature.

Throughout its history, Japanese architecture has embraced a fundamental relationship between the interior and exterior.
Yes, I think this is a characteristic of Japanese architecture. However, this quality exists in other parts of Asia too. There are two historical tendencies in architecture: one is human-centered with an extremely weak relationship to nature; the other has a strong relationship to nature. Modernism considers nature in the abstract.

Architecture has been greatly influenced by ecological thinking recently. However, in the West there is still a notable separation between architecture and nature in the way that buildings are constructed and maintained. For example, most contemporary office buildings have fixed windows, and occupants have no exposure to natural ventilation. This separation between inside and outside is obviously less apparent in Japanese architecture. How do you consider this threshold?
I don't really consider the relationship with the outside—it is not established.

Do you mean that you don't delineate the threshold as a hard line? I am reminded of your Halftecture projects at Osaka Castle, for example. There is a significant and intentional blurring between structure, skin, and interior space. In this case the blurring is relatively easy to achieve, since the interior space does not have to be conditioned. However, in the case of particular Springtecture projects, the exterior appears to flow into the interior and vice versa at the line of glazing. Although the materials appear to be the same on either side, the environmental conditions between inside and outside differ. Is it difficult to achieve this detail?
Air and water flows are a challenge. We have to conduct various simulation tests to ensure

Halftecture OR

Halftecture OO

that water does not penetrate the building. If the point of water absorption occurs outside the envelope, it is not as much of a concern. However, if it occurs inside the building, we have to modify the design to ensure that wind and water do not enter. We study this condition by looking at a physical model as well as a detailed, animated computer model. We then create a scheme and demonstrate how we will prevent negative circumstances, thus resolving any issues.

Do you conduct this simulation on your own, or do you hire engineers?

I perform the simulation with my staff here in the office. Engineers conduct simulated research on the structure, and we collaborate with them at various levels. The details, however, happen here.

Do you view this collaboration as important?

Yes, extremely. With Springtecture, for example, we had to make sure to work with structural engineers knowledgeable in wood construction. We collaborate with talented people—this is extremely important.

The highly collaborative relationship between architects and engineers in Japan is envied by many Western architects. The level of technological sophistication in Japanese architecture is highly regarded—especially the exquisite detailing. Is it difficult to achieve this level of detail in architecture? Does it take a lot of time?

There are two types of details. One type is represented in the ready-made product, which is already completely developed. Examples include franchise buildings like Uniqlo or McDonald's.[2] This type may really be considered a product, because the building is the same wherever you go. Although quality may be controlled, user satisfaction is low. Human beings desire variety.

The second type of detail is represented in original architecture. When details are created in new architecture, they take a lot of energy, time, and money. I create structured details, but they are extremely simple. Depending on the level of simplicity, the details take energy to develop, but I like to look for ways to lower construction costs. This is what defines architecture as opposed to craft. Arts and crafts are expensive, yet architecture is a little lower in price, and it is important for the creation of a positive environment. For this reason, I like to make architecture simple. I take time to create extremely simple details, as opposed to gathering many ideas as a composite.

---

2 Uniqlo is a popular Japanese clothing store. Its name is a shortened version of "unique clothing."

Springtecture B

In the last twenty years, the Japanese automotive and shipbuilding industries have increasingly influenced architecture, and the construction techniques used in these industries have been incorporated into various building projects.[3] How do you view this influence?

I think the influence has become very strong. Product design and car design are quite close to architecture. I think this is happening because of computer-based simulation tools and the fact that we are using the same software techniques. Therefore, the results are similar. There is freedom in material. Although materials used for products and automobiles are comparatively similar—metal and plastic, for example—the architectural equivalents must be stronger. Functional demands bring about different qualities in materials. These differing qualities lead to a positive variety in our physical environment. It is better to have a lot of materials in architecture.

Although you incorporate a variety of materials in your projects, metal appears predominantly in your work. When did you become interested in using metal in architecture and why?

I naturally liked metal since I was a child. No matter how it is used, metal is a heavy material—it weighs more than a person. So I became interested in this quality of gravity and weight from an early age. When I became an architect, metal was as expensive as concrete and glass. Metal is also extremely pliable—you can bend it, apply force to it, break it—metal's flexibility is a significant reason for my interest in the material.

Do you conduct thorough research to select the appropriate material for a project, such as aluminum or stainless steel?

At first I did not use a lot of aluminum or stainless steel—only plain steel. I did this because my ideas were extremely simple and steel has this quality. It can stretch, shrink, and rust. This potential for different possibilities makes steel a very interesting material.

Material resources have been a serious concern in Japan, and material and energy costs are likely to continue rising. How will this trend affect architecture?

---

3 For more information about the influence of shipbuilding on architecture in Japan, see Takafumi Suzuki, "Crossbreeding Shipbuilding with Architecture," on the *Pingmag* website: http://pingmag.jp/2008/07/07/crossbreeding-shipbuilding-with-architecture/.

Springtecture B

If you look at my lifestyle, you will understand architecture. The energy crisis will alter lifestyles—for example, encouraging people to get rid of their cars, walk more, and use less electricity. All of those things will affect architecture. My lifestyle is architecture. Architecture is not a purpose; it is a result. No matter how things change, I think architecture will be fine. To say that we don't need architecture is sad, but I think it is necessary to question its role. Architecture changes depending on the time, and this change is good, because different things are born as a result.

Japan has limited resources, and I think this situation will affect architecture in the future. Since there are few examples of this kind of change in history, a new architecture will likely emerge. As I mentioned before, paramodernism does not know what architecture is formally, because architecture is not a purpose. This is a healthy way of thinking. About one hundred years ago, we Japanese modeled architecture after European modernism. That was a form of stylistic mimicry—an objectification. However, it is unnecessary to make architecture a style. It should be a result of strong conceptual ideas.

I have noted your interest in expanding the scope of architecture into other areas, such as infrastructure. How is a project like Transtreet different or similar to your other architecture work?

That's right. Most basic streets are "outer" streets. However, if you make streets interior streets—like a living room or kitchen—it is quite interesting. Currently there is only one distinct function of a street, with its own separate meaning. I want to change streets so they don't feel like streets.

From this point forward, do you intend to create a new "-tecture?"

It depends on the recognition of a new program. We do not determine this; the client does. If a new program demands that conditions change, they will. In the last ten years, things have already changed. If we continue to look at things with clear vision, we can facilitate the change.

Matter in the Floating World   Flow

Transtreet G

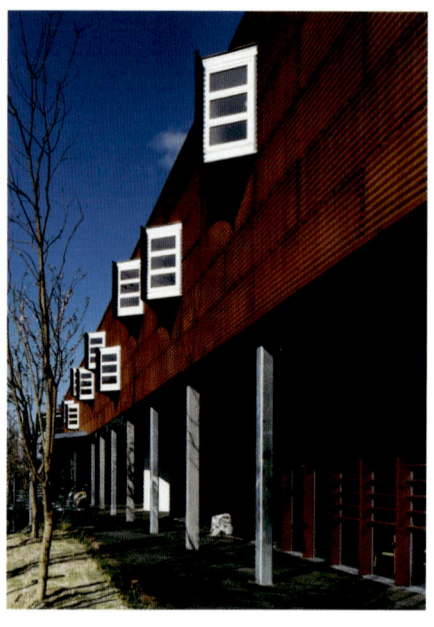

Slowtecture S

I like to make architecture simple. I take time to create extremely simple details, as opposed to gathering many ideas as a composite.

Rooftecture S

Architecture is not a purpose; it is a result.

Transtation O (top and bottom)

The Fluidity of Fabric

A conversation with Reiko Sudo, Nuno Corporation

Cofounder and artistic director of Nuno, Reiko Sudo has propelled traditional Japanese textiles into an unlikely realm. Although skilled in time-honored methods of fabric weaving and dyeing, Sudo also seeks to upset safe conventions in her craft and considers virtually any process fair game for experimentation. She has employed unusual treatments such as metal sputtering, blowtorching, rust dyeing, and three-dimensional weaving in order to achieve new possibilities in textiles.

Reiko Sudo was born in 1953 in Ibaragi, Japan. She studied at Musashino Art University in Tokyo and in 1984 was one of the founders of Nuno Corporation, a company and retail store that produces and sells innovative, functional fabrics. Acting as artistic director of Nuno since 1987, Sudo's visionary combination of complex technologies, traditional techniques, and new finishing processes has created remarkable visual effects that have revolutionized textiles within interior design, fashion, and art. Sudo's work has been shown worldwide, with exhibitions in the United States, India, and Israel. Her textiles are in the permanent collections of the Museum of Fine Arts in Boston, the Victoria & Albert Museum in London, the Philadelphia Museum of Art, and the Cooper-Hewitt, National Design Museum in New York.

Seal Skin (opposite)

184 Matter in the Floating World Flow

Green Fabric

It's good to learn from history, but at the same time we have to remember that the people who developed these traditional techniques were inspired by the same things that move us today.

Origami Pleats

Stainless Steel series

Kumosibori

The world of textiles has changed so much recently. There's a lot more experimentation, especially with non-petroleum-based resources.
That's true—but new synthetics can also be made without any new petroleum. There are new technologies for recycling postconsumer polyesters, new plastics developed from polylactic acid, and textiles that are wholly reclaimable. Without using new oil at all, we can recycle anything from shopping bags and raincoats to hospital uniforms; all kinds of polyester products can be recycled indefinitely.

It's a pity the Japanese rarely use *furoshiki* carrier-wraps anymore, especially considering the excessive amount of gratuitous disposable packaging today.[1]
Today's shopping bags can be considered a continuation of the *furoshiki*—carry them, flatten and store them, then carry them again.

What's this textile called?
This is Origami Pleats. It's made from reclaimed polyester in large panels, so it can be used to partition spaces in architectural applications. It's designed to be used in large quantities; otherwise it's pointless for the mill to invest the time in making it.

Can you incorporate non-petroleum materials like polylactic acid?
Sure, there's plenty of room in the threads. For one meter [three feet three inches] of fabric, we use from sixteen hundred to seventeen hundred threads, so there's enough interstitial space. It stretches like spandex and has highly overspun threads that contract to create a pattern, making the fabric more three-dimensional. Have you heard of sputtering?[2] It was developed by the automotive industry. This new Spattering Gloss in the Stainless Steel series is even more open.

Is it metal?
It's an alloy formed right on the surface of the textile. The threads are incredibly thin microfibers.

Can you make a shirt out of this material?
Yes, we have one right here.

Incredible—it's so soft.
It's soft, but it will set off an airport security alarm [laughs].

Where do you make these textiles?
We work with at least fifty mills around Japan.

That many? That must be difficult to manage.
Hmm….

---

1 Furoshiki are traditional Japanese cloths used to wrap and carry gifts, clothes, or other items.

2 Sputtering is a process in which thin metallic films are deposited when ionized gas molecules displace atoms of another material, and these atoms bond to a substrate. Sputtering is used for various commercial and scientific applications. According to research conducted at the Victoria & Albert Museum, this particular Nuno fabric is "made of polyester that has been calendered mirror-smooth and 'sputter-plated' with three powdered metals (chromium, nickel and iron). This gives it a metallic shine." http://www.vam.ac.uk/res_cons/conservation/journal/number_44/polyester-fabrics/index.html.

How did you first develop an interest in textiles?
I began drawing kimono patterns in college, which led to textile design.

Does Nuno attempt to combine traditional and contemporary approaches?
I have knowledge of traditional approaches, but I'm constantly thinking about how to modify or enhance them—like incorporating *shibori* into contemporary fabrics.[3] It's good to learn from history, but at the same time we have to remember that the people who developed these traditional techniques were inspired by the same things that move us today. Prehistoric people developed tools for knitting and cutting. We can marvel at their inventions—like thread—but did those people realize they were making a profound discovery? Today's discoveries are similar—we're not surprised to see people using computers or cars. It's the same thing.

You have been quite prolific in your textile creations. How long does it typically take to realize an idea?
I think of new textile designs and techniques every day. It may take just a minute to form an idea, but five to ten years to execute it. These things take time.

What kind of process is involved?
I have twelve staff members, all of whom are designers. They frequently throw out ideas. The sputtering technology is an example of an idea we wanted to test. We developed a large wall hanging called Deep Roots out of stainless steel and cotton for Mandarin Oriental Tokyo—the back is red and the front is gray. We made a stainless-steel mesh that we then burned by hand using a gas torch. The fiber was originally developed to strengthen radial tires, yet the knitted fabric structure makes it look soft. It discolors as it burns—like a stainless-steel frying pan [laughs].

The stainless steel and cotton are woven together?
Yes. We also made another "woods and water"–theme fabric for Mandarin Oriental Tokyo called Tree Rings. All the guest rooms and elevators are green. The client wanted the entrance to be dramatic, so the walls there are a deep red. The ballroom, main lobby, and restrooms are yellow. These fabrics look like paintings, because they're from hand-painted sketches.

Were they reworked using digital tools?
Yes, we painted three meters [nine feet ten inches] by hand and scanned the brushstrokes to create composite images, sometimes pairing two images to convey the sense of movement.

Repetition seems like a frequent problem in textile applications. The mind becomes fatigued by endlessly repeating patterns. How do you develop patterns that change?
If we're designing for a big space, we don't repeat. In the Mandarin Oriental Tokyo lobby, for example, we only repeated a pattern every six meters [nineteen feet eight inches]. It depends on the place. Small repetitions can impart a rhythm or sequence.

I can see repeating patterns, but they appear so natural. You use so many different materials. Are you always searching for new materials to incorporate?
Yes, everyone loves new materials. The Mandarin Oriental Tokyo is connected to the old Nihonbashi Mitsui Building, an important cultural property that has been renovated and enlarged to include a banquet hall, conference rooms, and offices. We finished the walls in a moiré-patterned fabric called Wood Grain derived from Japanese cedar planks. By weaving ridges into the basic fabric, then pressing in the grain, we created a natural moiré with no repeats over the entire wall. We get word of new materials from the manufacturers, but we also develop our own new materials here at Nuno. Anything's possible.

So everything was done by hand.
We call it an industrial product, but it required a lot of finishing by hand. We did a similar

---

3 Shibori, or *shiborizome*, is a Japanese method of dyeing cloth dating to the eighth century that involves folding, binding, twisting, and other physical manipulations.

Karadaki

We made a stainless-steel mesh that we then burned by hand using a gas torch. The fiber was originally developed to strengthen radial tires, yet the knitted fabric structure makes it look soft.

Moss Temple

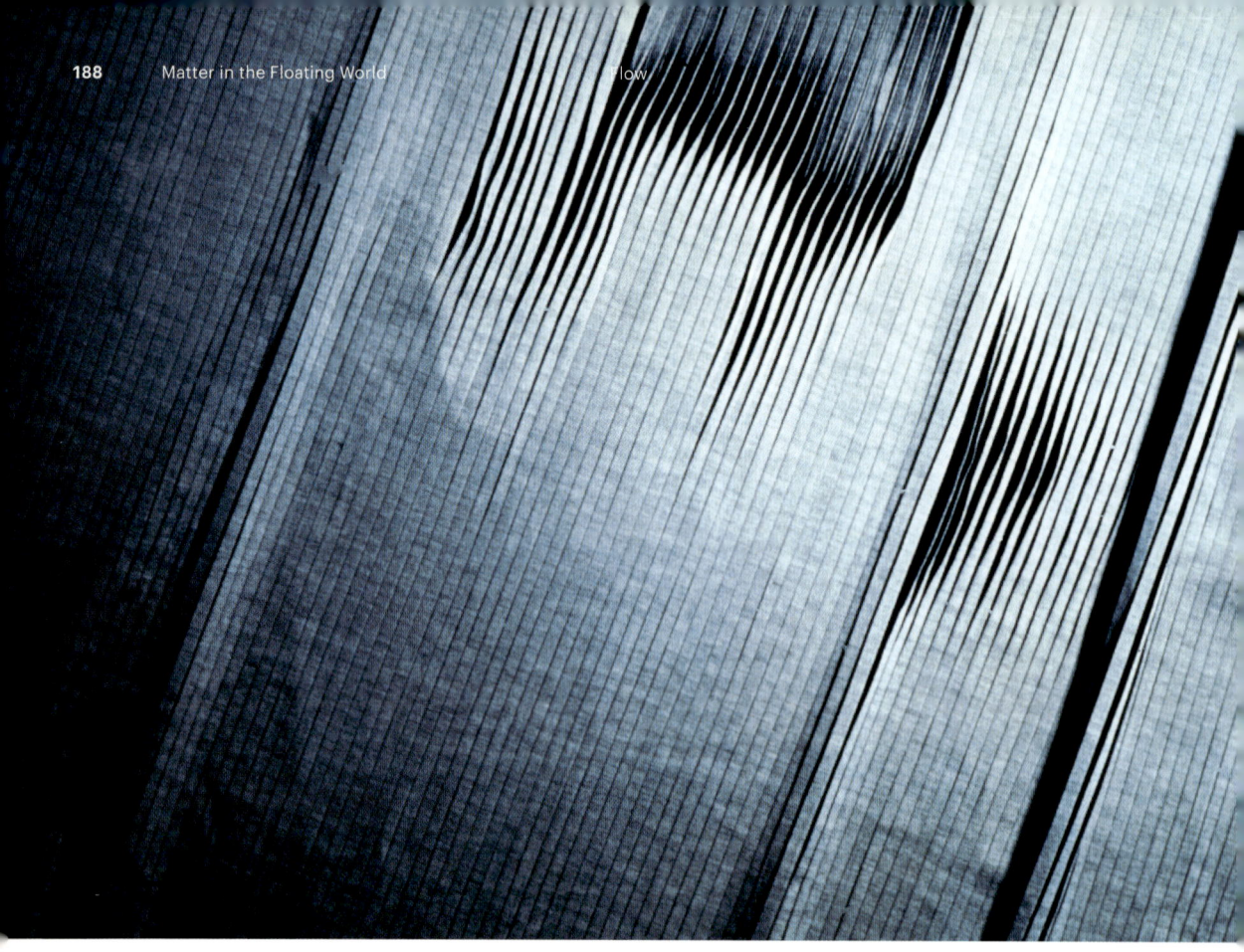

Bellows

Feather Flurries

Scrapyard Iron Plates

Circle Series

> Basically we create textiles out of anything that can be made into thread—natural fibers, of course, but also synthetics, metal, paper, even packaging tape.

Agitfab

Shifu

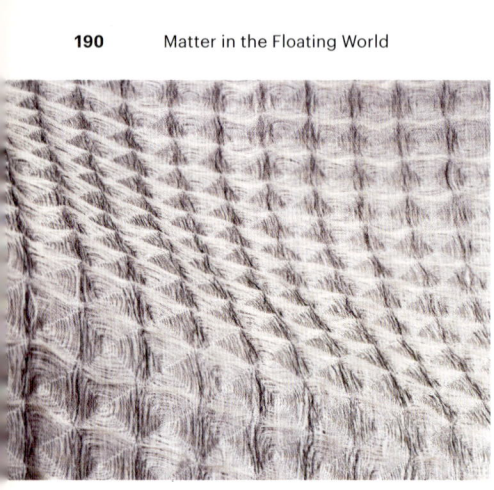

Jellyfish

Fabric is like water. It constantly responds to different forces—it's never static. Fabric isn't a rigid thing.

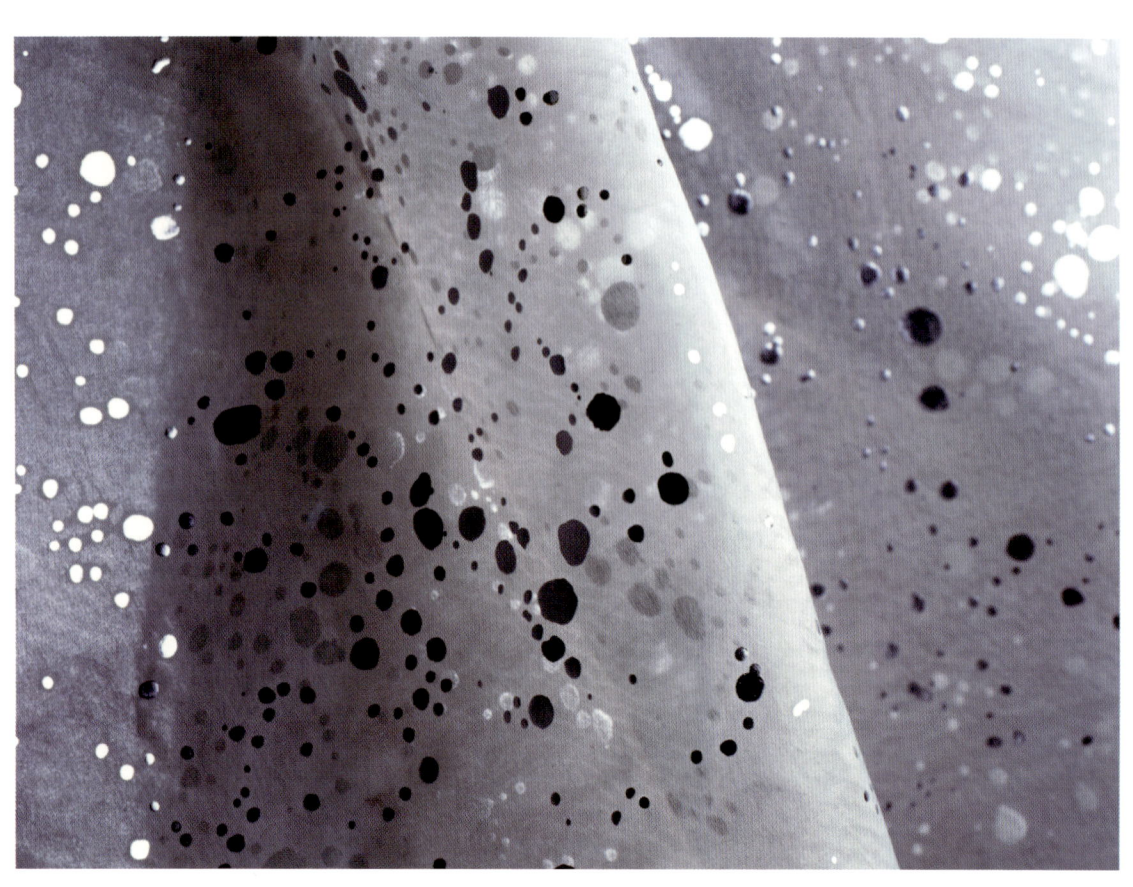

Mercury

moiré textile, but without the labor-intensive hand-finishing. Jun Aoki used this textile for his White Chapel in Osaka.[4] Aoki designed the basic plan and we realized it using a double-weave technique.

Do you have a particular attitude concerning the use of so-called natural versus synthetic materials?

We use them all. Basically we create textiles out of anything that can be made into thread—natural fibers, of course, but also synthetics, metal, paper, even packaging tape. Historically silk dates back to around 2500 BCE, and hemp to around 4000 BCE.[5] But it's only been seventy years since DuPont synthesized nylon and polyester from petroleum.[6] And now, with the possibility of recycling polyester over and over again, we're entering a new phase. It's something new for me to explore as a textile designer, because we can't reuse natural fibers like hemp, wool, or cotton—they deteriorate in the recycling process.

Right, downcycling—the fibers degrade.

Synthetics, as they say, have evolved to be fine as a spider's web, beautiful as silk, and strong as steel. These synthetics were initially developed to look and behave like natural fibers, but now we've pushed them so that they exhibit new properties and perform unlike natural fibers. This is even better.

What do you think about all of the new products being created today? Designers are enamored with new materials. Do you view these novel materials as important, or do they merely represent a fashionable trend?

I think they're important, but we should try to avoid making harmful mistakes with them. We cannot ignore new materials, but we also cannot use them uncritically. For example, a new kind of fabric could generate allergic reactions.

What about new processes, such as digital manufacturing? How do you decide what to automate and what to do manually?

There are things you can't do with a machine. We do what we can do by machine, then do what we need to do by hand. We're very pragmatic—we don't simply make things by machine in order to emulate manual techniques. Of course, it also depends on the textile.

You already make so many different fabrics, including designs for such diverse applications as wall coverings, tapestries, clothing, and bags. Is there a central philosophy that guides your work?

Fabric is like water. It constantly responds to different forces—it's never static. Fabric isn't a rigid thing.

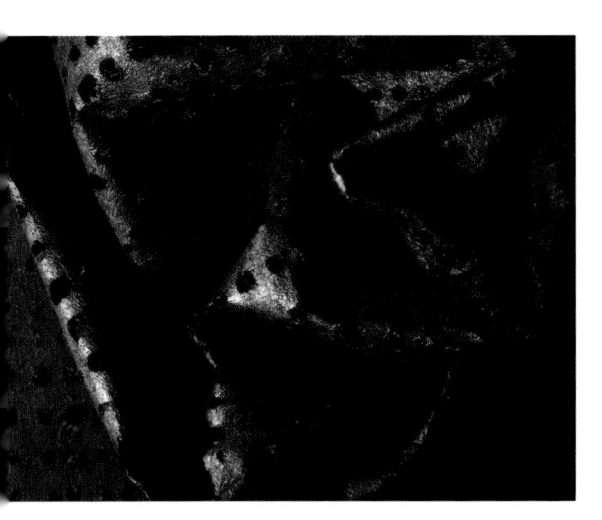

Amate

[4] See my conversation with Jun Aoki in this book, pages 149–59.

[5] Silk was developed in China during the Neolithic period, and parts of a loom dating back to 4900 BCE were found in Zhejiang province. Hemp has been cultivated for twelve thousand years. (Gerard C. C. Tsang, chief curator of the Hong Kong Museum of Art, http://www.asianart.com/textiles/intro.html; the North American Industrial Hemp Council, Inc.).

[6] DuPont's Wallace Carothers produced the first nylon synthetic polymer in 1935. DuPont produced the first commercial polyester fiber in the United States in 1953.

Liquid Architecture

A conversation with Sachiko Kodama, The University of Electro-Communications in Tokyo

Known for her provocative manipulations of ferromagnetic fluid (ferrofluid), Sachiko Kodama combines talents in both art and science to explore the innate qualities of an underrepresented material. Not only does ferrofluid's continuous shape-shifting capacity allow for the realization of dynamic sculpture, but Kodama's incorporation of environmental sensing technology also highlights the curious effects of responsive materials and environments.

Sachiko Kodama was born in 1970. After studying physics at Hokkaido University, Kodama entered the fine arts department of the University of Tsukuba in 1993, studying plastic art and mixed media. She then received a PhD in Art at the University of Tsukuba. In 2000 Kodama began working with ferrofluid and electromagnetism in the pursuit of dynamic sculptures that respond to environmental stimuli. Kodama's work has been exhibited at the Ars Electronica Center in Linz, Austria; the National Taiwan Museum of Fine Arts; the Tokyo Metropolitan Museum of Photography; the Wexner Center for the Arts in Columbus, Ohio; the Skirball Cultural Center in Los Angeles; the Science Museum, Tokyo; the National Art Center in Tokyo; and the Museo Nacional Centro de Arte Reina Sofia in Madrid. Kodama received the Grand Prize at the fifth Media Arts Festival in Japan (2001) and is currently an associate professor at the University of Electro-Communications in Tokyo.

Protrude, Flow *(opposite)*

What influenced you to develop sculptures using ferrofluid?[1]

I've always been fascinated by artworks that have aesthetic surfaces, including dynamic installations and kinetic sculpture. I also wanted to create a particular kind of sculpture in which all surfaces could move simultaneously. My teacher Yoichiro Kawaguchi created computer graphics art that simulated moving creatures.[2] These virtual organisms were very colorful and fascinating, and I was very affected by his work. I wanted to create similar works using real materials.

At first I tried using holography under the guidance of Professors Shunsuke Mitamura and Toshihiro Kubota. Holography is three-dimensional, virtual photography using lasers. Unfortunately this format did not convey the reality I wanted to achieve, because the holographic image is carried only via light. In fact, I felt that the distance between light and material represents a tremendous gap. Many artists nowadays use computer graphics and projection, for example, but I feel the impact of such media is weak.

Despite my interest, I thought it impossible to use real materials to achieve a truly dynamic sculpture. I therefore set out to appropriate typical animation and virtual reality tools to create works of art. I tried to generate many works, including holography and stereograms—which appealed to me, since they conveyed a sense of depth.

Finally my friend Minako Takeno introduced me to ferrofluid, which she was using to make experimental works. I was astounded and transfixed. After that Takeno and I collaborated on several works, including one that appeared to move and breathe based on environmental stimuli.[3] I introduced a computer to deliver electrical impulses to the ferrofluid based on audio samples of the exhibition space. I also employed a projection screen that enlarged the image of the material. In this way I wanted to focus on the difference between the real material and the virtual image—the sculpture and its projection.

When you first began to experiment with ferrofluid, what was your first impression? Were you surprised?

I was shocked when I saw this material, and its movement was very interesting to me. Photography doesn't convey the real charm of this material. Gradually the protrusion grows bigger and bigger like a galaxy, and many small spikes move in a spiral—it's really amazing.

Which form did you visualize first for the material?

The first form I imagined was that of a small urchin, and I developed a sculpture using this idea.

Did you want to create a larger sculpture after that?

Yes. This material is very interesting for everyone. Sometimes people say it's easy to make very successful artwork with ferrofluid and that my projects don't represent original work. They are correct in some aspects, I think. I agree the material is quite amazing. However, I am the director of my art, and the control of the liquid and lighting conditions is very important and difficult to achieve. The timing of the right movement is critical, including how and when each magnetic field is strengthened sequentially.

Could you discuss the installation entitled *Pulsate*?

That piece has philosophical meaning for me. Two people sit at a dining table, and in the middle is a bowl of ferrofluid. As communication between the two people takes place, the liquid is activated and moves. Technically, a microphone captures the ambient noise, and the computer analyzes the amplitude in order to control the delivery of electricity to the fluid.

---

[1] Ferrofluid is a liquid composed of ferromagnetic particles suspended in a solvent. The liquid becomes strongly polarized in the presence of a magnetic field.

[2] Yoichiro Kawaguchi is a computer graphics artist who teaches at the University of Tokyo. His most famous simulation was called "Growth Model."

[3] The most visible Kodama and Takeno collaboration was *Protrude, Flow* (2001).

Liquid Architecture — Sachiko Kodama

Protrude, Flow, 2008, at the Museo Nacional Centro de Arte Reina Sofia, Spain

Waves and Sea Urchins, 2003

Pulsate—Melting Time, Dissolving Time, for My Little Sea, 2008 at the Samuel Freeman Gallery, Santa Monica, California

Matter in the Floating World

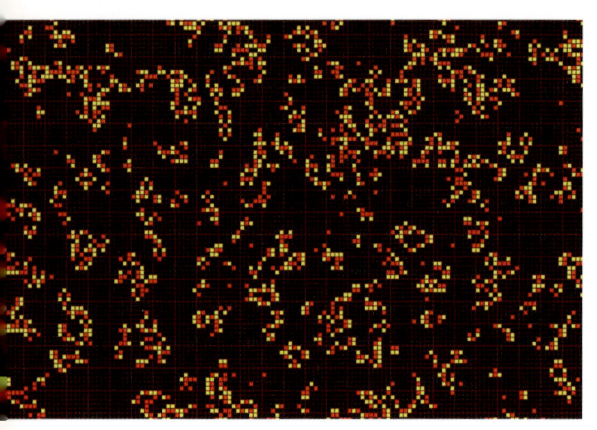

Mirek Wojtowicz's Mcell cellular automata program

Hiroki Sayama's evoloop program

I share your interest in materials whose properties may be quickly transformed. Today, when we think of high technology we typically consider large plasma screens or other sleek display tools. However, the images presented by such screens cannot compare with real, physical objects. I therefore wonder about the use of materials whose actual properties change, rather than a representation of transformation. There has been much discussion of intelligent buildings in architectural circles, for example, but such buildings are typically represented as having more sophisticated wiring and sensors behind conventional walls. I wonder why the basic material of the wall itself cannot represent intelligence. What do you think? Can you imagine constructed environments of the future possessing the qualities of your continuously transforming, intelligent sculptures?

I have a similar interest, and I have actually been working on something in the same vein. I'm a little shy to discuss it, but I have been developing a prototype for a new kind of carpet.

Really? Please explain.

Look at this computer-generated image. Do you know what this pattern is? This is a depiction of cellular automata.[4] The scientist Chris Langton developed a program to represent artificial life.[5]

Isn't that old?

This one is new.

It reminds me of the original "Game of Life" program created by John Conway.[6]

This cellular automaton program is slightly different [demonstrates another program]. I actually wrote this program based on Professor Hiroki Sayama's program. He developed an artificial life model called "evoloop."[7] Sayama introduced the concept of death to Langton's cellular automaton world. In Langton's version, cells spread all over the screen, and finally they become fixed. But this pattern is made and erased as cells touch one another. So when one cell meets another cell, it must die.

It's a beautiful pattern.

Professor Sayama wrote a Linux version of the program first, and I converted it to Windows. His graphics were small and monotone, and I made them large and colorful. I also wanted the program to be interactive for people. I thought it would be very interesting to make a wall or carpet whose surface pattern could

---

[4] A cellular automaton is a discrete mathematical model used to simulate biological processes according to programmed rules. According to website Wolfram Mathworld, it is composed of a "collection of 'colored' cells on a grid of specified shape that evolves through a number of discrete time steps according to a set of rules based on the states of neighboring cells." Eric W. Weisstein, "Cellular Automaton," MathWorld—A Wolfram Web Resource, http://mathworld.wolfram.com/CellularAutomaton.html.

[5] Chris Langton is an American computer scientist who coined the term "artificial life" in the late 1980s.

[6] John Conway, a British mathematician, created the self-evolving program called the "Game of Life" in 1970.

[7] Evoloop is a program that emulates natural selection, allowing various species to evolve.

change like this. So I created a physical pattern, but it was not a success, because we cannot recognize the solution.

So you want to create a physical surface upon which a pattern literally moves?

I have become interested recently in designers who experiment with wearable technology. I saw Ingo Maurer's clothing with embedded light and electronic devices exhibited at Tokyo Opera City.[8] The fabric is very beautiful, is it not?

I agree.

I have an interest in creating dynamic materials in a similar vein.

But this example is not actually dynamic, right? For example, could you incorporate LEDs, fiber optics, or photo-luminescent thread?

I thought about incorporating LEDs, but they are too big and would create a negative texture. Optical fibers might work.

Are you making any new materials?

I have been conducting experiments with students using rapid-prototyping techniques with 3-D printers.

In what way do you think truly dynamic and intelligent materials could be made? For example, clothing, building surfaces, and various objects that respond to one another as well as particular environmental stimuli? Do you think we would have a use for such materials?

Any kind of sensing technology can be applied, I think, to respond to sound, light, temperature, vibration, and so on. I select sensing technology that fits the purpose of my work. However, a typical problem arises when one considers the material itself. One has to design the system from the bottom up as well as from the top down, which presents an enormous challenge. However, it would be very interesting to accomplish. The use could come from the material.

It's like relating the pixel as a unit to that of the molecule or cell. What if a single thread of fabric could represent a kind of linear pixel, for instance?

It could be a pixel, but there is a discrepancy. There must be interaction between the pixel and the cell, a kind of reciprocal relationship. Like with the cellular automata program, in which adjacent cells interact, there must be an automatic response to context. The result is a kind of massively parallel computer, in which all calculations are calculated, everywhere.

It reminds me of Kevin Kelly's book *Out of Control*, in which he discusses the "hive mind" phenomenon in relation to the model of parallel computation.[9] He uses the example of bees working in concert toward a united objective.

I wonder if it's genetic? Of course, it's actually a little different. For instance, the queen bee and the worker bees have different roles. Their DNA is not the same. However, it is an interesting concept.

My primary interest related to the potential uses of parallel computing is increasing our understanding of human recognition. Since my childhood I have often wondered, "What is the visible world?" This is a very important problem for me. How do we process the language of images? The computer is a very sequential machine. A traditional computer runs one process at a time. However, I sense life directly, simultaneously, every part at the same time. Simultaneity is a very dynamic state of being, and for me the idea connects with Asian philosophy.[10] Despite the inherent difficulties, I want to create a tool that emulates the human response to the natural world in a comfortable way.

Speaking of the natural world, sustainability has become a fundamental concept in design today. I wonder if synthetic materials can learn from nature? Can we make truly dynamic, responsive materials that provide intelligent feedback? For example, could we create materials that indicate when air quality diminishes and attempt

---

8 Ingo Maurer is a German lighting designer and a pioneer in the use of new lighting technologies. The exhibition referenced here was titled "Ingo Maurer—Light—Reaching for the Moon," an exhibition held in Tokyo Opera City Art Gallery, Tokyo, Japan, July–Sept. 2006.

9 Kevin Kelly, *Out of Control: The New Biology of Machines, Social Systems, and the Economic World* (New York: Basic Books, 1995), 5.

10 See my note about *mono no aware* on p. 13.

Morpho Tower, detail

to improve it; or materials that try to harness energy from alternative sources when the power goes out? In the future I expect that our designed environment will be much more informative and responsive concerning local environmental conditions. Currently we have little or no access to how much energy we use for electricity or heating in real time, for example. Before long, however, we can imagine being surrounded by surfaces and devices that inform us of our energy use as well as many other important kinds of data. We will be able to interact with materials in many new ways.

We already have functional materials and devices that control humidity, temperature, acoustics, and so on. You mean something different, like materials with embedded computers? In my future vision, walls, ceilings, and floors will be no different from one another [laughs]. Buckminster Fuller's concept was that in a dome the ceiling is the wall and vice versa; so perhaps this concept already exists? However, I am more interested in kinetic surfaces. I need to be able to create surfaces with a large degree of movement using small amounts of energy. I call this concept "eco-movement," because little energy is required for a large response.

> When you conjure such a future in visual terms, what image comes to mind?

Water [laughter]. Another liquid! Water is an elemental substance and a natural interface for human beings. Imagine an existence within water, a floating life [laughter]. In such a life, we wouldn't need land; we wouldn't need to quarrel over artificially fixed constructs like property. Movement within water is very easy and requires little effort—speed becomes slow. Perhaps in this slow life we wouldn't get much done [laughter]. However, I like this image.

> Interesting! I can imagine the clothing you would design—it would slowly change colors based on one's mood or if it got wet in the rain—there could be many possibilities. Today, many people find luxury brands attractive, yet there is no relationship to the individual. Gucci or Prada, for instance, cannot match the unique qualities of each person. In the future, however, we may have a dynamic fabric whose properties can change almost like liquid in response to individual changes.

It could reveal one's skeleton—that would be embarrassing! [laughter]

Seriously though, there are current commercial needs for such chameleonlike fabric technology, such as military camouflage.

> Right. Fabrics that could actively harness energy from the sun, wind, or one's own body would be interesting as well.

I agree. Such materials would be fascinating from an ecological standpoint. It reminds me of a power-harnessing experiment that took place in Tokyo Station in which energy was absorbed from foot traffic as people passed through the turnstiles.[11]

> That was amazing. Unfortunately it's not a very efficient technology yet.

If it could work, it would unleash incredible possibilities. Once renewable power is readily available everywhere, then art can be propagated everywhere. Unfortunately the work I could contribute at this point would be too small due to a lack of funding [laughter].

---

[11] This experiment, conducted by the East Japan Railway Company, used piezoelectric devices placed under mats on the floor between turnstiles. http://techon.nikkeibp.co.jp/english/NEWS_EN/20081204/162357/.

> Since my childhood I have often wondered, "What is the visible world?" This is a very important problem for me. How do we process the language of images?

Morpho Tower

In addition to art, what could the possibilities be for architecture?

Architecture could change in fundamental ways. The architectural palette in conventional use is rather limited, but it doesn't have to be so. Take the structure of a building, for example. We view architecture as static, but natural phenomena such as earthquakes, wind, rain, and other forces that affect buildings are all dynamic. If we could develop dynamic, responsive structural systems—such as we see in tree branches, for example—they might perform much more effectively than our current models. To use another metaphor, if a building skeleton could act like a human skeleton, it might respond more effectively to a variety of loading conditions and weigh less. Future structures could also be self-healing, with materials that act like osteoblast cells in bone. In this way the buildings of tomorrow might take a cue from your work with liquid architecture.

Might the dynamic facade of Jean Nouvel's Arab Institute in Paris be a representative model?

Yes, if it hadn't broken.

It broke?

Unfortunately the electronically triggered "eyes" meant to control light levels were not working when I visited the building. As the saying goes, technology will always change, and it will eventually always fail [laughter].

It's a vicious circle. New technology is constantly being developed, and one can't stop using it [laughter].

Kevin Kelly is now writing a new book based on the idea that technology has its own consciousness. In it he asks, "What does technology want?"[12] For example, technology needs power, but it also requires clean resources such as water—much like people.

Isn't this a kind of determinism? Although interesting, this definition of technology is scary [laughter]. It seems that it could be used to justify technological needs without questioning. By defining technology like an individual, are we simply trying to make it more human? What is humanity, anyway? [laughter]

You make a good point. Perhaps it is inevitable that the made will become more like the born.

---

12 Kevin Kelly revealed his upcoming work in a lecture at the "Pop!Tech" conference in Camden, Maine, Oct. 2006.

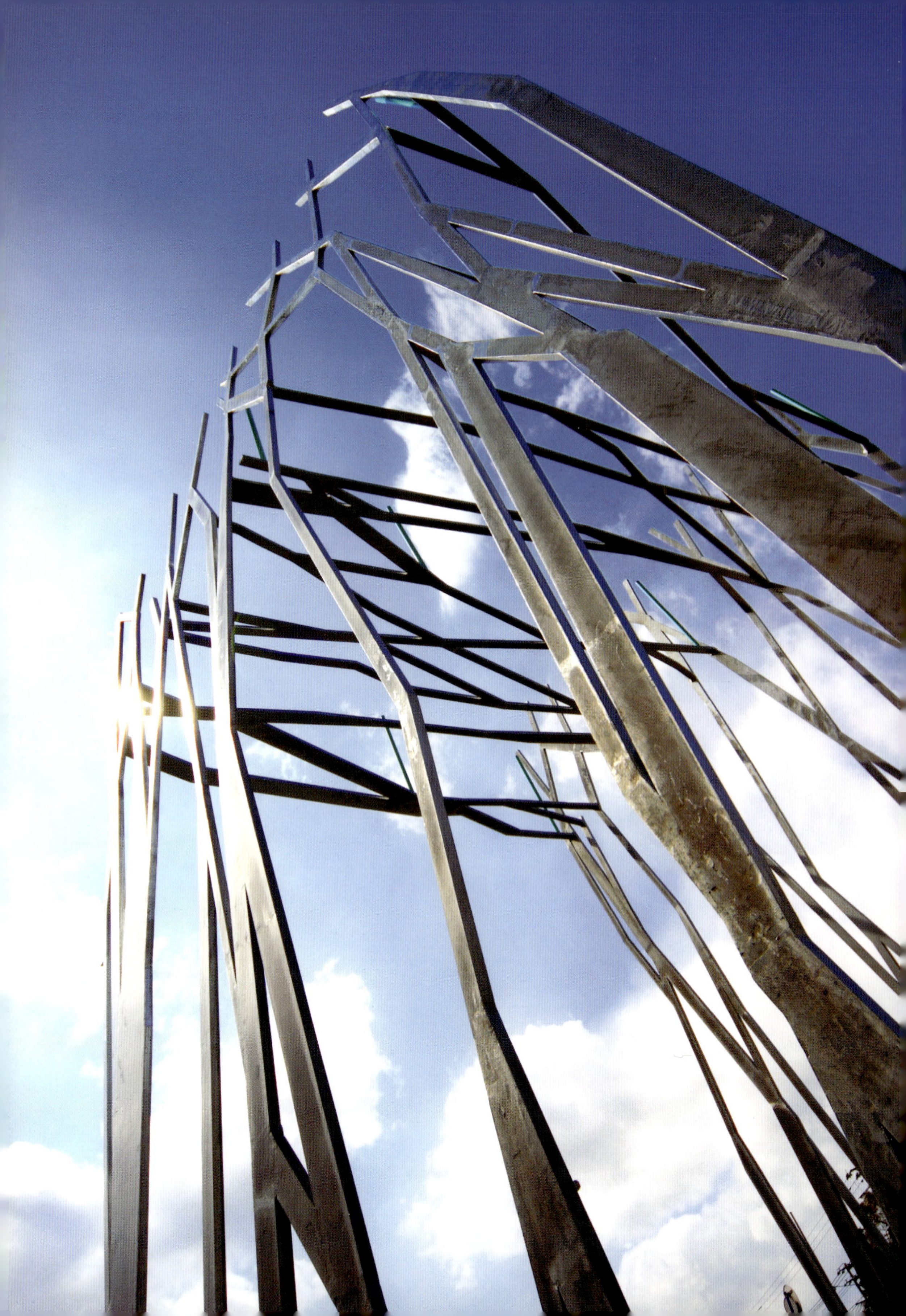

EMERGENCE

> I believe there is a primordial form from which things are derived.
> —Terunobu Fujimori

"Emergence" describes a state of becoming, a process in which the measurable materializes out of the immeasurable. It is a state of anticipation as much as a process of manifestation. Emergence is a concept deeply embedded within Japanese culture and is celebrated passionately with the annual appearance of spring cherry blossoms or autumn colors. Architecture often takes cues from natural processes of cyclical renewal, as evidenced in the centuries-old tradition of the Ise Shrine reconstruction. According to Arata Isozaki, "The rebuilding-and-relocation scheme of twenty-year cycles embraces a biological model of regeneration. In order to preserve life, forms are generated and regenerate isomorphically.... In the process, architectural and ritual impetus strive to preserve identity through maintenance of an archetypal form."[1]

In addition to cyclical renewal, emergence also relates conceptually to the process of deriving forms from nature. In recent decades notable Japanese architects and engineers have experimented with the formal and spatial opportunities presented by biological constructs, in an effort to escape the shackles of twentieth-century modernism. In his groundbreaking Sendai Mediatheque, Toyo Ito consolidated building services and vertical circulation into a series of bundled tubes resembling sea sponges or stalks

Shin Minamata Mon, *Makoto Sei Watanabe Architects' Office*

of seaweed. Recounting the design process of the Mediatheque, Ito says that "contrary to the historical order of architecture taking shape in nature, I attempted the reverse process: to induce nature out of built forms, as well as to inject materiality into 'Less is more' space, precisely in order to return some living reality to the void of economics and data."[2] Ito calls this new approach the "emerging grid," a "system by which a uniform grid is manipulated to yield a continuum with a three-dimensionally curved shell; a method for transforming simple regular spaces into complex spaces rich in variation, hard inorganic space into supple organic space."[3]

For Ito and other enthusiasts of biomimetic emergence, the computer has played an increasingly important role in achieving the complex shapes and indeterminate structures that result from such experiments. Mutsuro Sasaki, the structural engineer for the Sendai Mediatheque and several of Ito's other projects, employs techniques that "involve generating rational structural shapes within a computer by using the principles of evolution and self-organization of living creatures from an engineering standpoint."[4] Architect Makoto Sei Watanabe utilizes complex algorithms in software of his own making to determine optimal structural forms for buildings as well as cities. Employing an approach he calls "induction design," Watanabe hopes to seed the constructed environment with the intelligence of natural ecological systems. Computer scientist and textile designer Akira Wakita manufactures materials and assemblies that maintain an active connection to the digital world. Lifelike in their real-time response to contextual stimuli, Wakita's objects explore the liminal threshold between cognition and physicality.

Artist Tokujin Yoshioka applies a variety of direct physical techniques to conjure natural phenomena in material assemblies. In an approach he has dubbed "second nature," Yoshioka seeks to invest design with the emotive power of natural wonders—claiming that "we wish to explore what kinds of design appeal to human emotion, and to this purpose we are reexamining nature itself, which transcends the human imagination and possesses a primitive power."[5] Masayo Ave summons a variety of biomimetic forms within her designs for textiles, furniture, and light objects. Advocating a multisensory awareness of materials, Ave's main interest is "to discover the sensual and emotional value of the materials, which are often overlooked, and give them new life."[6]

---

[1] Arata Isozaki, *Japan-ness in Architecture*, trans. Sabu Kohso (Cambridge: MIT Press, 2006), 145.

[2] Toyo Ito, "The New 'Real': Toward Reclaiming Materiality in Contemporary Architecture," in *Toyo Ito: The New "Real" in Architecture* (Tokyo: Toyo Ito Exhibition Executive Committee, 2006), 32.

[3] Ibid., 38.

[4] Mutsuro Sasaki, *Flux Structure* (Tokyo: Toto Shuppan, 2005), 17.

[5] Tokujin Yoshioka, *Second Nature* (Tokyo: Yutaka Shima, 2008), 11.

[6] Masayo Ave, quoted in "Haptic Conversation 2," in *Haptic*, by Kenya Hara (Tokyo: Masakazu Hanai, 2004), 181.

The Emerging Grid

A conversation with Toyo Ito, Toyo Ito & Associates, Architects

After becoming one of Japan's most successful and thoughtful contemporary architects, Toyo Ito has embarked upon a new course in design. Originally enamored with the technological promise of lightness and transparency, Ito has since embraced a biomorphic approach toward structuring surface and space—an order he calls the "emerging grid." His recent works conjure an alternative state of abstraction, based on the incorporation of simple, pervasive geometric systems at a monumental scale. Based on this approach, Ito hopes to define a more substantive—and human—architecture.

Born in 1941, Toyo Ito graduated from Tokyo University's Department of Architecture in 1965. After working for Kiyonori Kikutake Architects from 1965 to 1969, he started his own studio, Urban Robot (urbot), in Tokyo in 1971. In 1979 the studio changed its name to Toyo Ito & Associates, Architects. From his early White U in 1976 and Silver Hut in 1984 (both residential projects) to the much larger Sendai Mediatheque (2000) and Island City Central Park GrinGrin (2005), Ito has shown himself to be one of the most radically creative and influential architects of his generation. Ito has won many awards, including the Arnold W. Brunner Memorial Prize in 2000 and the RIBA Gold Medal in 2006.

Mikimoto 2 (opposite)

Tod's (above and right)

I think the human body has changed, based on our varied and virtual world of today. For that reason, I think there might be a new abstraction. I call it the "new real" in architecture.

Since your early projects, your work has been defined by a profound sense of lightness and ephemerality. Yet recently you have shifted your focus away from transparency and weightlessness in architecture toward something more substantive. Why is that?

My early work was about lightness and delicacy. For the Sendai Mediatheque, however, I wanted to appeal to the strength of architecture. I wanted to design to architecture's best qualities. I had always been looking for public projects to design, but contemporary architecture does not have much societal meaning in Japan. When an architect is asked to design, people will say, "Oh, he/she is making something like that," or "It might be beautiful, but it's difficult to use."

You hear only these kinds of remarks. There has not been a kind of consciousness that an architect's existence is necessary in society; rather, architects have been thought to make pretty things. During the Sendai Mediatheque competition, I wanted to convince people that architecture has significance to society. Ever since, my work has developed a stronger character.

During the symposium held at the Haptic exhibition, you and curator Kenya Hara had a compelling conversation about the need for design that relates to multiple senses.[1] Is some level of abstraction required to realize haptic design thinking in architecture?

Until now abstraction in architecture was mostly visual. As Mies van der Rohe said,

"Less is more." The minimal spaces he designed are said to be abstract. However, I think the entire human body can sense this abstraction. These are the kinds of things I am thinking about. I think the human body has changed, based on our varied and virtual world of today. For that reason, I think there might be a new abstraction. I call it the "new real" in architecture.

Yes, like your exhibit by the same title.[2] You describe the idea of the emerging grid, which relates to the influence of virtual tools on physical space and materials. Why is the emerging grid important for architecture?

According to Terunobu Fujimori's theory about the white and red schools of architecture, white describes Mies, and red describes Le Corbusier.[3] However, I think this division is too simple [laughter]. If one pole is abstract and the other is real, I am interested in the middle space. For example, Mondrian took the basic pattern of a tree and gradually made it abstract. He could have generated a pattern at some point in the process, but he did not stop. He eventually arrived at the concept of the grid. However, the Tod's building adapts the complicated pattern of the zelkova tree as a structural frame. This frame is not a true grid. Thus, I think the middle of the process is the most interesting.

Many of your recent projects like Tod's have a biomimetic quality. Do you actively research forms and patterns found in nature?

No, not really. I don't really research natural forms, nor do I try to emulate nature directly. However, I think there is a kind of architecture that likens itself to nature without directly copying it. In the past two to three decades, design and construction have changed. Before now it was difficult to achieve this kind of complexity in architecture. We have since profoundly developed our ability to analyze structure, which has led me to consider the new possibilities inherent in the emerging grid.

The Sendai Mediatheque must have been the departure point for this conceptual direction. The idea to combine three simple elements—tubes, floor, and skin—is very powerful.

I can still remember the first time I saw your competition entry. How did you generate the idea for this project?

One idea comes from water. From the beginning I considered the architecture a metaphor. I wanted many things to flow into one another—moving figures with latent energy. Moreover, the opportunity here was to create a new library for the digital era. Depending on the network, people could connect to the world in the same way that water connects the world. We developed the idea of seaweed or marine life as this metaphor.

Also we reinterpreted the rules of the project, which stipulated a large proportion of office space as well as a 10-meter-tall [32-feet-10 inch-tall] gallery. For the office space, we created a dome, and the gallery space was inside this space too. At the same time, the structure would be one entire thing. I thought of the structure off the top of my head. The dome would be here, and the lower levels would be here [drawing]. Also the light would enter this way [drawing]. The elevators and stairs would be inside of this space. So I had this kind of drawing. If I made this with one floor, that would be enough, right? The structure could be built with this form alone. With this in mind, the image of a tube and an integrated lighting strategy emerged. So clarifying what people want is important in design.

For your Mikimoto 2 project, the idea of the plate transformed into a wall.

Yes. First there was the Serpentine Pavilion, which gave me the idea for the structure of Tod's. In the Tod's project, I tried to achieve this kind of beautiful network structure. For

---

1 Kenya Hara, *Haptic* (Tokyo: Takeo Co., 2004). See also my conversation with Kenya Hara in this book, pages 87–97.

2 Toyo Ito: The New "Real" in Architecture, exhibition held in Tokyo Opera City Art Gallery, Tokyo, Japan, Oct. 7–Dec. 24, 2006.

3 See p. 14 for a description of Fujimori's red and white schools of architecture.

Sendai Mediatheque
facade (top),
level one open square (middle left),
level two (middle right),
stair tube detail (bottom)

Serpentine Pavilion 2002 (above), detail (below)

Mikimoto 2, I designed the opposite—this was this, and the force is distributed in this way [drawing]. For that reason, if there had been no Tod's project, the Mikimoto 2 building would not have been possible.

> This kind of construction is quite rare. Buildings typically require a lot of joints—floor joints, panel joints, control joints, expansion joints, and so on. It is also common to see orthogonal regulating lines such as vertical columns in tall buildings. These types of joints and lines are not visible in the Mikimoto 2 project, making it one of the most unusual tall buildings in recent years.

There is a floor joint, and above that is a beam [drawing]. It is possible to construct architecture with just these two elements, but usually there are walls and plates [drawing]. This system distributes the loads, but in the case of the Mikimoto project, that is a little more complex. This kind of structure [drawing] enables the weight to be distributed, and it could be said that this is a beam and these are the plates. The relationships become obscure, and the result is a particular form. It's the same thing with Tod's, but when we were confirming the permits in the case of Tod's, people thought this was a beam. But there are no beams in the project; there are floor joints and then a plate system. It's here where the load is being distributed. We made decisions utilizing this kind of process so that it looked like the beams were not joined. We received permits for the first time for this idea. In actuality, the beams are supporting the load consistently throughout the space, but it's still a mysterious thing. If it were not done this way, it would not have received a permit. It's kind of a weird story.

> It is amazing to think that these types of complex, indeterminate structures have only recently been enabled with new structural software programs. One difference between the two buildings is that Tod's has visible joints and Mikimoto 2 does not.

This is because the steel cladding of Mikimoto 2 is directly integrated with the concrete structure, and the two materials have a similar coefficient of expansion. Therefore, expansion and contraction are tightly controlled.

> Obviously you work closely with talented structural engineers.

Right now the engineer whom I am working most with is Mutsuro Sasaki. I also work with Cecil Balmond and Arup. I have done one project with Masato Araya, and I have also worked with a younger guy, named Masahiro Ikeda. I am working with these four people. At the beginning of a project, I will get advice from them, and they will tell me if what I am designing is okay, and I give them feedback. This is the way we collaborate.

> With this kind of collaboration, does your initial form remain the same or does it change?

It changes. That happened with the Sendai Mediatheque, and with most cases I am wondering what will work. I don't always know the best solution; so I work on various things, consult with my staff, and eventually the form changes. After all, things that change are interesting. If you fix the design around a particular form from the beginning, there's nothing creative about the process. If you have a form that you initially select and it's realized, it's always the same thing. But if something comes to you during the process, it's a discovery, and that's interesting. For that reason, architects cannot do it alone. We need engineers and our staff—these people can offer various ideas. Once we don't understand the world, that's when we are creative. But there are a lot of people who don't like this [both laughing].

I think there are people who think that architecture is created by one person. I am not like that. I think that architecture is collaborative. When I do projects abroad, there are things that I don't know concerning the local area. When I was working on the Berkeley Art Museum in California, I didn't know everything, so I asked different people and then understood what things were about. Working in Tokyo is different—I am interested in something that can't be done. Little by little, I think it's good for architecture to be different.

211   The Emerging Grid   Toyo Ito

Mikimoto 2, retail storefront (right), nightime view (bottom left), sketches of Mikimoto 2 (bottom right),

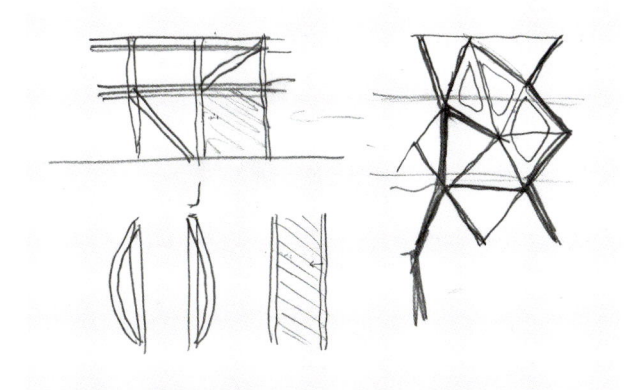

You not only believe that the design process should have a dynamic quality, but that architecture itself should also be dynamic in some way.

Well, we think of the human body as being perfectly symmetrical, but that's really not the case [both laughing]. There are left-handed and right-handed people, people who run differently, people with one leg longer than the other, and so on. Human beings remain in motion throughout their lives, except perhaps when sleeping—but even then they move a little. Humans always have a center of gravity, so when we move different things happen, causing a general state of instability. If we take one step, the next move requires a moment of instability. Architecture searches for its own instability in order to put things in motion. Today's society is an unstable society. If nature and the body combine, there will be balance.

For example, I use the form of a tree a lot. In reality, this form is not truly symmetrical, because it is affected by the wind, sun, and other forces. It is a depiction of instability brought to balance—I think this kind of architecture is interesting. I could not do this kind of thing in the past. Designing this kind of structure is very complicated. With new computer technology, however, instability can be designed and built.

The Torrevieja Relaxation Park strikes me as an example of instability brought to balance.

That is a very unstable project [both laughing]. The form is conceived as being fluid. The structure is akin to a series of arches, except that they are really spirals.

The form is like a seashell.

Yes, it is an open space. It has an inherent instability, as if suspended within motion. When you are inside the space, you sense the fluidity of the forms.

When I look at this project, I am immediately conscious of its materiality by the clear and direct way in which you use wood and metal. However, you have other projects that seek a level of abstraction, such as the Serpentine Pavilion or Mikimoto 2. Is this a difficult balance to achieve in your work?

As with your previous question, it is not about a difficult balance, but rather a new type of abstraction. Abstraction is definitely necessary. If there were no abstraction, what is real would become fabricated and artificial. With a new type of abstraction, modernism can be transformed into a fertile and rich territory.

For example, the Tod's building has a surface treatment in which the glass and concrete are absolutely coplanar, creating a flat surface. When the glass enters the interior of the building, there are shadows. There's a feeling of reality, and the abstraction disappears. This is mysterious. Abstraction occurs at various levels, like the emerging grid.

When I see the elaborate patterns that may now be realized with sophisticated software, I cannot help but be reminded of Adolf Loos's declaration that ornament is crime.[4] Are these patterns really ornament, or might we say they are something else?

Patterns do not have great depth, but they carry fun possibilities. As it was established, modernism eschewed patterns. However, a new abstraction could be a pattern—I think this is an interesting problem to look at. A new abstraction is attached to many things— it may convey visual interest like a pattern, yet it is still abstract. I don't have any confidence that I can solve this issue, but theoretically I think there are new patterns, and architecture is inherently part of the pattern-making. It's an intriguing challenge.

Another recent challenge for which modernism provided little guidance is the problem of dwindling resources and other environmental concerns. The biomimicry movement advocates the emulation of natural forms and processes in order to improve this situation. The emerging grid seems to share commonalities with biomimetic formalism, but could it harness biomimetic processes as well?

---

4 Adolf Loos, *Ornament and Crime: Selected Essays* (Riverside, CA: Ariadne Press, 1998). The original essay was published in 1908.

Torrevieja Relaxation Park (top), interior (middle)

When the glass enters the interior of the building, there are shadows. There's a feeling of reality, and the abstraction disappears. This is mysterious. Abstraction occurs at various levels, like the emerging grid.

Mikimoto 2, spiral stair

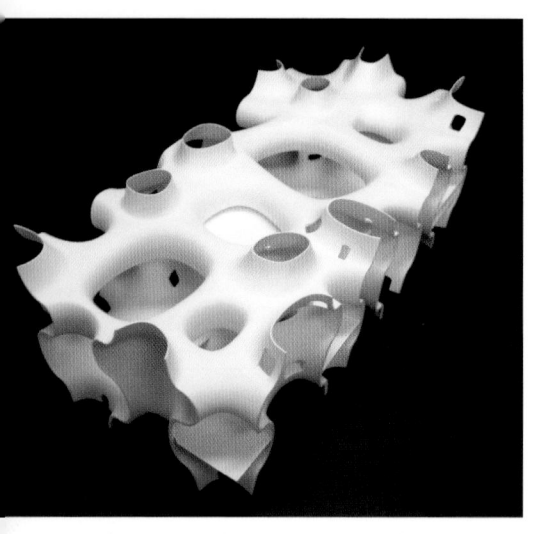

Taichung Metropolitan Opera House, analytical model

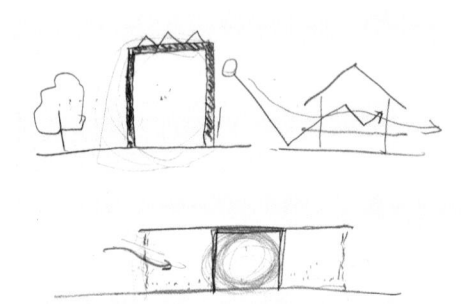

Sketches of soft architectural systems

> First the idea of architecture must be changed. Then architecture and nature must deepen their relationship by way of the emerging grid I described, which is a softer system of architecture.

Right now architecture is discussed in terms of energy. I use thermal insulation often, thus increasing the effectiveness of energy, as well as solar batteries. So architecture's relationship with nature breaks—it creates an artificial environment, which is different from the surrounding environment. This is a method for heating a wall [drawing]. Basically I am making a mistake in doing this—traditional Japanese homes have soft boundaries. Wind and light are able to enter [drawing]. I want to create this kind of relationship again. However, it's difficult to achieve. Our expectation is that spaces need to be cooled and heated right away.

First the idea of architecture must be changed. Then architecture and nature must deepen their relationship by way of the emerging grid I described, which is a softer system of architecture. Another more general thing is that, although incredibly difficult to achieve, half of architecture can be built with thermal insulation and the other half should have an environment closer to nature. In a country like Japan, there's not really a time during the year when it's really cold and really hot—it's only like that 10 percent of the time. We can use supplemental thermal controls during this relatively small amount of time. If this is done, things will definitely change. If we made every space artificially temperature-controlled, it would be unfortunate. If we decide to do what I am suggesting, more enlightening things will occur.

There is a natural logic inherent in the treelike structures used in Tod's or the Sendai Mediatheque, for example. I wonder what would happen if these structures actually communicated fluids and energy like a tree—adopting the idea of living processes?

That's true. There are many kinds of things that can be done.

Conventional notions of sustainable design often leave much to be desired—designing the prescribed overhangs, applying solar panels, and filling out environmental checklists. However, the idea for a kind of biomimetic

abstraction could open up a world of possibilities, and I think would be fully compatible with the emerging grid.

That's true. Nature and architecture should have meaning. If water is in a space, no one should wonder where it comes from—because of the meaning that is already understood. Long ago it was like that, people conducted their daily lives by the river—eating, doing laundry, and so on. Life could not be lived without the river; people were connected to it. Today, however, the meaning disappears. It's a very simple thing, but with today's buildings, where the water, energy, air all go—I think this detachment has changed people's lifestyles and it is happening before our very eyes.

When I was designing the Sendai Mediatheque, I looked at how much energy was necessary for building operations—I was told to design thinking about these things. I am realizing we have to think about these things more.

Do you think the public consciousness is changing as well? I am thinking of your essay "Architecture in a Simulated City," in which you denounced contemporary culture as being as vapid and thin as a piece of Saran-wrap film.[5] This kind of sterile, transparent packaging has been a powerful metaphor for the artifice and homogenization represented by contemporary lifestyles. However, ecological design has recently become a mainstream concern in Japan as well as in other countries. This concern will perhaps change people's attitudes about this kind of material use in a literal sense—people have begun to question plastic bags or bottled water, for example. Additionally, there is a possibility that people will question artificiality in a conceptual sense. What do you think—will the Saran-wrap culture disappear?

No, it won't. Perhaps if some ideas change a little bit, then architecture might respond accordingly. It's really a question of the nature of this surface, which is what makes artificiality possible. I don't think the situation will change, but perhaps we can hope for a gradual transformation of this surface.

Tod's interior

Za-Koenji Public Theatre, interior detail

5 Toyo Ito, "Architecture in a Simulated City," *Kenchiku Bunka* 46, no. 542 (Dec. 1991): 23–35.

Natural Logic

A conversation with Makoto Sei Watanabe, Makoto Sei Watanabe Architects' Office

Makoto Sei Watanabe is an architect who is also proficient in biology and computer programming. Based on research related to complex ecological systems and computer-generated algorithms, Watanabe seeks to liberate the design process from its typical intuitive, unsubstantiated approach, with tools that ensure the optimal performance of buildings and cities. By shifting the emphasis from style to performance, Watanabe redirects the point of control from the hand to the CPU—thus capitalizing on the computer's abilities to solve complex problems and generate more lifelike results.

Born in Yokohama in 1952, Makoto Sei Watanabe studied architecture at the Yokohama National University and graduated in 1976. He worked for Arata Isokazi & Associates until 1979. In 1984 he founded the Makoto Sei Watanabe Architects' Office in Tokyo. Watanabe is known for his work in algorithmically generated architecture and the development of software programs to design and structurally optimize buildings, infrastructure, and cities. His books include *Induction Design*, *Algorithmic Design*, and *Makoto Sei Watanabe: Conceiving the City*. Watanabe has received several prizes, including the Good Design Award (2001), the Architectural Institute of Japan Award (2002), the Environment Design and Equipment Design Award (2002), and the Japan Public Architecture Award (2008).

K-Museum, detail of ground surface (opposite)

Aoyama Technical College

Buildings are constructed, altered, and destroyed in a way similar to how plants grow, transform, and die. Thus, I view the context of design as a natural ecological system.

How did you become interested in the idea of ecological systems in architecture?

As a young university student, I had trouble choosing between architecture and biology as a major. Even though I selected architecture, I still have a strong interest in biology. For example, when I see a city skyline, I can easily imagine a grassy field. Buildings are constructed, altered, and destroyed in a way similar to how plants grow, transform, and die. Thus, I view the context of design as a natural ecological system.

Is this how your "induction cities" theory developed?[1]

Yes. I began writing software programs to simulate ecological systems in 1990. The first program was completed in 1994, and I called it "induction cities." The name came from my original interest in how these systems operate at urban and regional scales. However, I have also applied this program at the scale of architecture, so I added the phrase "induction design." Recently I adopted the name "algorithmic design" because of the growing international popularity of algorithmic design processes. Each of these three terms offers a slightly different perspective on the same process. The aim of this project has been to generate a new method for design.

The traditional design method is arbitrary in nature. For example, if we were to design a drinking glass, we would think about the form and feeling of the glass. We would make some models and drawings, and we would create various prototypes and change the form along the way. Finally, we would choose one form—a single line to define the profile. This would not just be any line, but one particular line selected by the brain and the hand. However, this process is arbitrary. Of course, we make many studies and compare different solutions—but at the last moment, we choose one line without any reason. And the person who can choose the best line is called a genius [both laughing].

So perhaps the real genius is the person who can create the best "software."[2]

Yes, yes. This is the point. In the traditional design process, not everyone can use the "software," because it is only the genius of the brain. This kind of design has good qualities, but I feel we may also find another way. We can instead use software that is accessible to anyone because its rules are

---

[1] Makoto Sei Watanabe, *Induction Design* (Basel, Switzerland: Birkhäuser, 2002).

[2] In this case "software" suggests the information logic driving a project, rather than a computer program.

transparent. After all, we have many criteria in the design process, which we might call evaluation points. If we can write down our requirements, then we can make a program, because writing involves logic. Not all design is driven by logic, so our criteria will only cover some parts of design. With the drinking glass example, we might dictate the profile, size, smoothness, and other features. Once we can describe these requirements, we can translate them into a program.

In terms of architecture, one challenge is that the architect does not always have all the information, such as particular structural or electrical code requirements.

Right—there are many requirements. The program changes the dimension; it translates design into logic. There are many benefits that can result, such as dealing with many requirements, but please don't misunderstand—this process also loses many things. Program considerations alone won't solve everything [both laughing]. It is best to take a reductionist approach and consider each requirement in turn. Then the program can help us solve each part incrementally.

It's unusual for an architect to develop software, especially at this level of sophistication.

Yes. When I started this process, I didn't try to address everything at once. I selected one requirement at a time and developed a simple code to address it. When we look at the scientific method, for example, we see a reductive approach in which experiments are conducted and examined in isolation. Removing unwanted influences is an inherent part of this process. So I wanted to apply this method to architecture. Architecture is not science—it is a much more ambiguous field. However, I've felt that part of architecture can benefit from the clarity and objectivity of science.

Algorithmically generated design has become increasingly popular.

Yes, you're right. However, I don't know any constructed works that have been generated in a truly algorithmic way. When I started this method, no one was doing it.

I think scale has been an impediment for realizing this kind of work. It's one thing to send a CAD file to a 3-D printer, but another thing entirely to construct an entire building from an algorithmically generated model. The bits-to-atoms transfer is a significant challenge. One needn't care much about the mechanical properties of cornstarch in a tiny 3-D-printed model, for example, but one certainly worries about the structural performance of material at the scale of a building.[3] The fact that you have integrated structural calculations within your design software is a major achievement, and I presume an essential factor in the realization of your own building-scale constructions using this method.

The other aspect that differentiates your work is your interest in ecological systems. Architects who employ algorithms to generate designs are often motivated solely by their aesthetic potential. In your case, however, I perceive an authentic desire to learn from nature. Do you feel that computers can enhance our understanding of natural processes? Can synthetic logic follow natural logic?

Architects, critics, and philosophers have long discussed the relationship between architecture and nature. Some architects consider natural forms, like the structure of a leaf. By way of contrast, the Metabolists were more concerned with natural processes.[4] Of course, they adopted a metaphor of a biological system, but I think there is another way—a more advanced way to use the system itself. Life runs on its own kind of software. We cannot know everything about this software, but we can learn some things and adapt them for use in architecture. I think this is the next age, one that regards the relationship between the natural and the artificial.

---

3 3-D printing produces models by depositing successive layers of material, such as cornstarch or plastic.

4 Metabolism was a Japanese architectural movement begun in the 1960s interested in notions of biological growth and renewal. Although it only lasted a decade, the movement is still influencing contemporary designs focused on emergent themes.

Emergence

Life runs on its own kind of software. We cannot know everything about this software, but we can learn some things and adapt them for use in architecture.

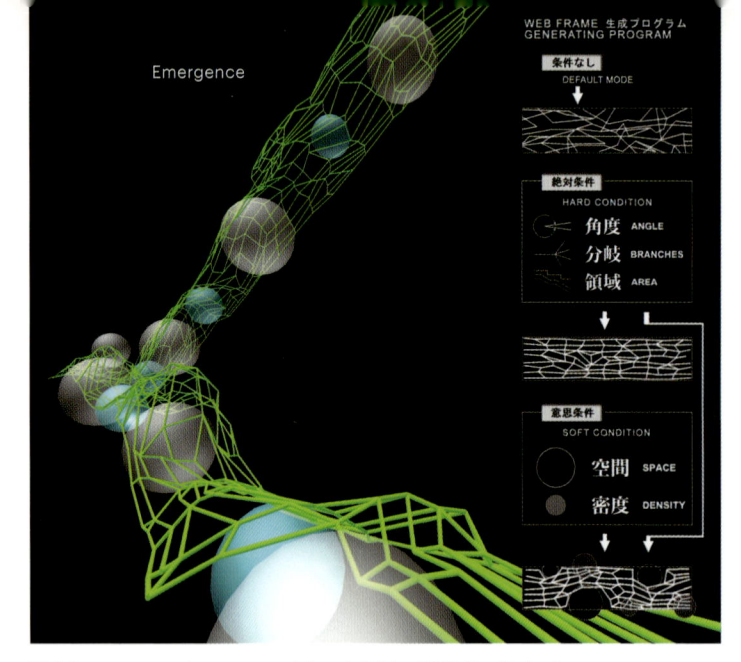

Web frame–generating program (above), Iidabashi Station (below)

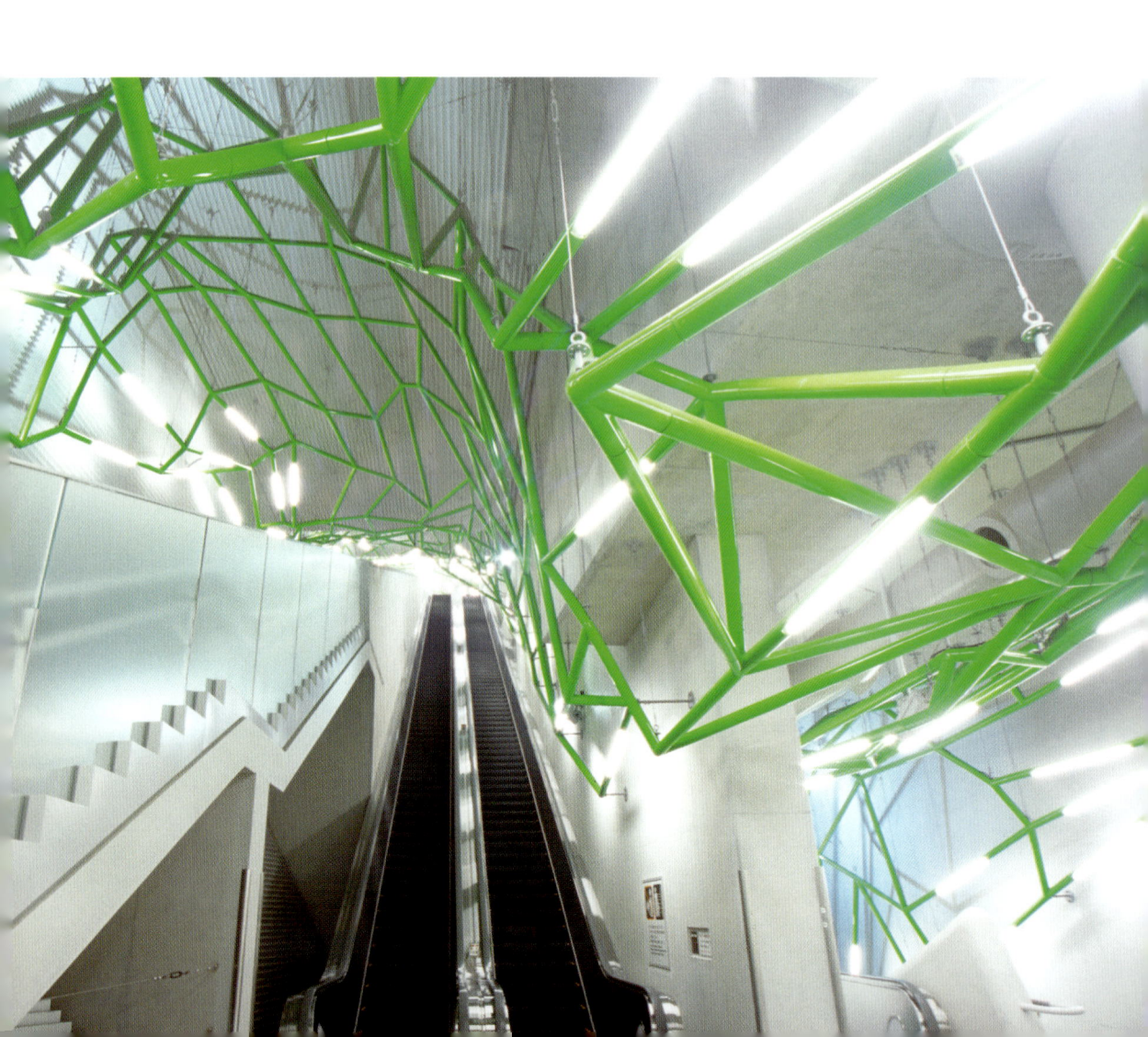

Your Shin Minamata Mon project seems to have emerged from biomimetic considerations for material efficiency. How do you generate form and structural intelligence simultaneously?

The software I developed has two processes, one for form generation and the other for structure optimization. First you enter programmatic requirements and the form is generated. Then you add any point loads that have not been addressed in general loading considerations. The software then calculates the structural loads and adds lateral loads to the calculations. Next the program modifies structural components based on three member sizes, adding and subtracting members as needed. So the result is different from the original generated form. Although the structural optimization process is separate, it is possible to employ a cyclical method between form generation and optimization.

Is this what you mean by your term "architectural seed"?[5]

I think that "seed" is a kind of metaphor. The seed is itself a program defined by DNA and supplied with some material. When I plant a seed underground, it spreads a root in search of water and avoids hard, compacted earth in the process. At the same time, the seed spreads upward in search of sunlight. The forms that emerge for the root and stem might seem random, but they are not random. There are very strict rules at work. Thus, I have tried to adopt a systematic approach to design. I want to create a seed that will work under this kind of self-centered system. I call it a "seed" because I think of our design documentation as a kind of DNA to generate architecture.

Hypothetically speaking, could you simply define point loads in space and have the program generate optimal structure to begin with?

It's not impossible, but it's not easy. Shin Minamata Mon was designed entirely by the software I developed, called Keiriki.[6] In this case I concentrated primarily on the structure, so I began with a simple form. The web frame at Iidabashi Station was generated with an earlier version of the software that lacked the same structural optimization process. Therefore, I spent more time on the form and relied upon a simple structure. I should mention that there is an iterative evaluation process with these programs. The first results are usually not perfect, so I tweak the parameters and run the program again and again until I have achieved the desired effect.

Is it a challenge that your software generates structural components and connections that are all so different?

Yes, there is no complete road map. Each project is quite different and I tailor the software to the specific requirements of each project.

What I mean is, many buildings make use of mass-produced components that are modular and predictable in order to save money. Is it therefore an economic challenge for contractors to work with a complex set of custom components?

Yes, you're right. A good example is Kashiwanoha Station, the facade of which is composed of many panels. For example, one panel is five meters [sixteen feet five inches] long and another is two meters [six feet seven inches], and there are over two hundred panels. Every piece looks different. If you have a very large budget, you can have these panels made by hand [laughter].

In the medieval ages, important buildings were made this way by large teams of craftsmen. However, the clients who could afford these projects were kings, popes, and so on [both laughing]. Mass production brought good quality products at low prices to many people, but the diversity was lost. So I want to develop a way in which we can achieve the diversity of medieval handmade crafts with the low cost of modern mass-production technology.

---

5 Watanabe, *Induction Design*, 11.

6 Keiriki is free software that may be downloaded from Watanabe's website, www.makoto-architect.com.

Kashiwanoha Station

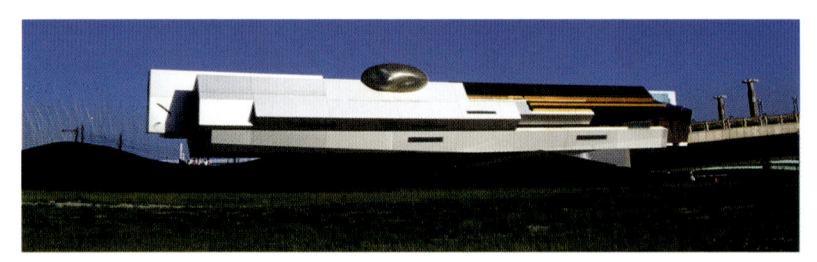

K-Museum

Iidabashi Station, corridor

I want to develop a way in which we can achieve the diversity of medieval handmade crafts with the low cost of modern mass-production technology.

Digital fabrication is usually celebrated as a means to this end. Do you believe this process can deliver the mass customization you describe? Could your software be used to construct future buildings, for example?

You mentioned the 3-D printer earlier. These days many architects and critics talk about the 3-D printer. When I visit universities in other countries, I find that many professors don't design by themselves—they suggest you can simply use a very big 3-D printer and make anything you like. However, I think it's a dream. As you said, it is possible to make architectural models with this process, but constructing a building is a different challenge. It is much harder to predict material strength, integrate complicated systems, and so on. However, we are on this path.

The idea of mass customization is intriguing because of the potential diversity it will enable. One might say that mass production has reinforced the idea of the monoculture—like we find in single-crop industrial farming or tract housing developments. However, mass customization promises to deliver polycultural environments that act as diverse, balanced ecological systems. Does this idea apply more accurately to your concept of the city as an ecological system?

It's a very good question. I have always felt that people can easily comprehend the form of the Western city. In European cities, building heights are strictly regulated, resulting in a uniform urban fabric. Japanese cities are quite different. Tokyo has a very different order that is less easily comprehended—some might say it is similar to chaos. There is an organic, biological quality to the form of Tokyo, and it is perhaps a more diverse system, like you say. However, I am not so confident it is a very good system [both laughing]. I am always trying to understand such systems so that we might develop models from them.

Form is one consideration, but how about materiality? The modern cityscape is dominated by a relatively small palette of materials, such as concrete, glass, and steel. I have often wondered if cities could become more diverse in terms of materials as well as material intelligence. Could greater diversity be realized via locally responsive materials that harness energy or clean pollution relative to their contexts, for example?

Yes, I understand. Materials and systems could be oriented to reduce energy consumption—perhaps they could lead to a new kind of design.

Material diversity can also be an effective tool for wayfinding in cities. Your Iidabashi Station project employs different visual and tactile material-based strategies to help direct subway travelers within an underground environment, for example.

I'll just say that the number of materials we can use in architecture is very limited. The reason has to do with the scale of architecture—many materials are structurally weak at the building scale. We must consider both strength and weight. A breakthrough would require some new technology, and we must develop a sprout of this technology now. There are actually many sprouts underway—for example, intelligent materials with self-repairing capabilities, or materials that change form under stress to support new loading conditions. These are exciting developments, but for now we will have to wait [both laughing].

I spoke to NEC researcher Masatoshi Iji about his recent innovation of a shape-memory bioplastic using kenaf fiber, for example.[7] Currently this material is used for mobile phone and laptop casings, and it is being developed for automobiles. We will have to wait for architectural applications, however.

Yes [laughing]. I hope it will be on sale during my lifetime [both laughing].

---

[7] NEC Corp.'s Dr. Masatoshi Iji has been developing several exotic flavors of bioplastics, such as flame-retardant bioplastic, kenaf-reinforced bioplastic, and intelligent bioplastic. See Blaine Brownell, *Transmaterial 2: A Catalog of Materials That Redefine Our Physical Environment* (New York: Princeton Architectural Press, 2008), 98, 102, 103.

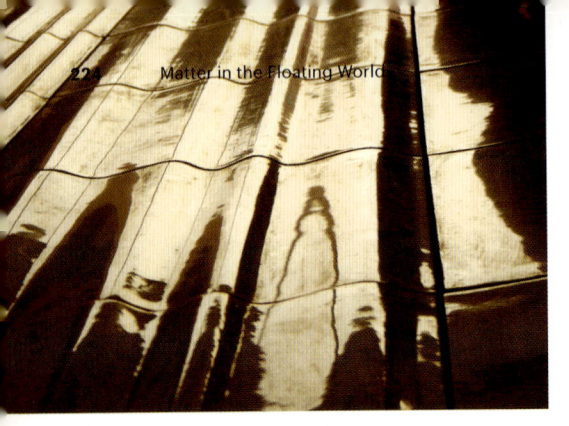

Tokyo House, wall surface detail

I think it's important to note, however, that innovation does not necessitate the use of exotic materials. We might argue that your work is innovative in terms of process, and in the way that you modify common materials based on algorithmically generated designs. We have discussed how these algorithms relate to static systems found in nature, but I'm also curious about how they relate to dynamic systems. You seem especially interested in waveforms, for example, as seen in the surfaces of your Tokyo House.

I'm intrigued by the tactile quality of rippling surfaces. When I see these surfaces, I not only sense their visual presence, but also imagine what they feel like. We might say that we touch them with our eyes. Science has shown us that the senses of sight and touch are closely related. So we have eyes in our fingers and fingers in our eyes. Whenever I design some form, I think about the visual and tactile qualities at the same time. I can't separate the visual from the tactile. Also architecture must take stable form, but I am enamored with things that change. So I try to impart qualities of flow or flotation to stable materials. Rippling water is my favorite, because water has no stable form.

It's a nod to fluid dynamics. Sometimes you write about architecture in terms of fluid dynamics—a condition of perpetual transformation. Programmatically this concept seems to relate well to transportation architecture. Conventional transportation space is made up of monotonous, elongated corridors and platforms for the movement of people. Yet the spaces in your transportation projects continually change, like the way in which a river continually changes.

Yes, you're right. Transportation architecture connects one place with another, but hopefully it also connects with another world. The system should not be fixed.

Of course, we're considering fluid dynamics in a metaphorical way here, but you have also designed work that literally moves—such as the *Fiber Wave* installations.

Yes, this is related to the theme we were just discussing. In this case, *Fiber Wave* emulates the natural movement of plants or grasses. When the wind blows, the plants change form; when the wind disappears, the plants return to their usual form. The plants are structurally resilient—they are moved by the wind, but they are unharmed by it. I think this is a very smart kind of structure, but very difficult to achieve in architecture because of the expectations for stability. For the *Fiber Wave* installations, I used carbon fiber that can resist wind speeds up to 40 meters per second [89.5 miles per hour].

What about the lights?

The tip of each strand has a solar-powered LED and a battery. So *Fiber Wave* collects power from sunlight during the day and emits light all night.

The effect is a kind of dynamic information field.

Yes—normally, wind is something you hear or feel but don't see. *Fiber Wave* allows us to visualize the wind.

Thus, the wind becomes a kind of participant in the design. You have applied this idea of natural forces participating in the design process to other projects. The Sun-God and Wind-God cities are conceptual works affected by natural elements, for example.

Yes, you're right. When we design a house, for example, we have many criteria related to the rain, wind, physical context, privacy, and so on. In the Sun-God City project, I selected only one criterion—sunlight. I then attempted to discern the maximum consequences of this criterion. The result is an idea about what kind of house we can design for sunlight.

225 Natural Logic Makoto Sei Watanabe

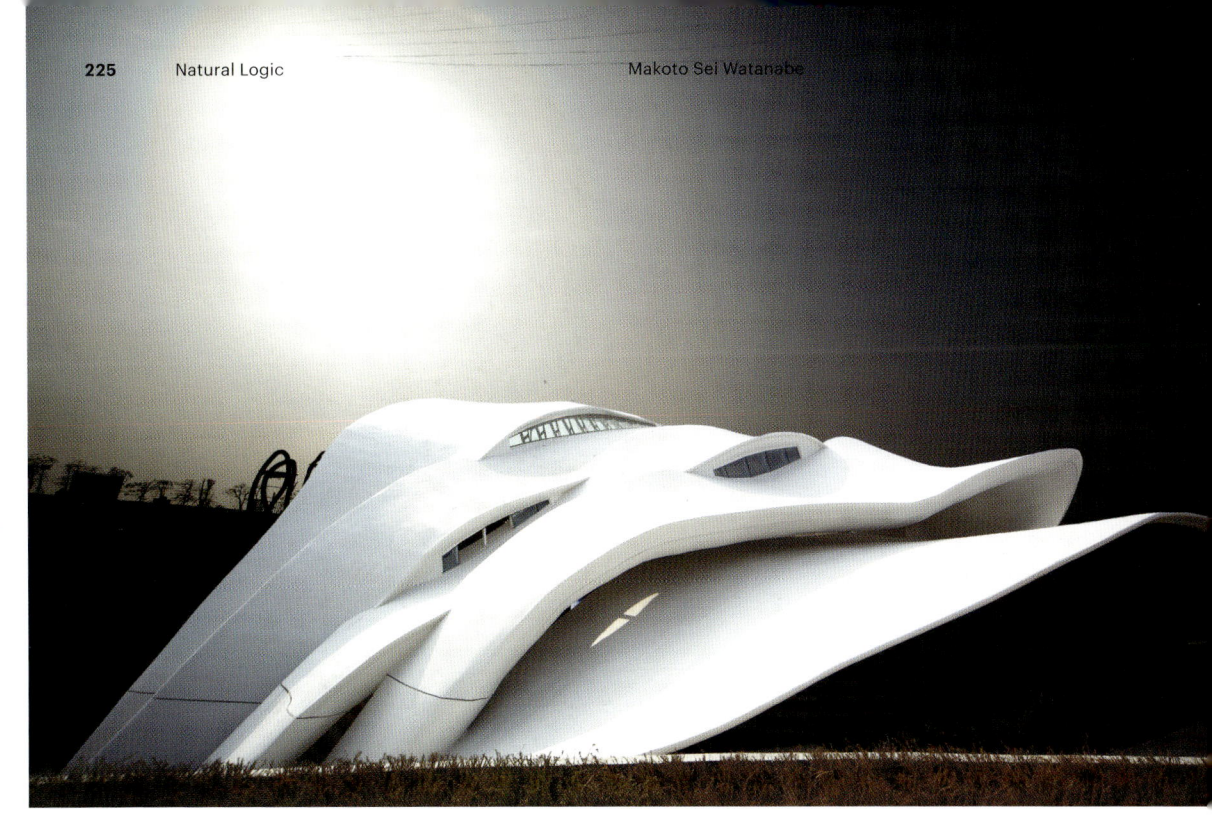

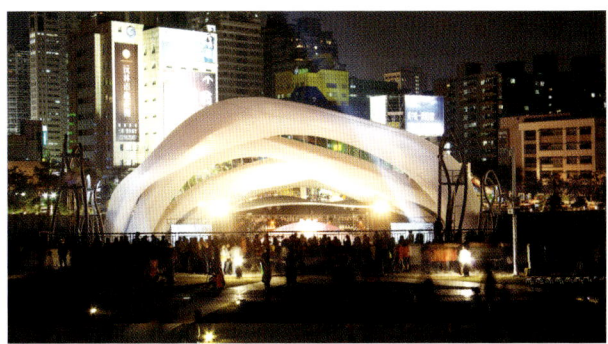

Ribbons (top),
Ribbon exhibition at the Kunsthaus Graz,
Austria (middle), detail (bottom)

226 Matter in the Floating World

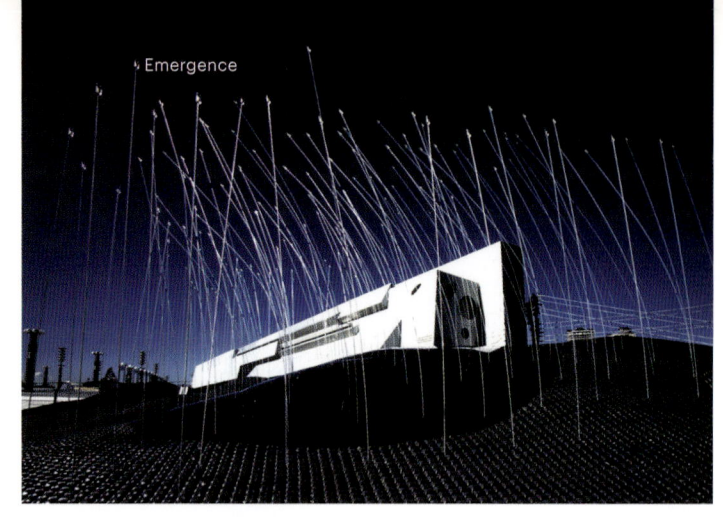

Emergence

Fiber Wave *installation at the K-Museum, Tokyo*

Fiber Wave

A small blade of grass represents a beautiful solution authored by nature, but that "program" took millions of years to develop. We only have a few decades.

Sun-God City, *diagram*

Wind wing, Iidabashi Station

I see. And you also tried this with wind?
Yes, sun, wind, and also road patterns.

Were these projects all generated by software programs?
Yes. I also had assistance from undergraduate students, since the programs are difficult to use.

I see [laughing]. I am intrigued by Google's ongoing efforts to construct a parallel, virtual Earth—as well as the desire to create new virtual worlds in Second Life, for example. It seems that these virtual realms would benefit from the incorporation of your software algorithms, because more intelligent constructed environments could be created based on a deeper understanding of natural forces. Given the broad applicability of your programs, what challenges remain for the realization of this idea?

It depends on the application. The program is a strong theme for me, and I want to integrate form-based and performance-based criteria more seamlessly in future programs. The real challenge is the evaluation component. You can write software to solve for certain requirements, but the result is not often beautiful. By beauty, I mean aesthetic beauty as well as beauty related to internal logic. We need beautiful solutions, but these are not easy to achieve. A small blade of grass represents a beautiful solution authored by nature, but that "program" took millions of years to develop. We only have a few decades [both laughing], so the challenge is how to develop beautiful solutions within the time we have.

Soft Interface

A conversation with Akira Wakita, X-Design program, Keio University

In a society increasingly fascinated with virtual environments and the internet, Akira Wakita seeks to make physical materials smarter and more responsive. Marrying fashion design and wearable computing, Wakita and his researchers at Keio University explore the potential effects of intelligent garments and communicating surfaces. Wakita aims to bridge digital and analog worlds via smart materials, arguing that the future physical environment could be composed of soft interfaces connecting bits to atoms.

Akira Wakita received a PhD in Computer-Aided Design from Keio University, Japan. A creator of virtual reality interfaces and interactive textiles, Wakita focuses on the research of smart materials, information technologies, and robotic technologies that connect the material world with the cybernetic world. He has exhibited at many conferences and art festivals, including SIGGRAPH, the European Media Art Festival, the Electronic Language International Festival, and the Graz Biennial on Media and Architecture. Wakita's awards include a Nikkei Architecture Digital Design Award (1999), a Multimedia Grand Prix Award (2000), and an Asia Digital Art Award (2003). Wakita is an associate professor at the Faculty of Environment and Information Studies, Keio University, where he is head of the X-Design program.

Ephyra (opposite)

I'm interested in the way your work navigates the intersection between digital and physical realms.

Yes, it's very difficult work, but we must solve the problem of bridging physical and virtual content. I believe that in the near future, we will develop an interface that breaks the wall between humanity and technology.

How did you develop this interest?

My background is quite complicated [both laughing]. Originally I was very interested in computer graphics and computer-aided design. I was an engineer for CAD software, and I developed mathematics for NURBS geometry—such as how to attach two NURBS patches without any distortion.[1] Then I became interested in the use of 3-D models on the web. At the beginning of the twenty-first century, the technology called Web3D was being developed, and I recognized the importance of the user interface—which is the visualization of an activity within cyberspace.[2] At that time, I met the architect Fumio Matsumoto, a former disciple of Arata Isozaki. We started a collaboration focused on the interface, and I shifted my position from an engineer to a designer as a result. I was a doctoral student then, and after graduation I founded a small design company targeting Web3D and interface design.

Two years later I was invited to teach at Keio University and establish a design curriculum. The dean asked me to change my focus yet again—this time to sociology. I was totally confused. I thought about this new research field for a while, and I realized that fashion is a field that exists at the intersection between sociology, technology, and design. I started researching wearable computing, despite the fact that I had no prior knowledge of circuit design or soldering.

That must have been quite a challenge. The early interfaces you developed—the Infotube, City Tomography, and Ryukyu Alive—are all quite spatial in nature. How did you design these interfaces?

I was interested in the visualization of information—how data could be projected within a simulated architectural space. Infotube was my first work in collaboration with Matsumoto, based on a technology called VRML.[3] We developed a virtual counterpart to the Motomachi historic shopping street in Yokohama.

It's interesting that virtual reality has found a foothold in commercial applications, since consumers typically prefer the physical presence of merchandise. Virtual interfaces therefore seek to overcome the alienating flatness of digital space. We see this tendency in operating systems that allow users to browse documents or media files as if they had dimensionality, for example.

Yes. With Infotube, we envisioned a kind of future shopping mall. However, the virtual form had no relation to the physical space.

Was this the case with City Tomography?

Yes. This project visualized the Ginza shopping district in Tokyo, based on the real geographical space in which we could attach information to the buildings.

Like Google Earth?

Yes, very similar to Google Earth. We wanted to attach customer evaluations and comments to the virtual stores, and these comments could be added by mobile phones on site. Ryukyu Alive addressed a completely different scale, using the metaphor of a galaxy in which one could access a massive digital archive developed by Okinawa Prefecture.

You then began work on physical interfaces, such as Activity Score and Key Transponder.

---

1 "NURBS" stands for non-uniform rational basis spline and is a mathematical model used to create sophisticated curves and complex shapes with a high degree of accuracy.

2 The Web3D Consortium was founded to promote open standards for three-dimensional graphics on the internet.

3 "VRML" is short for virtual reality modeling language, or virtual reality markup language, developed to represent three-dimensional graphics on the web. It has been replaced by X3D.

231　　Soft Interface

Infotube

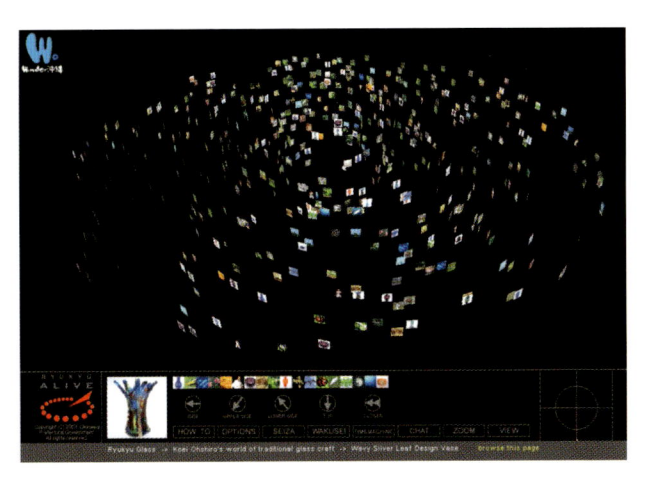

Ryukyu Alive

We must solve the problem of bridging physical and virtual content. I believe that in the near future, we will develop an interface that breaks the wall between humanity and technology.

Activity Score

Matter in the Floating World   Emergence

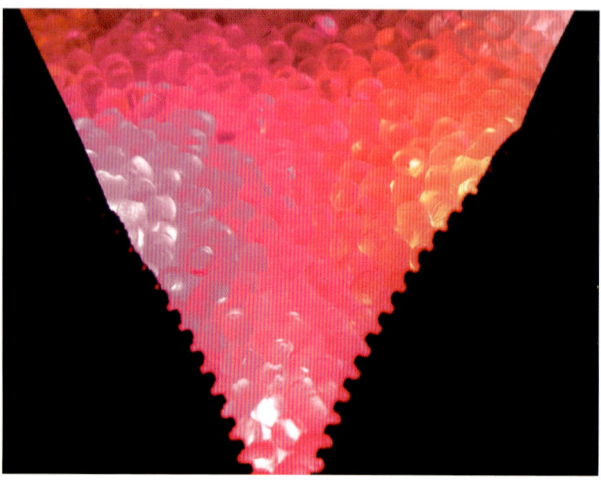

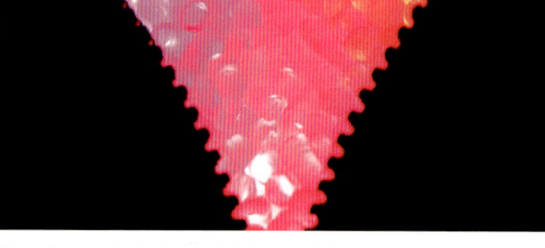

Wearable Synthesis (top and right), detail (bottom)

Yes. These projects utilized RFID technology to augment real objects with virtual information.[4] Key Transponder is a kind of social experiment. When someone comes to the door, he or she touches an interface and a signal is sent to every member of the group who holds a key. If there is a cute girl at the door, many boys will come to her assistance. However, if it is a boy, no one may come [both laughing].

Did Wearable Synthesis develop out of this idea for a social interface?

Yes, Wearable Synthesis was a leap forward. Typically we view live computer information via display or projection, but in this case I decided that the "canvas" would be clothing. After all, fashion is also a kind of visualization.

How did you develop the concept?

First we surveyed the relationship between fashion and wearable computing. The typical goal is to make wearable computing fashionable. However, we wanted to make fashion more effective by employing wearable computing. This is an important distinction.

We read many papers about fashion, and determined that the most important aspect concerns the coordination of clothing. If you go into a store to buy clothing, you think about the coordination of your potential purchase with your existing wardrobe—despite the fact that the clothes may be from another store. You are always thinking about the context. So I developed a technology such that one article of clothing may "speak" to another one. A shirt and shoes may communicate, for example, and maybe both assume the same color. This is one possibility of coordination using wearable computing.

So the "speaking" you refer to results in shifts in color and pattern?

Yes, and the one example where we have used synthesis is inner wear. These garments have temperature and humidity sensors, and the clothing changes color based on these readings.

So if I'm hot…

Yes—if you're feeling hot or aggressive, the color would be red. Or if you are cool or your mood is calm, the color may be blue. Other garments also respond in kind—a jacket will sense the color sensor of the inner wear, for example, and change its color to match.

I see. What about two people? Can their clothes communicate?

Yes, yes. In Japan, there is a term for people who dress in matching outfits called *peiruku*, which is short for "pair clothing." Individuals may wear clothing to match their child or girlfriend, for example, and this desire for pairing may be facilitated by wearable computing. Also if one wearer senses the presence of another via the infrared radiation sensor or RFID tag, the actuator on the other wearer's clothing will blink as if to say "hello." So if the wearer is a shy guy, this technology may be useful for him to visualize his feeling.

Wearable Synthesis is not limited to one or two people, however. A thousand people could wear clothing that senses the presence of others and changes color. For example, the color of my clothing could change yours and your neighbor's and the next person's, and so on. It could be a kind of fashion trend, or a way to log the spread of fashion trends [laughing].

Could clothing change color based on the weather forecast or the condition of the stock market, for example?

Maybe it's the next step, but difficult to develop. There are products that change color depending on this kind of information…very interesting.

Perhaps this could be one of the capabilities of Fabcell. How does this technology relate to Wearable Synthesis?

We presented Wearable Synthesis at a SIGGRAPH fashion show.[5] At the time we didn't have a model, so I played the role myself

---

4 RFID stands for radio-frequency identification, which involves tracking people, animals, or objects with tags.

5 SIGGRAPH stands for Special Interest Group on GRAPHics and Interactive Techniques, and is an annual conference on computer graphics and related technologies.

[both laughing]. One of my assistants was also a model for the show. We began to feel that LEDs were too crude for use in clothing. If I were to put on a shirt with many LEDs, you would probably think of me as a strange guy or mad scientist [both laughing]. We wanted to use a nonemissive textile instead of point light sources. So I thought we would have to develop the material itself.

This was quite a breakthrough.
Yes. Fabcell is composed of two kinds of fiber. One fiber is an ordinary fiber for the weft layer, made of hemp thread. The warp layer is made of conductive thread.

How did you weave it?
By hand. It's a very complicated task.

Yes, I can imagine. Wow.
We actually made a weaving machine just to produce Fabcell. When electricity is supplied to the conductive thread, the temperature of the fabric will change. Changes in the timing of electricity delivery will control the color temperature of the textile.

So you can achieve blue, green, and yellow. What about red?
I'm trying to realize red, which is difficult. We are using special ink called liquid crystal ink. This ink is limited in that it must be painted on a black surface. So blue appears clearly, but red does not.

How bright is Fabcell? Does it work outside of a dark room?
Yes, it's the same as ordinary clothes. However, the liquid crystal ink is heat-sensitive, so direct sunlight can change the color temperature.

I see. So far you've used the technology to make textile screens?
Yes. We are also making a Fabcell dress made of many small patches. The concept is that one may download internet-based images and display them on the body. You could change the image, color, pattern—everything. We can use Fabcell as digital wallpaper too, so we could change real wallpaper to match the desktop "wallpaper" of a PC [laughing].

What about carpet?

Oh yes, carpet is another example. By using Fabcell for carpet, we could employ real-space navigation by altering ground patterns to create pathways.

How long does it take to change colors?
It takes about ten seconds from black to blue—the color cycles from black, red, green, to blue.

And how small can the swatches be? You treat them like physical pixels, I presume?
Yes. Currently, the pixel is four to five centimeters [one and a half to two inches], which is very large. Now we are developing form-changing textiles—allowing us to control the actual feeling of the material.

Really!
Do you know the computer graphics term "texture map"?[6] Fabcell is a kind of physical texture map in that it allows the display of a pattern.

And you want to make a "bump map."[7]
Yes, yes, a bump map—a displacement map that changes the actual feeling of the textile. We can use artificial musculature or biometal for this application.

By biometal, do you mean shape memory alloy?[8]
Yes. Shape memory metal is used to change the shape of the textile.

What kind of shapes would you achieve?
There are two deformations—large-scale deformations and local deformations. The local scale is established by shape memory. It is just a concept at this point, but we use Nitinol fiber for the weft layer and small biometals on the surface of the textile.[9]

---

6 A texture map is an application of color, pattern, image, or graphic detail to a three-dimensional model.

7 A bump map is the simulated application of a surface texture on a three-dimensional model.

8 Shape memory alloys (SMAs) are metals that "remember" their cold-forged shapes, and this characteristic is utilized to create dynamic microstructures with no mechanical parts.

9 Nitinol is a shape memory alloy of nickel and titanium. It was developed by William Buehler and Frederick Wang at the U.S. Naval Ordnance Laboratory in 1962.

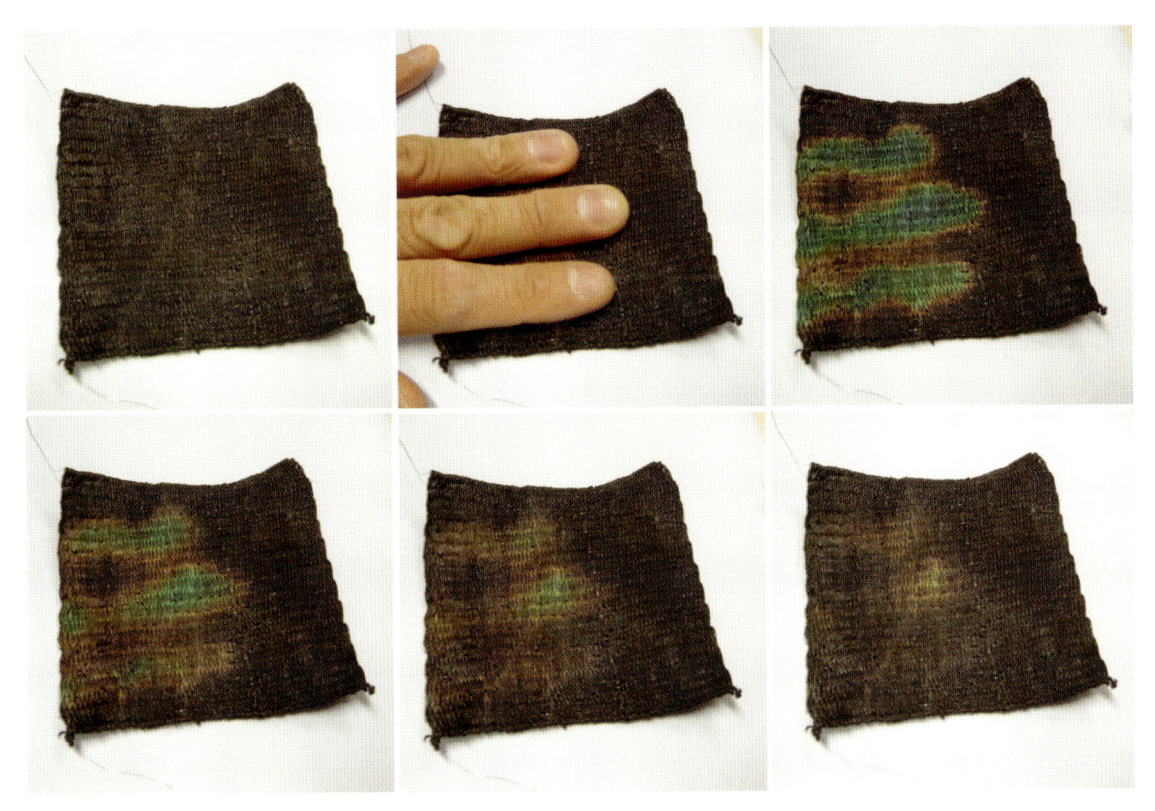

Fabcell

The color of my clothing could change yours and your neighbor's and the next person's, and so on. It could be a kind of fashion trend, or a way to log the spread of fashion trends.

Fabcell textile

Living Textile

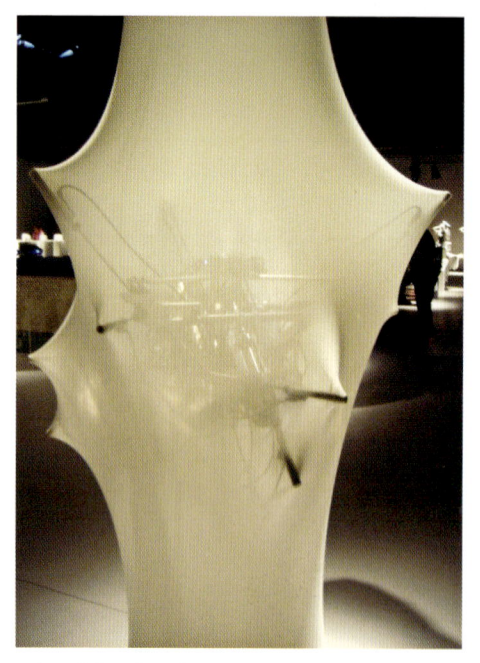

Ephyra (left and right)

The robot does not respond to inanimate objects—only the small static charge conveyed by human skin. The robot relates to the unique communication established between humans and machines.

With this composition we can change the surface of the textile. So my clothing could change shape with my mood.

Could it give you a massage?

Maybe, yes! [laughing] That would be a good application. We would like to move beyond the static textile. The living textile is our goal. In fact, we have developed a kinetic textile that deforms like a NURBS surface, and we call it Living Textile.

> **Amazing! Would it be possible to simulate Braille? A shape-shifting textile could bring a new dimension of communicability, whether in clothing or on a wall surface, for example.**

Ah, maybe—yes. Very interesting. If one touches the body, it could display a message.

> **It reminds me of an installation I saw at SIGGRAPH called Electric Touch, which gave visitors a small electric shock conveying a tactile image or texture.**

Yes, a haptic display.

> **Speaking of textile-based interfaces, perhaps you could discuss Ephyra—the installation you created with Shunji Yamanaka.**

Yes, it was a very good opportunity. Shunji Yamanaka once gave a guest lecture to my students and I showed him my laboratory. He remarked that the mode of production was similar to the one at his office, Leading Edge Design. After that, we collaborated on two exhibitions. For Ephyra we essentially developed a huge robot.

> **So it's a robot covered with fabric that you interact with.**

Yes. The fabric has no seams and is extremely tough. There is a tube supplying air to a hydraulic system. Ephyra is about four meters [thirteen feet] tall, and there is a circuit at the foot of the installation.

> **How does the interactive mechanism work?**

I used a sensor to respond to the static electricity conveyed by touch. In this way the robot does not respond to inanimate objects—only the small static charge conveyed by human skin. The robot relates to the unique communication established between humans and machines.

Amazing! And I heard there is a hidden command?

Yes. If you touch a sensor four times quickly in succession, all of the arms will retract immediately.

> **It's definitely not the conventional image of a robot.**

I like to think about what the future holds. Nowadays most products are rigid. However, the use of soft, elastic shells may be another solution—and closer to the nature of the human body itself. So I like to think about the skin of the product, which may be another means of conveying the electricity in wearable computing.

> **What about architecture?**

Yes, architecture. We are surrounded by hard materials. Perhaps walls could become soft. I would like to make a space that is completely composed of soft and elastic materials—using memory foam, perhaps.[10]

> **So this is the kind of interface that you imagine—a new kind of threshold between atoms and bits?**

Yes, a living textile. In the cyberworld we can make anything we want. So I'd like to break the wall between the cyberworld and the real world—with real textiles that convey texture maps and bump maps, and textiles that move independently. Textiles may then embody a kind of hybrid reality. In this spirit we can do more to awaken the latent possibilities within materials.

---

10 Memory foam is a viscoelastic polyurethane foam that is sensitive to pressure and heat from the body.

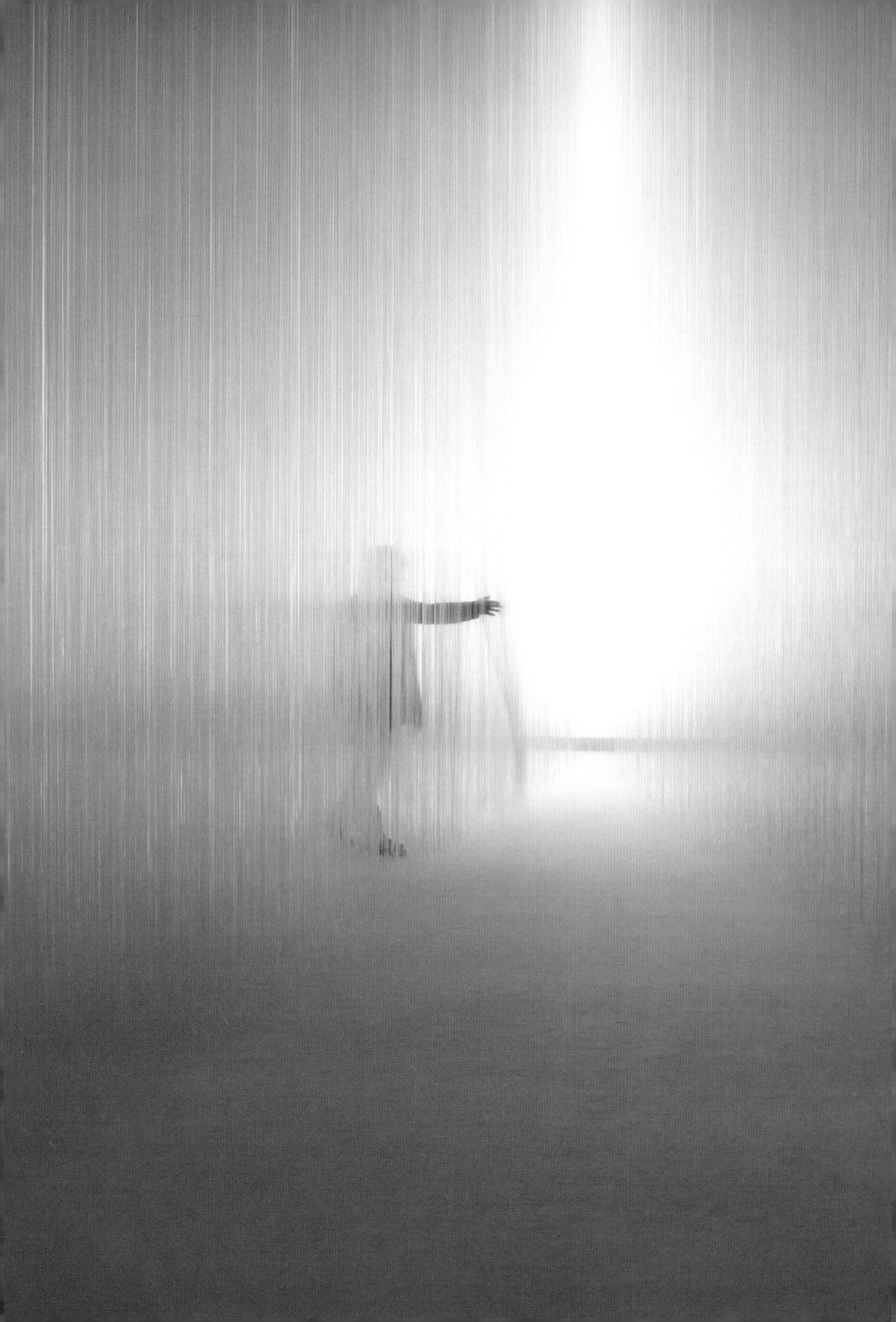

Summoning Nature

A conversation with Tokujin Yoshioka, Tokujin Yoshioka Design

Chairs grown in vats of fluid, cloudlike spaces enveloped by optical fibers, chandeliers made of suspended crystals, and furniture that "disappears in the rain"—these are the works of Tokujin Yoshioka, a provocative talent who represents the next generation in Japanese design. Yoshioka employs unusual methods of aggregating materials in the service of creating atmospheric, weightless encounters. His bold light fixtures, furniture, storefronts, and interiors shape experiences that evoke natural phenomena— a condition he terms "second nature."

Tokujin Yoshioka was born in Saga, Japan, in 1967. After working for Shiro Kuramata and Issey Miyake, he established his own studio, Tokujin Yoshioka Design. He has since become one of Japan's preeminent furniture, product, and exhibition designers. Yoshioka's Honey-pop paper chair, ToFU light, and other works have become part of permanent collections at the Museum of Modern Art in New York, the Centre Pompidou, the Victoria & Albert Museum, and others. He has received several awards, including Designer of the Year from Design Miami (2007) and the Design for Asia Award (2008). Yoshioka curated the exhibit Second Nature at the 21_21 Design Sight museum in Tokyo in 2008 and published his treatise on design, entitled *Invisible Forms*, in 2009.

Lexus L-finesse (opposite)

Your work is often characterized by the reduction of an idea to its simplest form, and it is obvious that you regard material selection very seriously. What is your general philosophy regarding the selection of materials?

I have a great respect for materials that have changed and the newest technology, but these become outdated as time passes. In recent years, I have tracked down materials that carry an intrinsic beauty and I am conscious of design that has this particular quality.

In your writings you have said that you select materials not because they are interesting or new—yet you rely upon materials to construct novel experiences.

The work, of course, starts with an interest. That is, newness and new technologies eventually become old within a year. What I recognize is that design up until now has had no history. Design is essentially about creating a fresh dimension that echoes human feelings. Therefore, I research and test things repeatedly in order to create the most provocative outcome. To this end, I think it is important to understand the characteristics of materials well. The materials I use may appear to be sophisticated, but I basically use mostly simple and everyday materials.

Would you characterize this approach as being particularly Japanese?

It is often said that my designs are Japanese, but my approach toward materials may be more similar to Japanese cuisine. Sushi-making is about choosing intimate materials and starts with learning about a relationship with the natural world—specifically, fish and the ocean. When sushi is eaten, it has achieved itself as a meal for the first time. For that reason, knife skills express the intimacy of cuisine.

Similarly even design that appears simple at first is created out of the pursuit of a thoroughly understood material.

The sushi analogy is an interesting one, because sushi-making requires careful and particular methods of assembly. Moreover, dishes like *chirashizushi* combine many ingredients together in one dish—like different pigments used to create a single painting.[1] I wonder if we could explore this analogy further? Assemblage art, for example, involves the aggregation of large volumes of materials in such a way that the field transcends the object. I cannot help but think of your Lexus L-finesse, Swarovski Ginza, or Moroso NY installations, for example.

These are not just about assemblage; I also try to employ the natural fundamentals of design. For example, in the Lexus L-finesse installation project, I attempted to harness the same fundamentals present in natural phenomena, such as clouds and snow. This piece did require the assembly of countless fibers by hand, with the help of one hundred college students. However, the aggregation of simple, clear fibers and their endless overlapping took on a particular whiteness, and an altogether foglike space resulted. In the case of the Moroso NY installation, an entire snowlike landscape emerged from the accumulation of simple tissue paper. Thus, although these installations were entirely artificial, I tried to create experiences that related to viewers' deeply embedded memories of previously witnessed natural phenomena.

Speaking of natural phenomena, the Venus Natural Crystal Chair offers a new approach to furniture fabrication, as it is grown rather than manufactured. Does this process herald a new strategy for you, or is it only for shock value?

I had been intrigued by the inherent beauty of crystals for many years before creating Venus. I challenged myself to create a completely new kind of chair based on a novel structure. I also wanted to create a counterproposal to the recent emphasis on the use of computer renderings to make virtual objects appear real, because I feel that the beauty of nature cannot be so easily emulated. I therefore sought to design a piece that embraced the awe-inspiring power of nature.

---

[1] Chirashizushi is an assortment of raw fish slices and other ingredients presented on top of a bowl of rice.

Summoning Nature   Tokujin Yoshioka

> Design is essentially about creating a fresh dimension that echoes human feelings.

Stardust

Stardust (detail)

Lake of Shimmer, Swarovski exhibition at Baselworld 2009

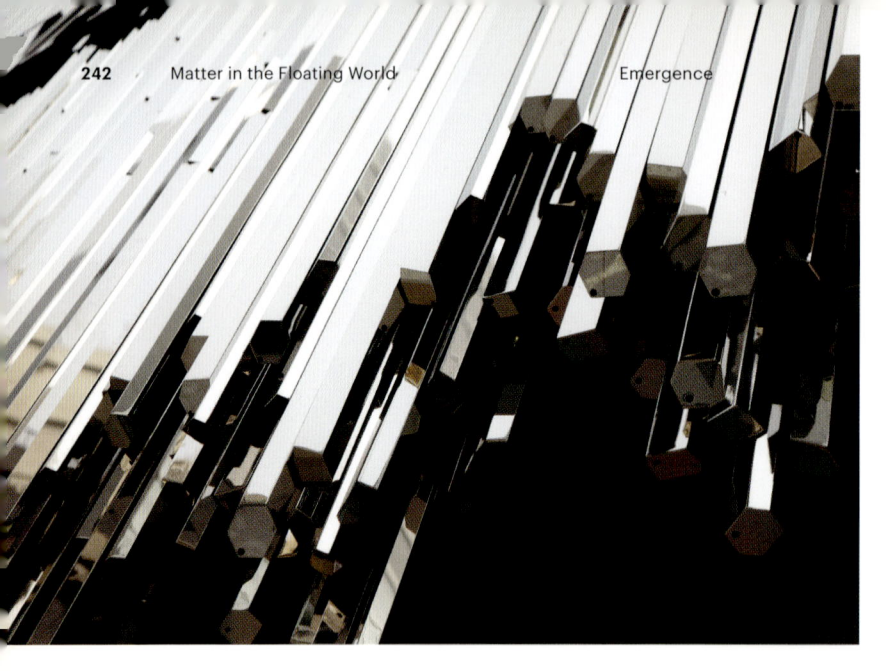

Although these installations were entirely artificial, I tried to create experiences that related to viewers' deeply embedded memories of previously witnessed natural phenomena.

Swarovski Ginza, facade detail (top), interior (middle)

Lexus L-finesse

How did you fabricate the chair?

The Venus chair was produced by two creators: I guided the initial stage of the process, but the remaining stage was led by nature. First I created a polyester fiber block to serve as the underlying structure of the chair. I then placed it in a large glass tank filled with a solution saturated with special minerals. Natural crystals began to accumulate on the fibers, and I let them grow for about one month before I deemed the chair to be complete.

Incredible. What implications does this process have for the future of design?

The fact that creation is not entirely controlled by human beings; beauty is born out of serendipity. The Venus chair effectively emerges out of nothing, and its form is governed by natural processes. This production method highlights the boundary between the physical world and the world of the imagination. In this sense, the process broadens the boundaries of creativity.

How do you reconcile this unusual method with your other works, in which you assemble static materials by hand?

I always seek to accomplish something that no one has done before. I want the work to transcend an ordinary, conventional state via a process of experimental layering.

How does one create truly unprecedented work?

My approach is to find the freshest dimension. This is not about finding form, color, or visual things, but rather a deeper dimension. For example, if I were to design a towel, it would not be about the shape being square or round, or white or yellow. If the towel is not the actual physical necessity, it might be good to consider a breeze instead. Meaning, I begin thinking about a larger approach connected to the basic function of something. My Honey-pop, Pane, and Venus Natural Crystal chairs have this meaning, and I think I was able to find a fresh dimension through these projects.

I should mention that work that is considered innovative at its inception simply because it utilizes a new technology or material will fade in importance with the passage of time. Therefore, I try to transcend such fads and achieve a fresh dimension in my work that will remain after one hundred years.

This kind of long view would suggest an emphasis on durability, yet you often use very temporary materials intentionally.

For the Paper Cloud, I used paper to express the concept more strongly, because of the prototype that was shown at that time.[2] I am planning to use cloth and leather for its production from now on.

With Venus, the project's function is a chair. In this case I was not only interested in the aspect of durability. I used natural crystals because I wanted to make a strong object that conveyed the message of an enduring history.

With the Honey-pop Chair, the purpose was to make a chair that appeared to be six pieces of paper material at first glance, and a structure made with a high degree of strength. This strength was achieved by unfolding many layers of precisely cut glassine paper.

This pursuit of a strong structure using weak materials is reminiscent of other Japanese designers, such as Shigeru Ban.[3] When describing your Fiber Architecture research, for example, you use the parallel of the Japanese art of Aikido, "in which the defender gains the resistance and strength by diverting the force through his graceful and circular movement."[4]

Is this a particularly Japanese modus operandi?

I am not conscious of approaching my work in a Japanese way. I think my work is more about the realization of natural principles rather than being Japanese. Fiber Architecture is a good illustration, because this kind of phenomenon can be seen in nature. If you look closely at plants, you will witness the accumulation of many fine fibers that create a strong network.

---

2 Yoshioka's Paper Cloud is a sofa made entirely of crumpled paper, which he designed for the manufacturer Moroso in 2009.

3 See my conversation with Shigeru Ban in this book, pages 68–81.

4 Aikido is a Japanese martial art developed to protect both defender and attacker from injury.

244 Matter in the Floating World Emergence

Venus Natural Crystal Chair, part of the Second Nature Exhibition at 21_21 Design Sight

Venus Natural Crystal Chair

Second Nature Exhibition at 21_21 Design Sight

This production method highlights the boundary between the physical world and the world of the imagination. In this sense, the process broadens the boundaries of creativity.

Paper Cloud

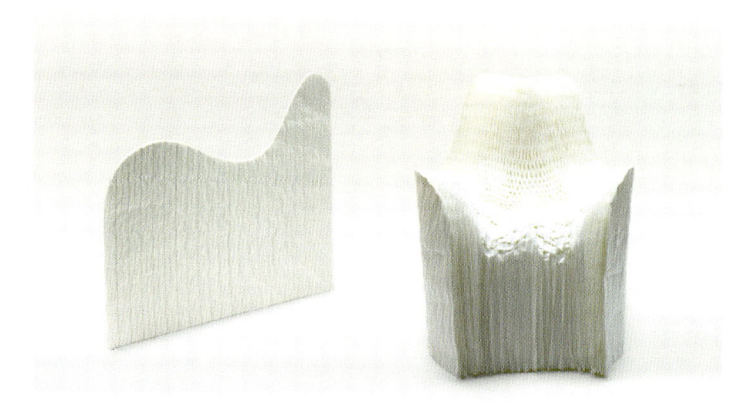

Honey-pop

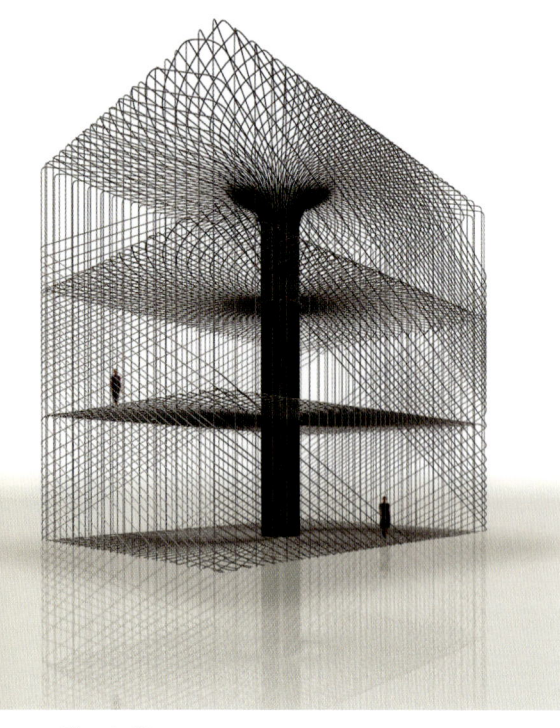

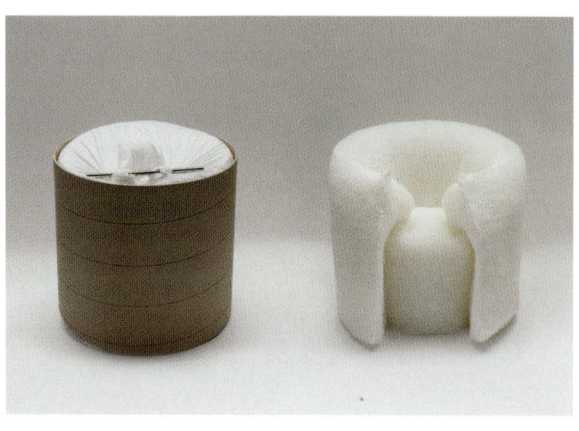

Pane Chair

Fiber Architecture

Another example would be the Pane Chair, which was inspired by the spongy, fibrous structures in baked bread that demonstrate a high capacity to absorb forces despite their softness.

Another type of dematerialization that you often employ is transparency—not only to reduce the solidity of a work, but also to impart it with an uncanny physical presence. Your Water Block bench and Chair that Disappears in the Rain, for example, are imbued with rippling textures that create a blurring effect.

When the shape of a lighting fixture disappears, only the light becomes visible. If one is left only with the feeling of sitting in a chair, then it must be a very unconventional kind of chair. In order to get closer to this kind of design ideal, I often utilize transparency. Also, I often have the desire to show the reflected light of something more than its inner color.

In terms of the texture and imperfections you mention, I am also interested in the overlapping of endless, transparent things that result in a white color—like a fog. I want to create work that changes its surrounding atmosphere.

Speaking of light fixtures—could you describe your general approach to integrating light and material?

As I said before, materials are like Japanese cuisine to me, because materials capture the chemistry of design. The Tear Drop and ToFu projects were based on the concept of designing light and were the result of this idea. The goal is not to make light fixtures, but to illuminate. Beyond focusing on a particular material, it is about the light.

Water Block bench

Remembrance window installation, Maison Hermès, Tokyo

When the shape of a lighting fixture disappears, only the light becomes visible. If one is left only with the feeling of sitting in a chair, then it must be a very unconventional kind of chair.

Tear Drop light

The Sound of Material

A conversation with Masayo Ave, MasayoAve creation

Masayo Ave is an embodiment of cultural and disciplinary synthesis. One of Japan's most intriguing design exports, Ave has practiced in Japan and Europe, and she brings expertise in architecture, product design, landscape, fashion, and lighting design to her work. In projects ranging from everyday objects to architecture, she seeks to expose the emotional value lying hidden within materials and has led a number of workshops focused on design-related material research. For Ave, design is a process of discovery in which she thoroughly studies a material in order to optimize its potential. She argues that design is a profoundly multisensory experience, and her ongoing experiments with haptic learning promise to break new ground for material applications.

Masayo Ave was born in Tokyo in 1962. She studied architecture at Hosei University and worked for Ichiro Ebihara Architect and Associates until 1990, when she moved to Milan to complete a master's degree in industrial design at the Domus Academy. In 1992 Ave founded her own design studio with offices in Milan and Tokyo. Ave received a grant from the Akademie Schloss Solitude, Germany, and launched her own collection, MasayoAve creation, in 2000. As the winner of a number of international competitions—including the ICFF Editors Award (2000) and the A&W Mentor Award (2006)—Ave has garnered international recognition within a variety of design fields and was nominated as a juror for both the Red Dot Design Award and Interzum Award in 2004. Currently based in Berlin, Ave has taught in Milan, Berlin, and Tallinn, where she was appointed professor and head of the product design department at the Estonian Academy of Arts in 2007.

Hattifatteners hanging light (opposite)

Throughout your career you have trained in a variety of design disciplines and established your base location in several different countries. As a budding designer, did you know you would embark upon such a colorful journey?

I had been aware that travel would enrich the quality of my design work, although I did not have any clear picture about how this would happen in the beginning. I have built a career by "sniffing and scratching," which is my intrinsic nature, and the wide range of activities I have engaged in as a designer is simply the result of small, incremental steps over the course of the last two decades.

I am interested in your first step—what inspired you to move to Italy from Japan?

I wanted to move to Milan in 1989 in order to join the experimental master's program in industrial design at the Domus Academy. I did not have any preconception about Italian design, mostly because I was educated as an architect in Japan during the mid-1980s—a period that predated the "Italian culture boom" there. I had a basic knowledge about historical architecture in Italy, but I was actually more interested in modern masterpieces by Scandinavian architects such as Alvar Aalto, or European design movements, such as the Vienna Secession or the Bauhaus. However, by experiencing Italy without any preconception—not falling blindly in love with Italian design from a distance—I was able to discover the true essence of Italian design purely with my own eyes. I could also analyze and value Italian design rationally within the wider context of European design culture in general. I considered Milan—where I lived from 1990 to 2005—to be a hub in which I could learn about other European cultures and engage the broader environment of Europe as much as possible. Since 2005 Berlin has become my new European hub, and I have also frequented Tallinn in Estonia for a two-year professorship. It has been fascinating to discover different parts of Europe in this way, although I feel that I am still in the middle of my colorful journey.

I can imagine that such a broad perspective derived from operating in different countries would greatly enhance one's work. I am also interested in your knowledge of multiple disciplines. How might your experience with architecture affect your design of a light fixture, for example?

I consider products to be mini-architecture, which I can build at 1:1 scale on my worktable. I think my design method is always based on the discipline of the architect. I also consider products to be part of the space in which humans carry out their daily lives. It is difficult for me to start designing a single product before getting a picture of the ambience in which the product will exist— not only the user's environment but also the temporary storehouse of the factory, shop, or even the space of the transport container. Throughout my career I have noticed that many trained designers can start designing once they have a clear picture of the user.

I wonder if this particular regard for "product space" in the design process is especially Japanese. Despite the fact that you have lived in Europe for many years now, would you say that part of your work is still inherently Japanese?

The answer is definitely yes! Something very Japanese always reveals itself in my design work and reveals my Japanese identity no matter where I am.

Interesting! On this note, I wonder if you could describe the fourteen-hundred-year-old Japanese art of *shibori*, or "shaped-resist" textiles?[1] How did you utilize this process to make your shaped-resist polyester products, such as the Hattifatteners hanging light or Ninni floor light, for example? In what ways did you modernize the process?

I studied the traditional Japanese shibori textile technique in 1993 and 1994. Meanwhile, I got to know about an advanced shaped-resist technique used to fix flexible

---

1 Shibori, or *shiborizome*, is a Japanese method of dyeing cloth dating to the eighth century that involves folding, binding, twisting, and other physical manipulations.

Toft cushion

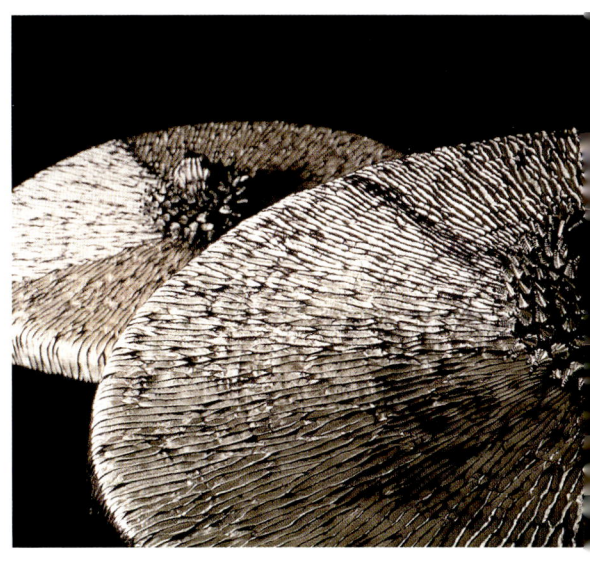

Filly table cover

> **It is difficult for me to start designing a single product before getting a picture of the ambience in which the product will exist.**

three-dimensional textures permanently within textiles. I became fascinated with the idea to apply this technique to interior items, as I felt that the texture could make products feel naturally alive, even if synthetic fibers were used in making the textiles. So I made a lot of experiments with shaped-resist textiles in order to understand how to achieve this quality of being alive. I recognized that this character could easily be killed, however, if manipulated in the wrong way. I knew that I needed to learn the best way to bring out the intrinsic character of the material—which is actually the key to approaching any material in design.

In the years that followed—from 1995 to 1997—I realized models of handicraft textile applications in lighting and furniture—such as the Mimura floor lamp, the Toft cushion, and the Filly table cover, in addition to Hattifatteners and Ninni. I realized the key to optimizing volume and handling light effectively by making models, and I also applied the method to create the Genesi light using open-cell polyester foam. Actually, I always consider Ninni to be the mother of Genesi. In my design process, low-tech practices often create the sparks that initiate work with high-tech materials, and that's why I always experiment with both methods.

Your description of products feeling naturally alive seems to relate to the striking biological character evident in many of your creations. Works like Corona di Muse and Toft cushions resemble sponges or coral, for example. Is there a benefit to emulating biological forms in design?

When I get an idea, I often start working directly on the volume model before making any drawings or sketches. I never try to make materials fit a form previously defined on paper. Rather, I explore a material as it is—searching for the best form that brings out a material's inherent potential. In this way, drawn lines cannot work against the true nature of a material. I simply follow the physical logic

252 — Matter in the Floating World — Emergence

Genesi Light (above), showing construction (right)

Materials have a soul, and they amaze and delight if you know how to study them, question them, and listen to them.

Corona di Muse

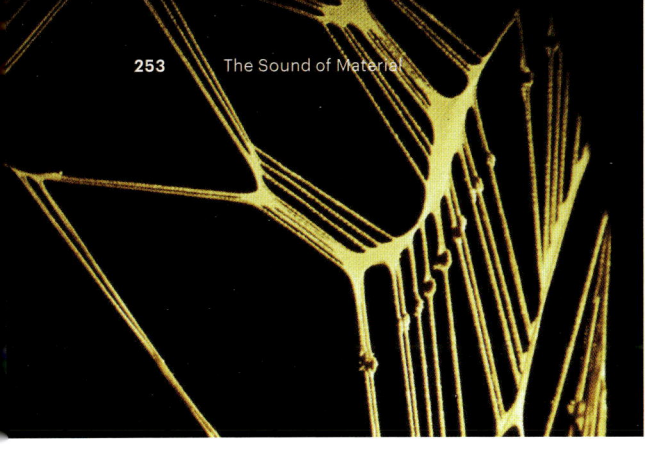

Sound of Material project

800 Dots haptic paperback book cover

and structure of a material, and if I am successful, the form automatically results in something close to what we have already seen in nature. The intrinsic character of a material should not be killed by a design operation—the operation should rather define an appropriate limit of exploration for a material in order to determine the best function. I work very much like an engineer, logically rather than emotionally. You will know that I am from the engineering faculty even though the final appearance of my work is often considered to be poetic or artistic. My ultimate goal in design is to realize an object that can silently express its intrinsic *anima* as peacefully as a sleeping cat on a sofa. I therefore endeavor to find the key, like a scientific secret that determines the perfect form created by nature.

> **Amazing—what you describe is a kind of presence that you impart to materials. Is this the approach you use for your Sound of Material work?**

Yes, originally "Sound of Material" was a title of one of my first experiments with synthetic materials and was awarded a young designer prize in 1991 at a competition organized by the Napoleon Bullukian Foundation in France. I gave the project this name because it was a challenge to listen to a material's "inner voice," in order to discover a new application that explores the material's true expressive potential. I conducted various experiments with the synthetic fabric Lycra, which is known for its exceptional elasticity and vivid color.

I pursued Lycra's intrinsic sensorial, emotional, and expressive qualities, and completed the experiments with possible applications in both fashion design and furniture design.

Materials have a soul, and they amaze and delight if you know how to study them, question them, and listen to them. I have been fascinated with this notion ever since beginning my career as a designer, so when I had the opportunity to conduct a design workshop for young students at the Ecole des Beaux-Arts in St. Etienne in 2001, I introduced this research in order to share my fascination. Since then I always give the title of "Sound of Material" to the series of workshops focused on this topic.

> **One of the topics I discussed with designer Kenya Hara was his 2004 Haptic exhibition, which showcased your 800 Dots tactile paper.[2] There is an obvious connection with your work in haptic interface design at the Berlin University of the Arts [UdK]. Why the recent interest in tactile-oriented design? Is this the origin of a significant movement?**

The experience I had discussing haptic design with Kenya Hara and Reiko Sudo for the Haptic exhibition and book was really inspiring. We all agreed that haptic design should not just be a seasonal topic found in a gap between different disciplines, but rather a genre of original significance located

---

2 Kenya Hara, *Haptic* (Tokyo: Takeo Co., 2004). See my conversation with Kenya Hara in this book, pages 88–97.

within a cross-disciplinary field of design. Coincidentally, the discussion occurred just before I received a three-year guest professorship at UdK, so I had the idea to establish the Haptic Interface Design Institute—an experimental institute specifically focused on haptic design research and development.

I also had another motivation for bringing this topic to the university. Through my experiences at previous workshops in academia, I realized that university students represent a sort of haptic-starved generation, as they have grown up with shiny and clean products covered in "do not touch" labels. The students are therefore quite keen on the topic of hapticity, and I anticipated that their hunger for this approach would exert a positive influence toward the development of this theme within design. I conducted a variety of research and development projects at the institute, including the creation of a *Haptic Dictionary*—a compendium of new onomatopoeic terms that express tactile emotions. The institute activities attracted a great deal of attention from students, not only at UdK but also from other European institutes. In three years, more than seventy students from various nationalities had participated in the project, and I really enjoyed working with them.

Could you describe some of the products that emerged from this endeavor, such as the Haptic Touch Panels?

Touchable! was actually one of the final projects realized at the institute in UdK. I developed it in 2007 with Beronika Bijarsch and Mareika Weber, who were participants from another art college in Berlin called the Kunsthochschule Berlin Weißensee. The basic aim for Touchable! panels was to create a new type of material sample that would appeal to our sense of touch. Ordinary material samples with adhesive labels bearing a code number and technical information seldom appeal to our senses. The haptic quality or materials changed a lot based on how the materials were processed, so at first we dared to select ordinary materials such as 80g A4 office paper, acetate, polypropylene tape, urethane foam, and rubber sheets, and we sought to make these materials haptically compelling by analyzing the potential of these materials in our hands. Even a sheet of 80g A4 office paper has a completely different tactile character depending on whether one touches its plain surface or its edge. We concluded this research with the creation of a series of touchable panels that would be very "appetizing" to touch. We expected that these haptically focused samples would stimulate the imaginations of designers and engineers better than conventional samples, and I am looking forward to realizing more of these panels for material industries in the near future.

I would certainly love to touch one. What about your Haptic Cushions?

Yes, we also created a collection of cushions filled with various soft materials—such as fluffy fibers of cotton, wool, polyester, fine steel, and so on—to be a sort of educational tool to help students discern the tactile difference between various soft industrial materials. The cushions also make different sounds when you touch and squeeze them.

Very interesting. This is a kind of knowledge rarely taught in visually focused design schools.

Right. Although our everyday life is surrounded by millions of different industrial materials, the level of general knowledge or multisensory consciousness of these materials is very low. I therefore believe that it is paramount that we create an opportunity to learn about materials within a basic educational curriculum—to build not only analytical knowledge but also sensory knowledge. I am very interested in working further on this Touchable! project in order to develop basic material literacy in children, for example.

A wonderful idea—not only must we enhance visual literacy, but also haptic literacy. After all, there are so many materials available for designers to work with today. Would you say

Cool Cushions

Haptic Touch Panels

that a diverse background is important for working with various materials and fabrication processes?

A diverse background can be helpful, but I think that the most important thing is to be curious about the background of each material from multiple points of view—such as technological, engineering, economic, ecological, and so on—in addition to personal artistic preference. Staying in touch with updated information released by experts in each field is so important, as the pace of new material development is so rapid today. The ability to focus and quickly discover essential information from within a pile of data will be important—as will the capacity to communicate with experts in other fields. For me, understanding fabrication processes is fundamental to the appropriate handling of materials in design. For this reason, I always follow the latest advances in industrial machinery with great curiosity. All of this information will not only help you learn more about materials, but will also paint a more vivid picture of the world in which we live and design.

Is the future haptic? What is the next step for the Sound of Material?

The Haptic Interface Design Institute continues to move forward with its research activities. I expanded the field of this research to include all five human senses, and I have also been considering the so-called sixth sense of intuition and its relationship to the imaginative power of design. The Sound of Material remains a primary focus, especially considering the significant transformations in material technologies and the sensory potentials that remain to be explored.

I have also started to develop a new method of training one's "sensory muscles" to be as sensitive as a child's. Being a workshop educator for a decade, I am keenly aware of the lack of such exercises in general education. Training the senses is the basis for material literacy, and I am convinced that it should not be an exercise offered only to professional degree students. I am currently developing simple training methods—named "sensorial calisthenics" or "design gymnastics"—that may be practiced as a sort of joyful play by children as well as adults. I have started using these exercises in my design workshop for children, as I believe this new generation will take the next significant step in design.

Image Credits

All images are the author's unless otherwise indicated.

10 (1), 18 (1), 38 (1–2), 40 (1), 41 (1), 144 (1), 159 (3–4), 163 (1–2), 164 (1–2), 167 (1–2), 169 (2), 171 (1–2): Daici Ano
12 (1): Raphael Azevedo Franca
12 (2), 120 (1), 127 (1), 129 (1–2), 130 (1–2), 172 (1), 175 (1–2), 176 (1–2), 177 (1–2), 178 (1), 179 (1), 180 (1–3), 181 (1–2): Yoshiharu Matsumura
12 (3): Salvador Busquets
15 (4), 132 (1), 135 (1–2), 136 (1), 136 (2), 137 (1), 138 (1), 139 (1), 140 (1), 142 (1–2), 143 (1, 3): Akihisa Masuda
22 (1), 25 (1–3), 26 (1–2), 27 (1–2), 29 (1–4), 31 (1–2), 32 (1–3), 33 (1): Katsuhisa Kida/FOTOTECA
23 (1): Takaharu and Yui Tezuka Architects
35 (1): James Gibbs
37 (1, 3), 125 (1–2), 126 (2), 127 (2): Satoshi Asakawa
38 (3), 34 (1), 39 (1–2), 40 (2–3), 41 (2), 43 (1): Mitsumasa Fujitsuka
44 (1), 46 (1), 47 (1–2), 49 (1–3), 50 (1–3), 51 (1), 52 (1–2), 53 (1–2), 55 (1–2): Makoto Yoshida
45 (1): Takao Sakai
54 (1–2): Takeshi Taira
56 (1), 57 (1), 58 (1), 59 (1), 60 (1), 61 (1–3), 62 (1–2), 63 (1–2), 65 (1–2), 66 (1–2), 67 (1): Nendo
68 (1): German Nieva
69 (1): Shigeru Ban Architects
71 (3), 74 (1): Xavier de Jauréguiberry
76 (1–2, 4), 77 (1): Emmanuel Dambrine
76 (3): Shigeru Ban Architects Europe/Artefactory
78 (1): Eresh Weerasurlya
86 (1), 87 (1), 90 (4), 93 (1, 3), 94 (1), 96 (1), 97 (1): Kenya Hara
89 (1): Kenya Hara, Tamotsu Fujii
90 (1): Naoto Fukasawa
90 (2), 94 (3): Panasonic Design Company
90 (3): Kosuke Tsumura
94 (2): Sony Corporation
97 (2): Hara Design Institute, Atelier Omoya
99 (1): Takashi Okamoto
103 (1), 109 (2), 152 (1), 154 (1–2): Laurie McGinley
110 (1), 111 (1), 114 (1), 117 (1–2), 118 (1–2), 119 (2–3): Tadao Ando Architects & Associates
121 (1), 123 (1–2), 126 (1), 131 (1): Eriko Horiki & Associates
128 (1): Seiryo Yamada
133 (1): Terunobu Fujimori
138 (2): Antoine Taveneaux
149 (1): Yoshiaki Tsutsui
157 (1): Isaiah King
160 (1), 161 (1), 169 (1, 3): Atelier Hitoshi Abe
166 (1–2): Shunichi Atsumi
173 (1): Shuhei Endo
182 (1), 183 (1), 184 (1–3), 185 (1), 187 (1–2), 188 (1–2), 189 (1–3), 190 (1–3), 191 (1): Nuno
192 (1), 195 (2): Yozo Takada
193 (1), 195 (1): Mario Martin
195 (3), 199 (1): Sachiko Kodama
196 (1): Mirek Wojtowicz
196 (2): Hiroki Sayama
200 (1), 217 (1), 220 (1–2), 222 (1–3), 224 (1), 225 (1–3), 226 (3): Makoto Sei Watanabe Architects' Office
204 (1), 205 (1), 209 (1–2), 213 (1–2), 214 (1), 215 (1–2): Toyo Ito & Associates, Architects
206 (1–2), 242 (3), 244 (2): Nacasa & Partners Inc.
211 (3), 241 (2): Toyo Ito
228 (1), 236 (2–3): Shunji Yamanaka and Wakita Laboratory, Keio University
229 (1), 231 (3), 232 (1–3), 235 (1–2): Wakita Laboratory, Keio Univerisity
231 (1): Fumio Matsumoto and Akira Wakita
231 (2): Ryukyu Alive Consortium
236 (1): Michihiko Ueno and Akira Wakita
239 (1): Masahiro Okamura
241 (3), 238 (1), 241 (1–2), 242 (1–2), 245 (1, 3), 246 (1–2), 247 (1): Tokujin Yoshioka Design
244 (1): Masaya Yoshimura
245 (2): Alessandro Paderni
247 (3): Masayuki Hayashi
248 (1), 249 (1), 251 (1–2), 252 (1–3), 253 (1–2), 255 (1–2): Ave Design Corporation